Street Dreams
and
Hip Hop
Barbershops

Tracking Globalization

Robert J. Foster, editor

Editorial advisory board:
Mohammed Bamyeh
Lisa Cartwright
Randall Halle

A list of titles in the series appears at the end of this volume.

Indiana University Press
Bloomington & Indianapolis

Street Dreams

and

Hip Hop

Barbershops

Global Fantasy in Urban Tanzania

Brad Weiss

This book is a publication of

Indiana University Press
601 North Morton Street
Bloomington, IN 47404-3797 USA

http://iupress.indiana.edu

Telephone orders	800-842-6796
Fax orders	812-855-7931
Orders by e-mail	iuporder@indiana.edu

The paper used in this publication meets the minimum
requirements of American National Standard for Information
Sciences—Permanence of Paper for
Printed Library Materials, ANSI Z39.48-1984.

Manufactured in the United States of America

Library of Congress Cataloging-in-Publication Data

Weiss, Brad.
  Street dreams and hip hop barbershops : global fantasy in
urban Tanzania / Brad Weiss.
      p. cm.—(Tracking globalization)
  Includes bibliographical references and index.
   ISBN 978-0-253-32594-5 (cloth : alk. paper) —
ISBN 978-0-253-22075-2 (pbk. : alk. paper)
   1. Young men—Tanzania—Arusha Region—Social life and
customs. 2. Urban youth—Tanzania—Arusha Region—
Social life and customs. 3. Barbershops—Tanzania—Arusha
Region. 4. Popular culture—Tanzania—Arusha Region.
5. Hip-hop—Tanzania—Arusha Region. 6. Arusha Region
(Tanzania)—Social life and customs. I. Title.
   HQ799.8.T34W45 2009
   305.242'109678'26—dc22
                                    2008042735

1 2 3 4 5 14 13 12 11 10 09

For Ezra Weiss

Contents

Acknowledgments

For this book, even more than anything I've written previously, I've depended on the support and generosity of a great many colleagues, friends, and family. It all started, in a roundabout way, with going to the Satterthwaite Colloquium on African Ritual and Religion during the 1990s, meeting regularly with anthropologists and historians from across Europe, and getting inspired to get back into fieldwork in Tanzania. I had been doing historically based work since leaving Tanzania—the first time—in 1990, and I found that the work of my colleagues (many of them now great friends) on media, new forms of religious experience, and transnational movements of all sorts got me itching to head back to Tanzania. In the winter of 1999, I was extremely lucky to get some of the best advice I've ever gotten when Dorothy Hodgson told me of her friends, Jo and Judith, who could put me up in Arusha while I explored the prospects for a new project that summer. I've stayed with Jo Driessen and Judith Jackson on all of the subsequent trips I've taken to Arusha over the last decade, in 1999, 2000, 2003, and again in 2006. It's no exaggeration to say this book would look nothing like it does today were it not for the extraordinary generosity of and the conviviality I enjoyed with Jo and Judith. I got to know a great many scholars in a wide array of fields who passed through Jo and Judith's, learned a lot about Tanzania, and shared some of the ideas presented here in their earliest stages in conversations set against their amazing views of Mount Meru. Even better, I got to know the staff who work for Jo and Judith, and I hope Yuda and Mzee Julius won't mind my thanking them by name. Eddie Lawasi became my very, very good friend, and I have learned a great deal about life and work in Arusha from my discussions with him.

The Tanzania Commission for Science and Technology (COSTECH) enabled me to live and work in Tanzania while I did this research. Financial support for the research and writing of this book came from a variety of sources. The College of William and Mary gave me funds to carry out research in the summer of 1999 and a sabbatical in 2000–2001 that allowed me to carry out more extensive research and writing, along with funding by a Small Grant from the Wenner-Gren Foundation. In 2003–2004 I was a Burkhardt Fellow at the National Humanities Center, an experience that helped me complete the first draft of this book (in addition to turning my world upside-down—in a good way!). I have presented chapters from this work in a wide range of settings. Probably the most important one was the Advanced Seminar on Youth and Globalization held at the School of American Research in April 2004. My thanks to Jennifer Cole and Debbie Durham for organizing the event, loads of comments on my contribution (a modified version of which appears here in chapter 6), and to all of the participants, especially Ann Anagnost and Barrie Thorne, for their helpful critiques. Editing the volume *Producing African Futures* provided a great opportunity to think through many of the themes of this work, and I thank Jean Comaroff, in particular, for her comments then, and for her continuing impact on this work. It has been a real pleasure to organize and convene the Symposium on Current Perspectives in Anthropology since 2001. The many participants in this symposium have read almost every word in this book, and I'm grateful for their many contributions. I'll single out Misty Bastian and Adeline Masquelier for their especially trenchant and detailed commentaries on many chapters.

Working with Indiana University Press has been a real pleasure as well. Bob Foster's enthusiasm for this project has been greatly valued. His invitation, along with Judy Farquhar's, to speak to the Society for Cultural Anthropology, was a source of great encouragement. Becky Tolen found great reviewers for me, and she offered sound editorial advice about how to rein in my occasionally florid prose. This book is a lot better because of Bob's and Becky's wise counsel.

My family deserves special thanks for their support over the last ten years of working on this book. I thank my parents, Marty and Debby Weiss, for—well, there are too many things to list. But they put us up for the summer of 2007 when I made final revisions on the manuscript and made our lives easy for two months. My wife, Julie Corsaro, has had more patience with the inconveniences, the absences, and occasional relocations my research has required—especially at some rather trying personal moments—than should be asked of anyone. But we made it! My son, Ezra Weiss, was just three when I started this research. He used to tell folks, "My dad's going all the way to Tanzania for work—and he isn't even seeing any animals!" In the hopes that I've earned some small measure of respect from him since then, and that maybe it's been worth it, I dedicate this book to him.

A briefer version of chapter 3 appeared as "Thug Realism: Inhabiting Fantasy in Urban Tanzania" in *Cultural Anthropology* 17, no. 1 (2002): 93–128.

Street Dreams
and
Hip Hop
Barbershops

Introduction

Popular Practices and Neoliberal Dilemmas in Arusha

The years since the early 1990s have seen unprecedented transformations in Tanzania. The extent of these upheavals can be described in the broadest of strokes. A nation-state celebrated for its one-party democracy has introduced and implemented multiparty electoral procedures, a process popularly known as *mageuzi* (Swahili for "changes"). A national press that was restricted at the beginning of this decade to two daily publications authorized by the ruling Revolutionary Party (CCM) has given way to the burgeoning production and distribution of newspapers, tabloids, comics, and magazines published in Tanzania. The single state radio company broadcasting from Dar es Salaam in 1990 has since been supplemented by a host of state-sponsored and private stations, most of them headquartered in cities beyond the capital. Until 1994, there was literally no television broadcasting of any sort in mainland Tanzania, while today the private network ITV (its slogan in 1999: "The only station available in the whole nation!"), part of the IPP media conglomerate owned by Reginald Mengi, broadcasts locally produced serials and newscasts, as well as cast-off American sitcoms and action series. A great many private residences and businesses also have access to cable and satellite systems that offer programming from across Africa, India, Europe, and the United States. Perhaps a single iconic pronouncement conveys the force of this dizzying array of activities. In 1992, the second president of the United Republic of Tanzania, Ali Hassan Mwinyi, announced that the state had rejected the Arusha Declaration, President Julius Nyerere's renowned program of sociopolitical engineering, calling for *ujamaa*—African socialism. In its stead,

Rais Ruksa, meaning "President Permit" (as Mwinyi came to be known), adopted the reforms of structural adjustment required by the International Monetary Fund (IMF) in order to finance Tanzania's transformation into a post-(African) socialist society. In an astonishing bit of neoliberal synergy, postsocialist Tanzania has become the leading site within Africa for capital infusion from postapartheid South African investors (R. Schroeder, personal communication). Predictably, the boom of investment in the first years of this transition has given way to a massive bust as inflationary pressures and unemployment today escalate to levels as perilous as any in the independence era.

These wide-ranging and rapid shifts in the policy imperatives and institutional ordering of the Tanzanian state have also entailed adjustments in the structuring of its citizen's subjectivities. Consider the following example: on a large commercial street in Arusha, in an area near the city's largest mosque, a prominent secondary school, a reliable Internet café, and the only cinema in town, sits a clean, airy barbershop—in Swahili, *kinyozi* (pl. *vinyozi*)—that goes by the name of Classic Hair Cutting. The staff and clientele at Classic are interested in much more than haircuts. They spend most of their time in the shop reading an assortment of daily and weekly papers, listening to music performed in French, Lingala (a lingua franca in much of the Congo), English, and occasionally Swahili, and watching satellite television broadcasts from the United Kingdom, South Africa, India, and the United States. The *kinyozi* is unmistakable from the street, its front door dominated by a larger-than-life portrait of Dennis Rodman. The social life and stylistic virtuosity of Classic evince a complex, contemporary social formation in urban Tanzania. To be sure, this particular configuration of media, technology, and labor is controlled by a relatively elite social class; but the forms and images that define this configuration are pervasive in Arusha. There are literally hundreds of barbershops in town, often more than a dozen in a single city block. Many shops are less than a hundred square feet in size, yet even the smallest must have a radio, if only to entertain idle barbers. Remarkable portrait art is a feature of even the most rudimentary shanty *kinyozi* constructed from scrap lumber. Such sites in Arusha seem unambiguously to proclaim the contemporary efflorescence of popular culture as an array of practices and performances through which Tanzanians establish their place in an explicitly global and spectacular flow of images, objects, and persons. In the modes of fantasy that constitute their popular culture exemplified by such microinstitutions, urban Tanzanians imaginatively articulate and act on a world remade.

Classic Hair Cutting

My ethnographic research on popular culture, hanging out in barbershops and bus stands, seamstress tables and video halls, was carried
out in the northern Tanzanian city of Arusha. Arusha is a city that, by
virtue of the aforementioned Arusha Declaration (delivered in 1967), was
closely associated with the socialist reforms of Nyerere, Tanzania's first
president (1964–85). The city was founded as a German *boma* ("fort")
early in the twentieth century. Colonial policy under both the Germans
and British was concerned with the ethnic categorization of the city, essentially attempting to assure a distinction between so-called urban and
rural populations of Africans. Swahili communities, which were associated
with Islam and trading, were authorized to reside and engage in commercial enterprises in the town itself, while the Maasai (or WaArusha)
communities, who were (meant to be) pastorialists and agrarian, were
prohibited from full participation in these urban affairs (Peligal 1999;
Spear 1997). Today, Arusha is officially the third biggest city in Tanzania
(following the capital, Dar es Salaam, and Mwanza, on the southern coast
of Lake Victoria), with a population approaching 300,000. The city itself,
however, is the site of work and activity for a vast periurban residential
population that probably reaches closer to one million people. Because

of its attractive location at the foot of Mount Meru, near the border with Kenya to the north, Arusha has also been central to numerous administrative bureaucracies, serving as a center for the short-lived East African Federation, and has served since 1994 as the site of the international war crimes tribunal for Rwanda under the auspices of the United Nations. The political economy of the town is, however, most clearly dependent on the tourist trade, which accounts for over 40 percent of foreign exchange earnings for Tanzania as a whole. Arusha is an easily accessible gateway to a number of national parks, including Ngorongoro Crater and the Serengeti to the west, and Mount Kilimanjaro to the east. Today, tourism is universally held to be central to the development of the region, to say nothing of the personal income and long-term aspirations of a great many young people in Arusha.

The fin de siècle in Tanzania—a millennial moment (Comaroff and Comaroff 2000; Allison 2006) in which the premises (and unfulfilled promises) of African socialism have been undone by the strictures of neoliberal reform—has also seen the flourishing of small, independent businesses, such as those that provide barbering and hair styling services. I found these businesses—*vinyozi* and saloons (the standard term for beauty shops throughout Africa), respectively—amenable spots to carry out research on popular culture for reasons that I elaborate on throughout this book. One of the primary reasons for my initial interest in them in the late 1990s was their sheer inescapability. The town of Arusha seemed almost overridden with brightly painted hole-in-the-wall establishments possessed only of a mirror, a chair, and a set of clippers. It is no exaggeration to say that there were hundreds of barbershops in the center of the city alone; even the myriad tracks leading up Mount Meru and down toward the Maasai Steppe had several, and in some cases dozens, of barbershops. In part, neoliberal conditions of the kind associated with structural adjustment help make it clear why an informal business with a necessarily flexible workforce (one that receives essentially no training in most, though not all, cases) that makes use of cheap imported goods (from cosmetics and hair care products to the clippers themselves), all in the service of developing elaborate new techniques of selfhood, should proliferate in Tanzania.[1] Beyond these economic constraints, places like barbershops and hair salons formulate an imagined sense of what global relations are like from the perspective of urban Tanzanians; and how activities like hair care provide a means not just of observing or appropriating powerful images of that wider world, but of actively participating in it.

A range of barbershops across Arusha

A concern with such imagining is one of the more compelling developments in contemporary social analyses. From the most spectacular fantasies to the most mundane reveries, imagining the world—as it is and as it might be—seems to be an increasingly popular activity. There are surely rich imaginative implications of contemporary Tanzanian economy and society for many young people living and working in range of informal business setting akin to barbershops across Arusha. How might we articulate the different dimensions of this remaking in urban Tanzania, and thereby explore how modes of consciousness like spectacle and fantasy are constituted and concretized under prevailing conditions of social, political, and economic transformation found in Tanzania and places like it? It is important, I argue, to place these fantasies both in the moment of the contemporary restructuring of global relations and in enduring conditions of modernity, of which the present is an ongoing part. In particular, it is vital to recognize that imaginative practice is central to the forms of spectacle like those that pervade a globalized Arusha today, as well as a vital feature of social action and the production of consciousness in any sociocultural world. As Comaroff and Comaroff (1999b: 295) suggest,

> The processes involved in the rise of novel forms of planetary integration and compression—especially in the electronic economy, in mass communications, in flextime flows of labor and capital, in the instantaneous circulation of signs and images, in the translocal commodification of culture, in the diasporic politics of identity—challenge us by representing the most fundamental question of our craft: how do human beings construct their intimate, everyday life-worlds at the shifting intersections of here, there, elsewhere, everywhere.

Contemporary social conditions may be characterized by a distinctive range and articulation of relations, places, values, and persons—distinct principally because of the innovative, proliferating media of compression that facilitate the widespread sense of a global totality. Such realignments of space and time have been much discussed in many analyses of neoliberal reform. The tensions of contradictions of these realignments have been described by Geschiere and Nyamnjoh (2000), who note that the explosion of mobility, inclusiveness, and market openness has been matched by the palpable imposition of new forms of exclusion, marginalization, and constraint. Moreover, it is vital to recall that the shifting intersections of here, there, elsewhere, everywhere are an enduring feature of sociality and of social analysis in general, not an unprecedented possibility ushered in by these conditions themselves. It is the imaginative engagement with these shifting intersections, confluences that both structure social action and are concretized in social experience in Arusha, that I explore across a range of popular cultural practices, from video watching and clothing styles to informal economic activities and commuter transportation.

Barbershops are especially productive spaces from which to examine a nexus of these popular practices. Not only Arusha but also other towns in Tanzania, taking their lead—according to folk theories of barbering—from trend-setting Dar es Salaam, or *Bongo* (Swahili for "brain"),[2] have seen a substantial increase in *vinyozi*. The explosion of these cosmetological enterprises can be linked to broad political economic restructurings. The constraints of structural adjustment in Tanzania, especially urban Tanzania, precipitated a dual move, one that is increasingly commonplace under global neoliberal regimes. Tanzanian society was simultaneously opened to media, goods, and ideologies never before available, while the decline of state services and subsidies led (after a brief flourishing of both the formal and informal privatized economy) to the collapse of a host of employment opportunities. This sudden crash on the heels of unprecedented and exhilarating possibilities—unrealized by the vast majority of Tanzanians as anything but possibilities—made it possible for a broad swath of people to desire the signs and styles of a global order while finding ever narrower means by which to satisfy them.

This widening breach between the actual and the possible has been forged by barbershops in Arusha. In their own accounts, the young men who work in and frequent Arusha's *vinyozi* will often refer to the historical character of these businesses; the same is true, in this thoroughly segregated commercial niche, for the women in Arusha's salons and beauty shops. As many barbers and clients told me, barbershops are a new social institution, plainly a part of the contemporary Tanzanian landscape. Although people have long been tending to their hair, barbershops are "things of today" (*mambo ya siku hizi*) unknown to "elders from the past" (*wazee wa zamani*). Some told me that barbershops were part of the changes that had been brought about in the last five years in Arusha and that they were explicitly created "for the sake of the youth" (*kwa ajili ya vijana*). The *vinyozi* are appropriate for the youth because youth are especially interested in the forms and fashions that circulate through this microinstitution, and because in times of tumult and uncertainty, they provide young men with a "chance," an "opportunity," or a "place" (all terms encompassed by the Swahili term, *nafasi*).[3]

The socioeconomic status of the young barbers who labor in these places laborers should be clearly specified. In my work with over fifty shops in Arusha, and my passing familiarity with hundreds more, I found that barbers were not among the most disenfranchised and desperate residents of town.[4] Indeed, almost all of them had at least some secondary education, and many of them spoke and read English better than the average Tanzanian. A number of them came not from elite families but from families who had once had some financial means but had found it increasingly difficult to—for example—pay the school fees of their children, or provide housing for all the members of their family. In terms of the particular dilemmas of neoliberalism I describe in detail below, it makes sense that those with some means to imagine themselves as active participants in global cultural processes should appreciate their imaginative possibilities and should most acutely feel the sting of the inaccessibility of full participation.

Let me move beyond these economic circumstances and offer a comparative sketch of some selective barbershops in order to provide an ethnographic framing for this work. I want to suggest these shops link to the wider neoliberal conditions prevalent in Tanzania and to the concrete particulars of social life in Arusha. These shops are not typical in any way, nor do they reflect the widest spectrum of shops and the possible social lives of those who work in and visit them. But they do exemplify processes that are relevant, in different ways, to the lives of many young people in Arusha.

It is all but impossible to know how many *vinyozi* there are in Arusha at any point in time because they are ephemeral and tenuous enterprises. Countless kiosks and *bandas*—small wooden shanty structures—can be found on vacant lots and in decrepit warrens of informal businesses that once housed barbershops, some for a few years, others for a few weeks. In 2001, the Arusha municipal government implemented a plan to clean up the city center, principally by moving the central bus stand to an area near the main open-air market. In the process, it leveled a number of informal businesses, many successful barbershops among them, both on the site from which the buses were removed and in the area to which they were relocated. In contrast to these shops, the *vinyozi*, which I will call Casino Hair Cutting and Bad Boyz Barbering, were located only a few blocks away from one another in the commercial center of the oldest Swahili quarter of Arusha. Casino was, and remains, by far the most successful *kinyozi* in town. The well-lit shop has four swiveling barber chairs in front of large full-length mirror. A long bench for patrons and resting barbers sits opposite the chairs, and clients, barbers, and passing friends (and anthropologists) come by to watch the satellite television broadcast throughout the workday. At the rear of the store, behind a plate glass window, is the office, with a small desk, a desktop PC, and a cash box where change is made for customers. In addition to the staff of barbers, Casino also employs several young women who keep the books, make change, and mind the office. There is almost always a steady flow of customers, two to three customers per hour on a normal day, with as many as six or seven per hour on a Friday or Saturday. Each barber takes his turn cutting hair, although regulars can request a barber they are familiar with if they are willing to wait for him. Perhaps the most remarkable thing about Casino is the fact that virtually the same staff of barbers worked there from 1999 through 2006; no other shop I was familiar with had the same staff from year to year from 1999 to 2000, or 2000 to 2003. The success of Casino is hard to assess strictly in terms of haircuts. The quality of the barbers in terms of their training or experience was not substantially different from most other shops, and prices throughout town are virtually standardized. It is impossible to get a really good deal or to pay extravagantly for a haircut at a *kinyozi*. Undoubtedly, the key to the economic viability of Casino is found not in the barbering business itself but in the financial backing it enjoys from the wealthy Chagga businessmen from Kilimanjaro who own the place. According to one of the women working in the office (all of whom over the last several years have been distant Chagga relations to the shop owners), the brothers who run Casino have many other businesses, primarily involving, as she put it, "bringing cars to the bush," or *porini*, a term that can mean anything from bringing transport to the tourism sector to working in the tanzanite gemstone trade in Mererani, itself routinely described as "the bush."

The barbers who work at Casino have found comfortable day jobs—indeed, that's almost exactly how one thirty-year-old barber described it to me. "This is a good job," he said. "You can get yourself a new shirt, or a new pair of pants every once in a while. And I can have my nights to work on music, which is what I really want to do." Here he neatly summarizes the perspective of the barbers at Casino—and the aspirations of barbers across town. They can get a bit of extra money ("better than living day to day" is how one described it), which lets them keep up with the ongoing currents of self-fashioning (a new shirt, a pair of pants) and aspire to more prestigious, cosmopolitan, and lucrative enterprises. Such enterprises might include the music business, the tourist industry, or gemstone brokerage, all of which are typical claims that young male barbers made to me about what they hoped to do in the future.

In contrast to Casino, the barbers at Bad Boyz were less professional in their attitudes toward their work. Whereas the staff at Casino had all come to Arusha from elsewhere—Moshi, Dar, Tanga—and found work as barbers while simultaneously pursuing other careers, the staff at Bad Boyz were younger men who had all come from the immediate vicinity of the shop. Most of them had gone to primary school together. The barbers had worked together at a now-defunct *kinyozi* in the late 1990s and began working at Bad Boyz soon after. Bad Boyz was established by one of the young men, Hassan, who lived in a run-down compound immediately behind the shop with his mother and a younger brother. He was able to fund the shop with capital from an older brother who worked as a civil servant in Dar, and it provided just enough funding to get a small shop going. Bad Boys was much smaller than Casino. It had two barber chairs, but the shop was extremely narrow, with barely room for the barber and his client inside the shop. It did have a bench and chairs outside for clients and barbers (essential to the spatial form of such shops, as we'll see). Bad Boyz also had some fine artwork, including a few large, iconic paintings on the shop front, door, and inside, but it was largely decorated with a vibrant pastiche of pictures cut from the pages of *Vibe, Essence,* and whatever other glossy magazines were at hand. The men working at Bad Boyz were all much younger than the staff at Casino; most of them still lived at home with their parents or extended kin. Yet they described their futures in ways not very different from the staff at Casino. They, too, aspired to work in the tourist trade or as gemstone brokers (never diggers), two of the most visible regional enterprises. Unlike Casino, though, the staff at Bad Boyz was not entirely stable. Even though the employees had known one another for years before working at the *kinyozi,* they began to quarrel over wages. Some accused Hassan, who ran the shop with family financing, of withholding wages or lying about earnings (which were much lower than the wages paid at Casino, although not nearly as paltry as many *vinyozi* in town), and so left the shop to find work as barbers elsewhere. By the end of the summer of 2000, less than two years after it opened, Bad Boyz shut down for good. Hassan couldn't rely on his absent brother for regular remittances. He thought he needed to find other work to support his mother, and he especially wanted to secure school fees for his youngest brother. Hassan left Arusha that year to find work in Morogoro, where he could stay with relatives, and the staff members at Bad Boyz went off to find their fortunes elsewhere. Most of them remained in Arusha, often with family.

As I suggested, Casino and Bad Boyz are neither typical nor extremes of the spectrum of *vinyozi* prospects. Rather, they exemplify the ways that such shops reflect the logic of aspiration and what I will call the dynam-

Bad Boyz interior

ics of exclusion and inclusion characteristic of contemporary Tanzanian popular practice. Barbers depended on external supports to sustain themselves, like Hassan and his brother, or the Chagga entrepreneurs running Casino. More than one barber told me how the decline of what was once a comfortable family circumstance had compelled them to work as a barber. In my view, this does not make barbershops sites of desperation so much as locations that foster exactly the sorts of fantasy that suffuse popular culture practice across both Tanzania and much of the world. As I suggested, all the barbers I knew saw themselves working in the future in more cosmopolitan, prestigious (to say nothing of lucrative) positions, which their meager earnings as barbers allowed them to struggle toward in the meantime. Barbershops are places where the gap between the actual and the possible are deeply felt. In practice, it is the barbers' lot to try and translate the diffuse and alluring possibilities of globally mediated celebrity imagery into concrete circumstances—that is, their clients' very bodies. The relative knowledge, insight, and resources that most barbers possess make it possible for them to aspire to recreate and refashion their existence, often in unpredictable ways. The dilemmas of these aspirations—the fact that barbers (and not only barbers, of course) are both able to recognize the values of a wider world they found uniquely compelling and yet feel almost completely incapable of realizing the potential of those values in their lives—and these conflicted fantasies shape much of popular cultural practice in Arusha today.

The Dynamics of Neoliberal Reform:
Framing Popular Practice in Arusha

The forms of sociality and value that are cultivated in the general milieu that barbers and hairstylists, street hawkers and tourists tout across Arusha provide rich evidence of the way that young people, especially young men, imagine their futures and fates in the world at large. But these values have an ambiguous prospect. In my view, they alert us to the inordinate inequities in the world today, but they should also remind us that even those who suffer under these very real constraints still often find the world a place of possibility, even hope. Throughout this book, I describe the circumstances of inequality and the lived experiences of constraint that generate this proliferation of barbershops (and similar locations of cultural production) in Arusha. In what follows, I offer my perspective on the dynamics of these political and economic circumstances, the specific character and qualities of neoliberalism that both enable and constrain Arusha's popular cultural projects. My contention is that a specific neoliberal dynamic configures the particular structure of values and social interaction prevalent in Arusha's informal economies, and that it is performed in its popular practices.

Let me demonstrate this dynamically by way of a brief ethnographic illustration. The setting is not a barbershop but a family compound in June 2000, where parents, children, and guests are gathered around the television to watch the 1985 blockbuster action picture *Commando*. The essential plot of the spectacle is straightforward. Its narrative arc pursues one simple yet highly cinematic question: how many people can Arnold Schwarzenneger kill in the course of ninety minutes? By methods that range from dropping his foe off a cliff to pitching a lead pipe through his nemesis's chest, the future governor of California (at the height of an era presided over by a one-time California movie star) kills several dozen people. In the final scene, Schwarzenegger's character, Commando John Matrix— who has heretofore used such decidedly low-tech objects as a pitchfork, an ax, and a machete along with his gargantuan body as weapons—arms himself to the teeth with AK-47s, belts of ammunition, grenades, and a rocket launcher in order to exterminate the irregular militia of the vaguely Central American deposed dictator who has kidnapped our hero's beloved nine-year-old daughter. The outcome is never really in doubt.

I watched *Commando* on video along with the members of a family, whose numbers in that particular audience in 2000 included a man in his mid-thirties along with two of his children, a three-year-old girl, and her six-year-old brother. Even though no one in the family spoke English, they had no difficulty understanding the film, and they watched with rapt pleasure, commenting on the action, sympathizing with the characters, and appreciating the images. At the dramatic climax of the film, Schwarzenegger moves out of the shadows of the shed, where he has been hiding, and appears bare-chested, camouflaged with body paint, sporting an enormous arsenal ready to confront his daughter's captors. At this sight, the young boy watching with us burst out in astonishment, "Wow! It's Osama bin Laden!"

The interjection on the part of this young video fan is a fairly complex commentary. It exemplifies some of the unanticipated allegiances, and their characteristic tensions, that attend to the global dissemination of media, consumer goods, political ideologies, and religious discourses. Note, for example that this viewing took place in the summer of 2000, before September 11, 2001, but two years after Tanzanians experienced the bombing of the American embassy in Dar es Salaam. Remembering events like this one, familiar to every Tanzanian schoolboy, through the spectacle of Hollywood action indicates the irregularities and unpredictability of these global processes as diverse histories are generated in the encounter of spectacle, religious innovation, and geopolitics. Critics of the imperialist implications of the globalizing tendencies of mass mediation and consumerism emanating from the American culture industry might see in this boy's exclamation an equation of the glorification of military might with the rise of transnational terror, and so take his response as evidence of a kind of resistance—as though Western media were to be rejected (equating Schwarzenegger with bin Laden) for their banalization and, of course, commodification of violence, brutality, and suffering. In my view, though, this young viewer's spontaneous response—and commentaries and practices across urban Tanzania that take a similar form—is a good deal more ambivalent than this hackneyed model of rejection suggests. We might ask, for example, whether the excess and sheer force of extraordinary power mediated by such representations is something viewers feel should be constrained, or whether it is something they might desire. Does this young boy's assertion subvert the value of these remarkable images, or might it actually sustain and confirm their meaning for him? Moving beyond this single child's reaction, we might ask this: do urban African audiences and consumers for the media, goods, and ideas promoted by dominant agents and forces of global capital feel themselves to be oppressed or enabled by the potency of these cultural forms? As ordinary people in places like Arusha engage with such forms and thereby imagine the contours of a globalized world, do they understand themselves to be subjugated and marginalized by its forces, or might they experience a sense of belonging and inclusion in its apparently novel possibilities? Or can we find models and methods for addressing the multiplicity of the possibilities that a great many people around the world feel in such contexts? In what ways are the tension between open-ended prospects and repressive limitations managed and lived in everyday experience?

In my assessment of these questions, I hope to push beyond what has become the standard anthropological take on the investigation of globalization, and more particularly of neoliberalism. Rather than catalog the extent to which these transnational forces have been incorporated into "local" worlds of meaning and social life, what I hope to do is reframe that problematic, so that neoliberalism cannot be thought of as a realm of external relations to which communities "respond." The changes generally understood as neoliberal, with their emphases on consumption, thoroughgoing individualism, rapid circulation of goods, services, and persons, and the tying together of capital and the control of information in the creation of new financial instruments, have transformed the scale of social life around the world in ways that make terms like *local* and *global* highly problematic (Piot 1999). I suggest that looking at popular practices that have become pervasive under globalization, both promoted and dispersed by this neoliberal order, can reveal the character of these wholesale changes on many levels. Most importantly, we can ask, what are the forms of value that emerge under these contemporary conditions? How is that value produced and grasped? Further, I want to consider the constitution of neoliberal realities, and in so doing ask what sorts of sociality this order might generate. How is participation in this order recognized and affirmed?

These are the political and economic questions that I confront in this ethnographic interrogation of the practices and values of young men and women in Arusha. I can offer no simple answer to these dilemmas. Rather, I aim to demonstrate that a wide range of activities and imaginings in Arusha—and undoubtedly many other parts of Africa as well as the world—are shaped by these contradictory prospects, the simultaneous sense of inclusion and exclusion, that pervade the contemporary global political economy (Geschiere and Nyamoja 2000; Shipley 2004; Makhulu 2004). My contention is that these tensions are vividly realized in forms of spectacle and pleasure through which these contradictions are lived and felt, and so I give special attention in this work to the imaginative practices—and performances—of style, attitude, and everyday sociality through which Tanzanians come to inhabit the New World Order as they understand it.

Much of the work of forging connections between the creation of new modes of belonging and the production of value, especially in the neoliberal moment, is carried out by consumption, and so I interrogate problems of consumption, a concern I have examined extensively in my assessment of the history and culture of rural northwest Tanzania, a region quite different from Arusha (Weiss 1996, 2003). The contradictory character of the commodity is well understood, and there are many analyses of popular culture and value production in Africa that focus on the dissemination of commodities and the ways that their uses and appropriation both confirm the appeal of modernity while also challenging many of its fundamental assumptions (Comaroff and Comaroff 1993; Burke 1996). The insights drawn from these assessments are especially relevant in the current era, where value is increasingly understood as a capacity for consumption and production is increasingly defined and realized through processes of self-fashioning (Comaroff and Comaroff 2001; Liechty 2002; Cole 2008). What is less well understood but absolutely central to the account I offer here are the ways that this self-fashioning can blur the boundaries between consumption and production, again in ways that confirm the salience of the tensions between inclusion and exclusion.

The complicated connections between, for example, production and consumption can be shown to be essential to creating the intersection of elite and common modes of practice with global and local stylistic forms. If we look at clothing styles, we find that in the last twenty years, *mitumba*, used clothing, has become available in every community across Tazania (Hansen 1999). The social and cultural effects of these cast-off commodities have been enormous: used clothing sellers dominate public space in urban areas, and economic avenues proliferate (and marginal returns decline) as large bales of clothing are parceled out into smaller and smaller piles for sale. Debates rage about the effects of Western fashions on African consumers (Stambach 1999). At the same time, part of the direct effect of this consumer revolution is felt at the level of production, for now local tailors and seamstresses create their fashions—often in collaboration with their customers—with an eye toward the styles, cuts, and labels of the *mitumba* market. An array of tensions is manifest in these practices. Local producers find their work simultaneously marginalized by the availability of cheap, cast-off imports, but these imports also stimulate local production, in part because these imports need to be tailored and repaired, but especially because they create models that can be profitably imitated—not as a means of counterfeit and deception (which, as we shall see, is a pervasive concern surrounding the consumption of imported goods more generally), but as a way for consumers to grasp an even more affordable means of participation in this global trade. "Women in Arusha like to keep up with the times," a young tailor told me as he sewed Gloria Vanderbilt labels into the outfits he had just made from cheap Indonesian cloth (*sukari,* "sugar," in local parlance, a term derived from the grainy feel of this material) that his clients had brought to him for refashioning. In consuming these global styles, local clothing workers are also consuming the relationships and models that will guide their productive practice. This will in turn be consumed by their customers, whose tastes and sense of style are integral to their productive practices. In these ways, consumerism has also generated modes of production through the command of stylistic virtuosity now required of producers who help to create the terms and forms of their global interconnection. Consumption, then, at once a means of marginalization and a mode of participation, can be grasped as a process for generating value and sociality.

In contrast to prevailing views that see consumption as replacing production as a mode of value formation and as a social process more broadly, under global neoliberalism, I am interested in the ways these processes articulate in novel, popular configurations. But what do we make of neoliberalism itself? A term like *neoliberalism* is notoriously slippery and contentious. What is its real use as an analytical term, and as a historical phenomenon with respect to Africa? We might ask, for example, whether there is anything truly distinctive about the present era, or whether the New World Order is simply an amplification of structures and conditions that have long been in place in Africa and elsewhere. It seems that each passing African generation has been found in most social scientific assessments to be in crisis, so it is difficult to determine whether the current moment is distinctly different or a recurring structural predicament. Underlying these question are debates about whether neoliberalism itself is merely an academic invention, as opposed to a real social process. Although I do not anticipate that I can resolve these debates—and I think it's a worthy contribution to the literature simply to clarify the nature of the questions— there is a widespread sense in Arusha, and certainly elsewhere (and not only in Africa; see Comaroff and Comaroff 2000), that there have been momentous changes in social, cultural, and economic life since the latter decades of the twentieth century.

Beyond the lived experience of momentous upheaval, it is clear that a profound set of material, institutional, and extralegal transformations can be identified in the case of Tanzania in particular. Tripp's detailed work, both ethnographic and institutionally based, makes it plain that the course of liberalization during the 1980s and 1990s is central to urban social processes in Tanzania (Tripp 1996). What is crucial to recognize, Tripp notes, is that formal liberalization in this erstwhile socialist state was preceded by informal socioeconomic activities that became commonplace across a wide swath of Tanzanian society. State attempts at social regulation, most notoriously the *ujamaa* policies of collectivization, were imposed erratically and often brutally in ways that undermined Tanzanians' ability to sustain themselves. The restraint on private enterprise of any sort, combined with dire economic conditions throughout the 1970s and early 1980s, led to the growth of informal economic activities. Even salaried party officials ended up working to enforce regulations they found restrictive, as most needed to supplement their income through participation in small "projects" (*Biashara ndogo ndogo*).

This popular movement laid the foundation for official liberalization policies adopted by the state and party in the late 1980s and 1990s.
These programs of structural adjustment overseen by the World Bank
and IMF, beginning with the Economic Recovery Program of 1986–89
under President Ali Hassan Mwinyi, followed by the Poverty Reduction
and Growth Facility of 1996–99 under President Benjamin Mkapa, had
predictable (and dire) consequences. Today, Mwinyi is remembered as
Rais Ruksa—President Permit—for his willingness to agree to almost any
form of private enterprise—along with the tacit understanding that his
cronies would benefit from inducements offered in exchange for said
permits. The Mwinyi regime is recalled with some fondness, for the early
1990s in Tanzania was a period of economic growth and rising levels of
employment as private ventures expanded. Within a few years, though,
Mwinyi's successor, Mkapa, was said to preside over *Ukapa*, an unhappy
pun on his name that means "bankrupt," "empty," or "decline." The
overall effects of these reforms are succinctly summarized in the following gloomy statement:

> The early false indications of . . . prosperity following the liberalization of the
> economy experienced in the 1980's has proved short-lived. In the second phase
> government under President Mwinyi (also referred to as the "Ruksa" era), Tan-
> zanians enjoyed what is now clearly understood to have been a false prosperity.
> Record high government expenditure, combined with printing money to finance
> deficits, and smoothly flowing donor finance, gave Tanzanians a false sense of
> prosperity because money was everywhere. From 1995 to 1999, the loopholes
> have been curtailed and the atmosphere is one of very low liquidity in spite of
> the fact that imports have jumped to 36% of GDP while exports remained at 22%
> in 1997. Low liquidity ("Ukata"), disappearance of the "money everywhere,"
> occurs while shops are filled with cheap (escaping taxes) but unaffordable low
> quality imported consumer items. This situation (also called "Ukapa") has gener-
> ally increased desperation among the people. (Due et al. 2000: 8)

What is important to note here is the particular character of the
structural reforms introduced in the late 1980s and early 1990s. In part,
structural adjustment meant the collapse of state-supported enterprise
and led to steep declines in employment as a consequence of reductions
in the civil service and the elimination of over 400 parastatal enterprises.[5]
This led in turn to the growth of private enterprise and to the increasing
expansion of a host of informal practices as Tanzanians looked to sustain
themselves by any means available. Beyond the formal (de)regulations
introduced by structural adjustment came the concomitant social and
political set of transformations that have had profound consequences for
the dynamics of urban popular cultural life in Tanzania in particular. In

a breathtakingly short period of time, much less than a decade, an array of media, from cable and satellite television broadcasting to international magazines to tabloid comics, became widely available. At the same time, a kind of consumer revolution, strongly supported by this expanding mass media, was wrought under Mwinyi: suddenly, cheap but still unafford-able low-quality imported consumer goods could be found in every town in Tanzania. What's crucial is that the reforms implemented in Tanzania in the 1980s and 1990s were not just modes of liberalization. They had a specifically neoliberal character in that they linked ideas of growth and development to the expansion of consumer markets.

In practical terms, in urban areas like Dar es Salaam, Mwanza, and Arusha, this long-term proliferation of informal economic activities, coupled with new modes of consumption, has had a very specific set of consequences. With the transformation in the character of production to a system focused on processes of creative self-fashioning facilitated by consumerism, the enterprises of Tanzania's urban informal economy began to focus on services that promoted these new forms of value. Used clothing—*mitumba*—began to be imported in much greater volume in the late 1980s (see Hansen 1999 for a comparable case in Zambia), and this had clear multiplier effects in everything from the promotion of local tailor-ing, which creatively fabricates facsimiles of global fashion houses, to the proliferation of small shoeshine stands on street corners and bus stands. This same period saw an influx of commercial media—cassette tapes, then radio and television broadcasts—that made rap music, videos, and hip hop culture more generally available to Tanzanian audiences (Perullo 2005).

Domestic consumer goods like televisions and VCRs have established a significant market, but so have less high-tech cottage industries like hand-hewn furniture manufacture. The two coincide in the production of large cupboards created to hold the new goods now available: drawers for textiles and clothing, display cases for china, a TV niche. In Arusha, I was struck by the number of modest, even dilapidated, homes and apart-ments that had such cupboards, even if they sat empty, as though they were the minimum requirements for participating in an order of value driven by domestic acquisition.

One final point relevant to neoliberalism more broadly, and to the particulars of barbershops: several observers have noted that the crisis of neoliberalism is not simply a form of rupture but a specific problem of social reproduction (Comaroff and Comaroff 2001; White 2004; Ngwane 2004). Under current conditions, massive retrenchments, the rise of consumer-ism, and the recruitment of flexible labor have resulted in a decoupling of processes of production from reproduction.[6] Hyperindividualistic processes in domains as diverse as electronic children's toys (Allison 2006), legal code ~~...2003)~~ and Pentecostal Christianity (Meyer 1998b) have made it i~~...~~ a sense of mutual belonging essential ~~...~~ cing social forms. Under such conditions, ~~...~~ idioms of gender identity, in terms of which reproduction more generally is grasped, come to the fore as points of tension and conflict. In the case at hand, the exaggerated masculinity of barbershops and their denizens, with their pretensions of membership in a global hip hop nation, bespeak an attempt to give purpose to male bodies and relations in a world where the men's productive capacity is extremely tenuous (see also Buford 1993; Dyson 2001; Perry 2004). Women are simultaneously finding relatively more opportunity in both the informal sector and the formal service sector that attempts to find a more flexible workforce, yet they also find themselves subject to greater scrutiny. They are plainly more vulnerable as the gendered terms of production and social reproduction are grappled with.

It should be clear that almost all of what I discuss, with its specific implications for urban life in Arusha, is also a global phenomenon. Tensions surrounding social reproduction and the fraught character of gender relations in a world where the solidity of social value is up for grabs are evident in phenomena as diverse as legal battles over same-sex marriage across North America, to Pentecostal Christians' concerns about the importance of righteous marriage in current spiritual warfare (Bastian n.d.), to British football hooliganism (Buford 1993). The terms in which these tensions are articulated are always contingent and highly particular forms of local expression, and this book is nothing if not a demonstration of the centrality of problems of meaning production to issues of social (re)production more broadly. But these particulars clearly lend themselves to comparison on a global scale.

1   Themes and Theories

Popular Culture in Africa and Elsewhere

Hairstyle posters in barbershops throughout Arusha are a compelling place to begin an examination of the stakes involved in popular cultural practice. They certainly sparked my initial interest in barbershops and salons in town. These posters are made up of a pastiche of images and typically include photographs of African models with contemporary hair and clothing styles; photographs of African American celebrities, either posing in fashion shots or captured by journalists; hand-drawn illustrations of scenes of barbershops with clients getting their hair cut; the name and logo of the company sponsoring the poster, often for a hair care product but occasionally for some other consumer good, like beer or soda; and always a date—sometimes an annual calendar—that confirms that the styles represented are "keeping up with the times," as they say in Arusha. Most of these posters are printed in the city of Onitcha, Nigeria, which has a long history of mass-producing cheap commercial print media, and they are regularly displayed in shops alongside hand-painted signs and among an array of images taken from the pages of popular magazines and newspapers, most of which have an international circulation. In effect, these barber posters provide a kind of exemplar for the shops themselves because the shops' aesthetic organization (its multiple pastiche images) tends to resemble these posters. This example illustrates the ways that everyday forms of popular practice in a place like Arusha are mediated by images from European and American sources, assembled and distributed through a decentralized set of producers (here, West African), and intended to appeal to a wider African audience.

Interior of a *kinyozi*

Popular culture is clearly a vehicle through which an awareness of the interconnectedness of peoples and places is cultivated. It is central to those modes of creative self-fashioning often seen to be central to neoliberal value production and to the ambiguous division between production and consumption that this generates, especially in informal economic activities of the sort I examine in this book. Yet at the same time that circuits of images, goods, and persons contributes to a sense of global interconnection, they also promote an uneasy feeling of what Ferguson (1999) calls "global disconnect." If a global distribution of value adheres in processes of consumption while (most pointedly in Africa) a declining percentage of the population has access to the resources required for such self-fashioning projects, a sense of inadequacy and exclusion from these potent forms of value has become widespread. People in Arusha are increasingly familiar with the details of the lives of people around the world, from the clothing styles and brand names made popular in African American communities to the kinds of soap operas and films watched by South Asian audiences. But at the same time, in their own accounts of the world as they see it, they

"laws, prohibitions, and restrictions" (1998: 251)—it may be the case that certain varieties of popular performance and particular modalities of practice have concrete spatial and temporal qualities that make them plausible and productive in particular historical eras. There is no doubt, for example, that Bakhtin's understanding of the carnivalesque takes much of its force from the historical context of the Middle Ages, with its focus on such consecrated institutions as the monarchy and the church. How might the forms of familiarization shift in a world dominated, as is our own, by commodity circulation and mass media? How, we might ask, do the "crowning and decrowning" rites that Bakhtin finds at the heart of the temporally circumscribed carnival offer insight into the now ever-present material prospects of boom and bust that are so often attended to in contemporary popular practice?

These two related dimensions of familiarization—a grounding in hierarchies now (perhaps distinctively) constituted on a global scale and the range of forms that familiarization takes in specific contexts—point toward more general questions of sociality and value that are at the core of this ethnographic argument. How is value produced in the contemporary globalized order we inhabit, and what kinds of meaningful intersubjective relations do these forms of value both generate and depend on? In Barber's discussion of the ways in which African popular performance forges novel connections that often cut across class, ethnic, religious, and other social divisions, she asserts that Eurocentric characterizations of the distinction between high and low culture are of little relevance in the African context. She writes that in Africa, "the 'high' if it exists at all, is not the prerogative of an ancient ruling class, but a fragmented, precarious, conflictual new elite, defined by its proximity to an outside power, but nonetheless bound up with local populations by innumerable ties of kinship, language, community membership and patronage" (Barber 1997: 3). For Barber, popular performance provides a potent symbolic space for reconfiguring these multiple bonds of interconnection.

There is much to be said in support of Barber's assertion about the innovative social possibilities of African performance, and her assessment of the links between audiences and performers is clearly insightful. It is certainly the case tha[...]sha by the way that people of disparate [...]s, education levels, and ethnic origins, to [...]s of differentiation) could gather in salons, barbershops, bars, and corners—as they might put it, *kijiweni*, "at the little stone" (a term discussed at some length below), or places of routine, informal interaction—and engage in activities and discussions in terms that would be familiar to all. I also regularly heard elites like businessmen, NGO workers, and even policemen greeting one another and their friends using the same vernacular forms and idioms typical of young unemployed and underemployed men and women across town. Some of this commonality is undoubtedly linked to Tanzania's postindependence embrace (and perhaps invention) of African socialism, the policies of *uja-maa*, and their embodiment in the humble personage of the nation's first president, Julius Nyerere. The public culture of Tanzania has clearly and strongly been suspicious of all forms of social inequality, and this vigilance continues to be influential in the country today (Askew 2002). I do not, however, mean to suggest that the expression of a shared set of cultural forms entails either a common social condition or even much in the way of collective solidarity in actual social practice or lived experience. Indeed, as I will describe, it is increasingly the case that young people in Arusha are aware of, and characterize their lives in terms of, such social processes as oppression, hardship, and conflict. In part, this contemporary expression of conflict is related to the modes of popular practice that are tied into globalized forms of culture, from South African soap operas to Swahili hip hop, global forms that (not so incidentally) Barber explicitly avoids discussing as forms of African popular culture. But aside from the shifting empirical content of African popular culture, it is also the case that power and inequality are increasingly the theme of popular practice and social interaction. These practices raise troubling questions about the nature of authority and legitimacy, as the Schwarzenegger/bin Laden parallel I mention in the introduction suggests. Popular modes of familiarization suggest that social legitimacy is not merely aspired to; it is explored, critiqued, and reinterpreted even as its effects are disseminated.

In my view, a discourse of citizenship can only dimly capture the sense of fulfillment and satisfaction that attends to the appreciation of images that abound in pop culture iconography and style—images that are saturated with displays of social power and prestige. At the same time, these are often also images of unbridled, typically amoral potency. Yet in engaging with these dimensions of excess and unrestrained fantasy, and in seeing themselves both as suppressed and allured by these forms of excess, I also argue that the many youth who participate in these practices in Arusha come to forge new understandings of belonging. Here I would concur, again, with Barber in recognizing how popular modes of performance construct sociality, generating for participants a collective sense of how they fit together and ideas about the kinds of bonds that connect them, as well as a creating a broadly shared understanding of their place in a wider world. But I would add that the value of these relationships, the meaningful content in terms of which these relations are lived and felt, is often one of oppression, frustration, and exclusion. The sense of belonging that emerges, as I aim to demonstrate throughout this work, is riven with simultaneous feelings of antagonism and conflict.

Some Approaches to Urban African Popular Performance

Attention to these matters has a distinguished, if neglected, history in African studies. There is certainly nothing new about urban life in Africa or the cosmopolitan sensibilities[1] of urbanites and emigrants adroitly incorporating diverse cultural forms as they forge dynamic social practices. Nor is the social scientific, and specifically anthropological, exploration of these projects a wholly contemporary phenomenon. As Ferguson (1999) and Schumaker (2001) have discussed in detail, the Rhodes-Livingston Institute (RLI) produced valuable studies of social transformation in urban Central Africa, where questions of cultural innovation are plainly at the fore. As Fabian notes, in spite of its overt interests in "relations, networks and classes in which urbanites were caught up, not in what people living in towns created" (1998: 7), Mitchell, Epstein, and the Wilsons, among others, with the RLI offered essential glimpses into the importance of the role of style, value, and imaginative action in the production of urban popular culture in the Zambian Copperbelt. Mitchell's study of the Kalela dance (1956) in particular has proven to be foundational for future explorations of such phenomena as ethnicity, social movements, and stylistic appropriation more broadly (Ranger 1975; Vail 1989; Argyle 1991; Matongo 1992; Ferguson 1999; Hansen 1999; Schumaker 2001).[2] Mitchell's work is relevant to mine insofar as he addresses the intersection of African urbanites' sense of exclusion regarding the colonial color bar and their simultaneous, and in many ways contradictory, enactment of what he calls "European lifestyles." For Mitchell, Kalela exemplified the ways that Africans sought "prestige" through a form of "reference group behavior" (1956: 14). In effect, African dancers on the Copperbelt made use of elements of European practice—in this case, "the most obvious and visible symbols of prestige" (Mitchell 1956: 14), namely clothing—as a standard against which to evaluate one another on a scale of prestige. There are, of course, innumerable difficulties with such a model of emulation, or "reference group behavior." Magubane (1971) is right to point out that in the political context of colonial Zambia, Kalela could not easily be seen as one that promoted emulation; yet his alternative contention that Copperbelt workers of this era had little choice but to dress in a fashion dictated to them by their colonial masters can tell us nothing about the particulars of why they should dress in the specific ways that they did. It is one thing to observe that dominant modes of dress (or patterns of consumption more broadly) were part and parcel of colonizing culture on the Copperbelt. It is quite another to account for why irregularly employed urban Kalela dancers would have devoted such time, expense, and collective interest to the cultivation of a tidy, smart appearance that is deployed in a highly competitive, public, agonistic dance performance.

Ferguson (1999, 2002) has grappled at length with the conundrums posed by questions of style, performance, and prestige as it played out in the RLI literature and Magubane's critique of it. At one level, he argues for a more performative understanding of style. The model he proposes does not depend on a strict divide between such evidently entangled social groups as Europeans and Africans, and he does not make the normative assumption that only European lifestyles are sources of prestige that those who do not pursue such practices will simply fail to acquire (Ferguson 1999). A panoply of cultural styles is available on the Copperbelt, as they are in Arusha or almost any urban community, and each of them is motivated by distinctive criteria of appropriateness and desirability. At a second level, Ferguson is concerned to ground the performance of style in a political economy of what he calls "abjection," one in which Zambians feel themselves to have been "thrown aside, expelled, or discarded" (1999: 236) in the (only apparently) newly globalized economy. In this way, the performance of emulation is less about the desirability of cosmopolitan cultural forms than it is about asserting "claims to the political and social rights of full membership in a wider society" (Ferguson 2002: 555). Ultimately, for Ferguson, the significance of cosmopolitan performance styles is determined by the strictures of this political economy[3] and embodies the efforts of Zambians—and, we must assume, other marginalized communities left abject by the "neo–world order" (Comaroff and Comaroff 2004)—to establish their rights to inclusion in global society.

Neoliberalism has had a demonstrable impact on the way people around the world perceive themselves and their prospects for the future (Comaroff and Comaroff 2000; Weiss 2004). Yet the varied forms of consciousness that have emerged under these late twentieth-century conditions are rarely expressed as appeals to a set of rights or as questions of citizenship. I take Ferguson's emphasis on rights as indicative of a wider vision of sociocultural practices. For example, the juridical notion of "membership," as Fabian (2002) points out, overly constrains the modes of belonging that are asserted in urban African (and other) social and cultural milieus. Ferguson's approach to performance—particularly his recognition that meanings are realized in practice as a kind of "know how" (1999: 98) and rarely articulated as propositional claims—offers a more nuanced way of addressing the diversity of practices on the Copperbelt than does the dualistic assumption of situational selection that characterized the Mancunian work of the RLI. Nonetheless, it shares with that work a fundamental assumption: the distinction between society as an order of material relations and culture as a realm of meaning and signification. Thus he writes, "I use the term *cultural style* to refer to *practices that signify differences* between social categories" (1999: 95, emphases in original). The modes of performance that embody such styles are enactments of underlying social categories. Cultural performance is ultimately a performance of difference, a way for actors to situate themselves in relation to social categories (1999: 96). As important as the signification of difference—or distinction, as Bourdieu (1984) has put it—are the ways that social relations are culturally constituted. Popular cultural practice, such as stylistic performance, grasped as a form of social action does not simply position actors with respect to an order of relations; it can also work to generate, organize, and above all establish the significance of these (often global) relationships.

To see power and material structures as sources of restriction and overdetermination while meanings and values are labile and indeterminate simply reproduces the untenable distinction between society and culture. In fact, cultural practices like composing rap lyrics, commiserating at barbershops, and pursuing fashionable cast-offs are explicitly communicative. They work to forge connections, to persuade, to permit struggle toward some sense of belonging, and to define the terms of that belonging. In short, the collective exigencies of producing and defining meaning have their own sets of constraints, their own histories and conventions. In this book, I work to define the lineaments of meaning production in Arusha and to specify how these are articulated within sets of sociopolitical relations that are themselves meaningfully constituted.

In concrete terms, this means that the very question of Africa's marginality or its abject condition—the circumstances that motivate so many of the debates about emulation, prestige, mimicry, and the like—is not simply a material circumstance with which African people's practices contend. Rather, the specific meaning of social relations (the margin, the modern, the local, the cosmopolitan) are themselves formulated and engaged in the course of popular practice. Far from being simply a deprived or disengaged position, margins, I argue, may be highly productive spaces from which to examine, critique, and even actively participate in a totality of relations (Lowenhaupt-Tsing 1993; Foster 2002; Axel 2002; Das and Poole 2004). This brings us back to one of Mitchell's original tensions: the simultaneous exclusion of Africans from the social world of Europeans—a form of marginalization now writ large in a neoliberal world order—and urban Africans' creative efforts to incorporate global forms of popular culture into their lives. We need to problematize the nature of this relationship by asking how it is that those on the margins grasp their relationship to that wider whole and understand their own place in what they themselves plainly take to be a globalized world. In other words, and more specifically, what kinds of consciousness of oppression and exclusion are taking hold in urban Arusha today? How is that consciousness of power put into practice, and so realized in the everyday lives and struggles of young men and women in town?

The position of the oppressed is often celebrated as much as it is lamented, and those who are relatively well-off may be even more inclined to embrace the condition of exclusion than to reject it. This set of problems has also been addressed in work that is even closer to home—that is, in urban East Africa. In his study of *beni ngoma*, another competitive dance that Mitchell and others have seen as an antecedent of Kalela, Ranger also addresses questions of power, domination, and cultural imperialism. *Beni* ("band"), which emerged in the Swahili coastal towns of Kenya and Tanganyika in the late nineteenth century, was a dance form in which teams attempted to "reproduce the effect of a military brass-band" through the use of military instruments and drills, elaborate uniforms and paraphernalia, and a hierarchy of officers with European titles (Ranger 1975: 5). In spite of this apparent emulation of powerful colonial forces on the part of these East African dance teams, Ranger insists that *beni* cannot be explained "in terms of adaptation to absolute power" (1975: 14). This is so, says Ranger, for one very solid historical reason: *beni* did not originate in those areas of the Swahili coast that were most directly under European domination (that is, the freed slave villages and mission schools), but rather in urban centers that were relatively less subject to colonial control in this period. This particular point exemplifies Ranger's more general theoretical claim: creating a successful, enduring cultural practice requires "a sufficient degree of autonomy from European control" so that colonial cultural forms may "be made use of rather than merely adopted" (1975: 15). Specifying the significance of this distinction between being "made use of" and being "merely adopted" remains profoundly important to an examination of the theoretical problems, ethnographic models, and sociocultural practices characteristic of so much of African popular culture.

Avoir Raison en Afrique: Emerging Perspectives on the Popular

The challenge of analyzing African modes of making use of diverse cultural materials has been taken up by Bayart and Mbembe in a very particular but suggestively fruitful fashion. In contrast to the pervasive imagining of Africa as a kind of nullity, a form of existence that embodies only lack and want, Mbembe insists that his work is an attempt to comprehend African political, social, and cultural realities in "relation to nothing other than themselves" (Mbembe 2001: 5, citing Bayart). How can we assess African— or any—social practices in "relation to nothing other than themselves"? At first glance, this might seem to be a willful turning away from history, a refusal to see the consequences of centuries of colonial and postcolonial exploitation on African life worlds, or a rejection of Africa's modernity. In fact, according to Mbembe, the problem is not that African studies has failed to deal with the entanglements of African societies and the West, but rather that this scholarship has tended to fixate on this encounter in terms of a fundamental divide between those who wield "power" and their "targets," and consequently to view African social realities "on the basis of dichotomies that hardly exist" (Mbembe 2001: 5). Thus, African subjects are objects of both celebration and sympathy. They are lauded for their capacity to contest and resist oppression; they are pitied for their efforts to have their humanity acknowledged by a heartless world.[4] In either case, consciousness seems but a reflex of material conditions, and it is this instrumentality that reduces African existence to a form of nothingness (Mbembe 2001: 4). As Mbembe (2001: 6–7) notes, "The criteria that African agents accept as *reasons for acting,* what their claim to *act in the light of reason* implies (as a general claim to be right, *avoir raison*), what makes their action intelligible to themselves: all of this is of virtually no account in the eyes of analysts" (emphases in original). For Mbembe, then, the challenge is to ground of African subjects in social practices "imbued with meaning" (2001: 6).

So how do we comprehend and characterize the *avoir raison* of agents without seeing them simply as "others" to more dominant projects? How do we avoid the Scylla and Charybdis of instrumentalism and culturalism so that we can see Africans as subjects for themselves while never losing sight of their enduring and indelible connectedness to Europe, the West, and the world? One commonplace response to this issue is to "problematize everything in terms of how identities are 'invented,' 'hybrid,' 'fluid,' and 'negotiated'" (Mbembe 2001: 5). Such assertions of the fluid and flex-ible are legion in Africa; it is a characteristic claim, for example, of many works interested in Swahili identity (Fair 2001; Askew 2002; Glassman 1995). There is a certain empirical obviousness about the fact that cultural forms have diffused in recombination across the world. Yet analytics that emphasize the hybrid are as much about a reluctance to offer analysis as they are critical observations about social life. As others have noted (Comaroff 1999b; Friedman 2000), the framework of hybridity is at root a rejection of claims to determinacy, a counternarrative to the overdeter-mination of master narratives of history. Methodologically, this produces a kind of extreme historical particularism. In and of itself, the observation of cultural mixing tells us little about why social life assumes the manifold forms it does. Moreover, if the mode of social practice is identified as one that is fluid and negotiated, the motive for that flexibility is usually held to be the pursuit of some limited good. In the Swahili case, prestige and status, however these are defined, are the ends to be maximized through the flexible adaptation—that is, hybrid production—of transnational cul-tural forms and practices (Fair 2001). Here, the instrumentality of such theorizing is usually evident.

What is needed, then, is some way of linking together various levels of experience and practice—the particularities of East African motiva-tions and forms of intelligibility (that is, of making meaning, *avoir raison*), the global distribution of cultural forms, and the restructuring of value production processes under the aegis of neoliberal reform—in a way that does more than simply focus on the fact of linkage itself. My contention is that popular cultural practices both permit and constrain people in spe-cific social milieus (like an East African town) to establish relations and forms of interaction among themselves and with respect to a wider, now globalized world. That wider world does not form the backdrop to the im-mediate presence of these popular practices; nor is it a general resource to be appropriated, absorbed, or reacted to. It is, rather, the very situation in which those practices are produced, and indeed, the specific character of that situation—the nature of the linkage itself—is part of what is defined and established (that is, constituted) through these popular practices. The processes through which social life in Arusha is imbued with meaning and the forms of value production that have gripped the world since the latter decades of the twentieth century are part of a common purview.

The End of Mimicry: Global Aspirations

In popular cultural practices throughout Arusha, social relations are both formulated and acted on. Gender relations, for example, reflect men and women's understanding of the way that social reproduction in the current era is rife with the possibility of deception and dissimulation. Relations forged and fought between young, intermittently employed men in town—in barbershops, but also in minivan transport, the tourist trade, and other jobs in the service sector—are characterized by the production of social values that are informed by the sense of their status as marginalized global, social actors, even as these values work to recast the very meanings of marginalization and global interconnection. That is, the meanings of social relations are defined in the concrete specificities of cultural practices even as these practices are produced by the social and material conditions in which they are situated. It is thus impossible to reduce the nature of these highly reflexive processes to terms like *emulation, reference,* or *mimicry* because even as people in Arusha grasp globalized forms of cultural production as sources of value, these actors' engagement with those forms is designed to transform, never simply to reproduce, that value by situating it within specific social contexts—for example, by remaking the meaning of world religious movements like Islamic reform and Pentecostalism within the context of rap music performances. These engagements with popular forms also redefine the relations of people in town among themselves with respect to the wider world, so that, for example, that status of a disreputable *muhuni* ("thug") is recast as a celebrated figure who commands respect and wealth in the signifying practice of hip hop. There is no doubt that coercive interests, whose power resides in the hands of an infinitesimally small cadre of producers and distributors, have exerted their efforts to ensure the global dissemination of a narrow set of cultural styles. But it is also the case that the concrete forms and representations that have gained the widest currency commonly embody the position of being outcast and degraded; these representations also present a pose that is overtly critical of those who hold power. Far from aiming to endorse or emulate the values of a global cultural elite, they call into question the distinctions between the elite and the powerless, and they turn subversion into a form of solidarity.

In short, the one-way model of the "status holding group" in relation to those who "copy/mimic/refer to" them, as well as the notion of marginalized Africans demanding rights for all of the privileges of global citizenship, are overly simplistic; they exemplify "dichotomies that hardly exist" (Mbembe 2001: 5). The popular practices of Arusha's young men and women are not just attempts to reproduce the sources of value in the wider world or pleas for full recognition by global society. Rather, they are attempts to transform the world so that what qualifies as value and belonging can be defined and established by these social actors themselves.

Rather than consider these processes in terms of emulation or pleas for citizenship, it is much more productive to recognize in them the performance of exaggeration and excess. Consider (one of) Žižek's take(s) on excess. He writes:

> "truth" resides in the excess of exaggeration as such . . . the harmonious balanced totality is not the "truth" within which particular exaggerations, deprived of their excess, must find their proper place; on the contrary, *the excess of "exaggeration" is the truth which undermines the falsity of the balanced totality.* In other words, in the choice between the Whole and its Part, one has to choose the Part and elevate it to the Principle of the Whole—this "crazy" reversal introduces the dynamics of the process. . . . [T]he subject emerges in the event of the "exaggeration," when a part exceeds its limited place and explodes the constraints of balanced totality. (1997: 92, emphases in original)

Žižek recognizes the dynamic character of excess as structured by the Part/Whole relationship of balanced totalities. Excess, therefore, derives from the dominant totality; indeed, it assumes a role as the "Principle of the Whole." Yet, and for the same reason, it calls into question the very notion of totality as such. Applying this insight to actual social practice is notoriously difficult (witness Žižek's idiosyncratic and delightfully inconsistent efforts at cultural analysis), but it does seem relevant to urban African popular cultural processes. The excess and exaggeration of hip hop posing, as well as Kalela's fastidious attention to a smart appearance, clearly take part of their force from the prevailing sociocultural orders in which they are performed. The styles appropriated and elaborated in all such instances resonate with a wider, powerful order of signs. Even if their objective is not to pose a challenge to that order, through mockery, mimicry, or overt resistance, the mode of exaggeration itself unsettles the assured stability of this same "balanced totality" by focusing on formal elements—or parts—that are elevated to a level of equivalence to the order as a whole. This has the potential, as Žižek notes, to "[explode] the constraints" of the totalizing system.

Once the constraints of the whole have been dislocated in this way, we can understand the kinds of popular practice I address in this book, not as emulation or imitation, but rather as forms of aspiration (Appadurai 2004; Comaroff and Comaroff 2004; Argenti 2005). Aspirations invoke a clear,

naumwa!'" (And if the white man said "I feel sick" [lit., I feel pain], the House Nigga replied, "I'm hurting!"). Staf added, "But the Field Nigga, he didn't live with the white man, and he didn't care about him."

Today, both continued, there are House Niggas and Street Niggas. And, added Ahmed with great emphasis, "that's us, we're Street Niggas." Here, he departed, if only slightly, from the African American context and pointedly proclaimed, "We're Street Niggas. We don't go to work for the Indians (*Wahindi*)! We don't have a 'boss' who tells us '*Kaa chini!*' (Sit down!). We don't depend (*hatutegemee*) on anyone else. We have our own work (*kazi*), and our own house (*nyumba*). We have our freedom (*uhuru*). We don't have a 'boss' (*Hatuna 'boss'*). It's only the House Nigga that goes to work for the *Wahindi*."

This disquisition offers a remarkable concatenation of contexts and places, persons and memories. These sometime barbers, still in their teens, knew the verses and felt their resonance. Ahmed and Staf are, as they put it, "mental," or "conscious" (both English terms in the vernacular) of their environment (*mazingira*).[2] Their expression of this consciousness proposes an entire history in microcosm, a history of an African diaspora, inflected back, as it were, through Africa, a history of which Ahmed and Staf are a part, and which they continue to make. Moreover, the threads of these assertions intertwine with the town of Arusha itself, its localities and identities, past and present. Arusha began as a colonial garrison, forged in the slave trade and its aftermath, and this origin has left its legacy. Still, the neat fit of plantation bosses and Field Niggas, with Tanzanian *Wahindi* and Street Niggas, is complicated by the fact that the caravan trade of the nineteenth century, which German and British administrations came both to depend on and dominate, consisted of a complex mixture of Asians and Africans in Arusha. Many Africans (including, by their own accounts, the ancestors of both Ahmed and Staf) acquired important currencies of respectability and reputation through their collaboration with agents of the slave trade, including Asians, Muslims, and Swahili (Glassman 1995; Peligal 1999). In the colonial era, Asians came to enjoy relative, but only relative, privilege, explicitly under the German administration and implicitly under the British, constrained as they were under the terms of their mandate. This privilege, in Arusha at least, was perhaps most acutely felt with respect to housing and the control of space in this densely settled and desirable highland town (Peligal 1999). And so the force of a claim to "our own house" is a powerful evocation of colonial inequities still inscribed in the street. To take this concordance further, the language of these young men's declaration draws directly on the discourse of decolonization, with its demands for freedom (*uhuru*) and self-reliance (*kujitegemea*). These were indisputably the most central tenets of Julius Nyerere's African socialism, a philosophy and program indelibly associated with the Arusha Declaration. The guys at Bad Boyz Barbering worked each day literally in the shadow of the towering torch monument to Nyerere's pronouncement.

It is further telling that this exquisitely particular testament to Arusha's oppressive prospects is articulated as a historical consciousness, the terms of which are disseminated by means of electronic media with a truly global distribution. This translocal presence, simultaneously enacted and embodied in the immediacy of interpersonal relations (*Naumwa*! "I'm hurting!"; *Kaa chini!* "Sit down!"), offers a potent means of enabling and legitimating these young men's claim to entitlement. Such claims, though, are inevitably linked to new forms—and especially a new consciousness— of exclusion and rejection, which are expressly rooted in the same globalized processes that expound emancipation. Thus, the friction between Asians and Africans has clearly been exacerbated by the movements of capital and the expansion of market forces ushered in during the era of neoliberal reform, which continue to radically reshape Tanzanian economy and society (Tripp 1996). This conflict thus exemplifies the paradox that Geschiere and Nyamnjoh (2000: 423) ably describe: "Political liberalization seems to have strengthened a decidedly nonliberal tendency towards closure and exclusion." The explosion of privatization and mobility that makes possible the expansion of Tanzania's informal sector, and the modes of consciousness that characterize it, has also made palpable the antagonisms and restraints in this new world order.

As crucial as the entanglements of memory, person, and translocation embedded in Ahmed and Staf's discussions with me may be—and I do not wish in any way to diminish their significance—their commentaries are not simply symbolically rich discursive forms. The assertive claims like those that these young men readily made to me are proclamations that fly in the face of an analytical stance. Though they pose as interpretive schemes, the force and meaning of these declarations derive from the insistence with they are affirmed at least as much as from the information they report. As the visceral energy of Ahmed and Staf's accounts show, these exchanges are intended as challenges and provocations. They cannot simply be taken as ideas or commentaries, because in effect, they foreclose further discussion. Surely the truth with which they are conveyed cannot be countered or disproved in discursive debate. In this sense, they are performances, and what is more, they are enactments of violence of a particular sort. They emerge through a situation of confrontation that is simultaneously recollected and anticipated, retrospective and prospective. As Ahmed and Staf's cross-referencing of Field Niggas and barbers, bosses and *Wahindi* exemplifies, the violence that characterizes these confrontations is also often a violence done to others that is made to live in the violence of contemporary and immediate conditions. Considering the enactment of violence in this way—violence as eminently social and shared, and as the definitive and potent force of that sociality—permits me to engage encounters like the one described less as the outcome of encompassing politicoeconomic shifts, or even as the lived experience of widespread social upheaval, but rather as themselves constitutive actions through which the nature of reality is made real and consequential. If social practices like these are more enactments than arguments, I cannot hope to persuade readers of their truth through my own analyses. My ambition is to describe crucial, characteristic dimensions of these performances in the hopes of conveying the viability of the world in which these young men in Arusha actively participate, and so confirm the truth of the claims they proffer.

Presence, Provocation, and the Subject in Performance

When I went back to Bad Boyz the following week, I met up with Ahmed and a few of the other young men who had been there on Saturday. Sitting in a barber's chair in his Manchester United jersey was a guy, a little younger than the rest, who I hadn't yet met. He was Shabani, a younger brother of one of the regular barbers in the shop. I was quiet and probably too self-conscious when I arrived, pleased to have found the company of these guys who seemed as happy to have me around. Shabani regarded me a bit warily. Falling into the familiar habit of playing ethnographer with him, I looked across the shop walls and asked him what he made of one magazine photo. The picture showed the rapper, Eazy-E, now deceased but once a member of the seminal gangsta rap group, N.W.A., pouring out a forty-ounce bottle of malt liquor on the curb. Here was a generic performance I recognized, an oblation for the dead, and maybe, I thought, an act that Tanzanians would appreciate as a kind of ancestral libation, another global icon looping its loops back to them. "Why is he doing that?" I asked Shabani. He answered in plain English, "Maybe it's because of his pain." I nodded hesitantly, and asked him what kind of pain this might be. "The pain of racism in your country." Here I nodded a little less sheepishly, "Yeah, that's true. That's possible." Shabani now rose from the barber chair, "*Unakubali?*" (You agree?) he asked. Whether he was irate or shocked, I could not yet tell. I nodded once again—and this time Ahmed and his friends pitched in, too, confirming for Shabani that we had just had a conversation over the weekend in which I really did denounce racism and economic injustice in the United States ("Just listen to the verses," I told them). Shabani smiled broadly and firmly shook my hand.

What had happened here? Clearly, the tenor of this face-to-face encounter, jammed in the narrow confines of this shop, was confrontational. The aloof questions I posed were entirely inappropriate to the venue and to an as yet indeterminate association with Shabani that I had barely initiated. Idle chatter thus became the occasion for provocation. My appearance in the shop, my pursuit of a particular purpose, my attempts to elicit responses from others, my inquisitive detachment—in short, my *presence*—were antagonistic. This mere presence was clearly not a neutral position, for it posed an affront to the different modes of substantiating presence available to the guys in the *kinyozi*. The provocative character of Shabani's response to me discloses these modes of establishing presence in an urban element, modes that exemplify struggle and strife and so depend on the commitment of all those who inhabit this element in order to endure it. There is literally no room in this place for those who do not vigilantly insist on their claims to it.

If provocation, as I am suggesting, is characteristic of the way that presence is established in milieus such as these, it is crucial to recognize that these confrontations are not simply recalcitrance and resentment. They are also highly productive. Shabani's claims in this moment derive a good deal of their power from the way they refer immediately to my position in his world. Apathetic observations on images of celebrity were received as challenges that cut to the core of a person's substance, his pain. Again, this substance inescapably implicates my presence; Eazy-E's pain makes me, and certainly my country, culpable. This direct reference to, and grappling with, my presence suggests that provocation is enacted here as a means of inclusion. By meeting my distanced comments with direct confrontation, Shabani produced a situation that incorporated me (my exemplary status as an *mzungu*, my citizenship, my authority as a speaker of both English and Swahili) into his assertions about what really mattered in this scene. My presence demanded an acknowledgment of his assertions: either my acquiescence or my refutation would surely be proof of American racism. In this way, my participation in this encounter, shaped by Shabani's unmistakable incitement, could be taken as evidence of his entitlement to his own position, to his own presence. All of the performative features of this clash, our footing detached compared with committed interlocutors (Goffman 1981; Hanks 1995), the counterpoise of questions and proclamations, were deployed by Shabani in a highly productive fashion so as to affirm a conception of the world, which I was required to share, and our place in it.

The scenes of conflict—not so much confrontations, perhaps, as defused skirmishes—are plainly performances, and like all (successful) performances, they not only draw on a presumed, shared reality, they also work to bring about the truth of the reality they enact (Austin 1962). The antagonistic style emerges out of and demonstrates the intrinsic tensions of a contentious world. This constitutive potential is a general characteristic of performance, as many scholars have shown (Hymes 1974; Bauman 1977; Bourdieu 1991; Hanks 1995). But more particular to the performances I have described is the way that they configure the subject of the performance, the active agent who motivates the interactions and tells the tale. Ahmed, Staf, and Shabani offer potent and provocative assertions about the nature of the world, but it is crucial to recognize that they do so from a position that they hold to be one of dispossession. In effect, acknowledging their claims to entitlement and belonging entails conceding the deprivations to which they have been subjected. The force of these young men's assertions lies, to a significant degree, in the conviction that their ability to make assertions on their own behalf has been denied to them. Moreover, the pain of racism, or the brutality of slavery, like the abject position of a Street Nigga, are seized on as highly valued attributes. These young men's performances indicate that subjugation may be grasped as highly compelling means of creating social coherence. In such a turbulent context, the authority of the subject who speaks and professes to propose valid, even irrefutable, contentions is confirmed by their fractured, marginalized position.

Invincible Genres

This production of agency amounts to much more than an individualistic act of self-construction on the part of young men. Rather, it is a central, dynamic tension in performance that organizes a framework of relations, strains, hierarchies, and practices through which constructive interaction is facilitated. The interplay of dispossession as a legitimation of entitlement is itself a kind of genre in a range of performative encounters in Arusha today. It is a recurrent theme not only in the practices of young men in barbershops, but also in the antagonistic exchanges of any number of people in a wide range of contexts. My interest in this generic feature of commonplace performances might be seen to raise problems of normative description or cultural uniformity. It should be clear that there are multiple voices at play in Arusha's street life. This is self-evident when we appreciate the indispensable role that conflict plays in this world and in these encounters. Confrontational engagements patently presume multiplicity; indeed, they are incomprehensible without it. This is not to celebrate heterogeneity or to show the difference of innumerable voices (Abu-Lughod 1991; but see Lamb 2000:37 for a lucid critique of such an approach), but to show how a world can be synthesized and even given ontological weight, to be made compelling, to have a hold over those who act on it and within it. This synthesis is often achieved by means of "social typifications of framed interaction" (Lewis 1999: 540)—that is, shared, routinized genres of performance.

If we move outside but just alongside the barbershop, we can find an example of a performance genre in Arusha that reveals how such typifications can achieve a form of compelling truth. That genre concerns the stylistic form of minivan (*daladala*) transport. The world of minivan drivers and passengers is remarkably complex. Although most businesses in Arusha cater to a clientele that is more or less predictable (it is unusual, for example, to find young girls without any independent income spending much money in hair salons—and one absolutely never finds men getting their hair cut in a salon), minivans carry literally everyone in Arusha, young and old, the relatively well off and the virtually destitute. In a town that is rapidly expanding to include vast periurban residential zones, the *daladala* are virtually the only means of affordable transportation available to everyone.[3] Further, minivans lie on the uneasy border between official and informal sectors of Tanzania's economy. They require, for example, licensing for the drivers and permits for the owners of the vans. Fares must be clearly posted in the vehicle, and passengers actually enforce these prices by coming to the defense of fellow riders who claim to be cheated. I was surprised in the summer of 2000 to find that all of the minivans in Arusha actually complied with the district regulations requiring each van to paint a color on its side that corresponded to its officially sanctioned route; in the same period, I knew that many other informal businesses were shutting down (or taking long lunches) in order to avoid paying revenue collectors for business licenses. It will also be obvious to anyone who has ever ridden on a Tanzanian *daladala* (the name derives from what was once the standard fare, a large five-shilling coin, in the vernacular a *dala*, "dollar") that this official compliance is belied by the entire experience of driving and riding in the vans. The bench and bucket seats of these (mostly) Toyotas and Nissans are ripped out so that the vehicles can be fitted with extra rows of benches, each adorned with a flimsy fold-out seat attached to the end, all of which ensures that every *daladala* will be overflowing with passengers and cargo. Vans may have their routes painted on their sides, but this does little to prevent crews and drivers from surreptitiously traveling down alternative routes when they suspect they may come across more passengers (and fewer traffic cops). *Daladala* drivers, licensed or not, are also notorious for continuously smoking weed (*bhangi*), which Tanzanians say helps to maintain alertness and sustain their nerve for the grueling hours and the breakneck pace needed to turn even a meager profit in this fearsome business.

The ferocious competition of these *daladala* is extremely public—much more, for example, than the competition between barbershops—and is eagerly publicized by their crews and drivers. The conductors must loudly advertise their destination ("Kijenge! Kijenge! Kijenge! Kijenge!" or "Sakina! Sakina! Sakina!"), usually hanging out of the open sliding doors to attract pedestrians and would-be passengers. Drivers routinely cut one another off at passenger terminals along the main road, hoping to be in position to load up the greater number of paying customers. The larger buses that travel regularly back and forth to Moshi (about 100 kilometers to the east) are especially known for their efforts to get passengers from one town to the other as quickly as possible: winning conductors in these races can be seen hanging off the bus, belittling their competition as they pass. Not surprisingly, traveling in minivans, while convenient (if you aren't claustrophobic) and cheap, is seen as inherently dangerous. I would emphasize, though, that the dangers of this practice, which evidently derives from the intensity of entrepreneurial competition, are really only exaggerated, more desperate illustrations of what is recognized as a wider characteristic of economic activity, and even sociality more generally, in Arusha as a whole. The unkempt boys who shout from the open side doors of minivans live a life more tenuous than the idle Street Niggas at Bad Boyz, whose routines are yet again more rough-and-tumble than the lives of cooks and carriers that work for safari companies—jobs to which many *daladala* crews, as well as barbers, often aspire. But each is characterized, even lauded, for the way that it embraces competition, and in particular the conditions that make them tough, fierce, and implacable and so permit them to endure hardship.

There is much stylistic similarity, broadly shared and readily comprehensible, that cuts across a wide socioeconomic swath in Arusha. This stylistic repertoire, which also permits a wide range of variation, is further exemplified, in a highly revealing fashion, by an important set of discourse genres (Hanks 1995) that are especially associated with *daladala* transport. This genre is the decorative signs and slogans that are painted on the windshields of these vans. Already recognized as an important genre of everyday life elsewhere in Africa (Lawuyi 1997; see also Weiss 1999), these slogans are apt expressions and enactments of the social concerns I have already described. There is, to be sure, a degree of variation in the form that these slogans take in Arusha, but I feel justified in focusing on one particular category of such signs that, I argue, is exemplary of a common perspective in Arusha. The slogans I am describing as a genre here consist of a simple English-language phrase frequently combined with a name that functions as the *daladala*'s motto. It is the meaningful characterization of one's self as a recognizable type of subject that is especially arresting about these mottoes. To give one example, a *daladala* that I regularly took was emblazoned with the words "West Coast" in a decal on the top margin of the front windshield; across the rear windshield was the name "Carlos the Jackal" above the image of a pistol; all words and images were cut from the same silver foil. "West Coast" refers not just to places like California in the United States, but also to the style of gangsta rap that, as all aficionados in Arusha recognize, is associated with this region. Carlos the Jackal, guns blazing, is the notorious international assassin who was finally arrested in 1994 after eluding capture for decades. This example is a complete version of this genre, including, as it does, both a slogan and a name. These elements are also complementary: "Carlos" exemplifies the fundamental qualities of hard-core gangsterism associated with "West Coast." Similar examples include "Pain in Me" as a slogan paired with the name "Milosevic," and the phrase "On My Own" linked to the name "Pol Poty" [*sic*].

Even more common than these complete forms is the simple naming of buses and minivans. In 1999 and 2000, some of the more common names were "Sani Abacha" and "Cosovo" [*sic*]. It would be difficult to think of these signatures as advertisements designed to attract customers to the services of minivan transport; one large bus that shuttled tourists from the Kilimanjaro airport to downtown Arusha a few times each day bore the name "OSAMA" in large black lettering atop its rear windshield— hardly a moniker to assuage the apprehensions of safari-going visitors to Tanzania. And lest we think these mottoes codify a simple anti-Western reflex (and tourists be damned!), I would point out that "Monica" was an exceedingly popular name, although "Clinton" and "Bill" were perhaps the most prevalent of all.

Keeping in mind the performative context of intensely competitive entrepreneurialism in the course of recklessly dangerous transport that is the occasion for these names and slogans, how can we assess these minivan poetics? I asked Samuel, himself a professional painter who had painted more than a few such *daladala* mottoes in his time, what he made of these terms. As Samuel put it, *vijana* (that is, teenagers or youth, but especially young men[4]) like to show that they are in the know, that they keep up with international events and follow reports of global celebrity. But, he added, the kind of celebrities they particularly embraced and identified with were those who were recognized for (or, more accurately, were notorious for) their *ujeuri*, loosely translated as "invincibility"—loosely because the invincibility so admired in the qualities of one who possesses *ujeuri* (that is, a *mjeuri* [sing.] or *wajeuri* [pl.]) is certainly not the result of having ab-solute power or exercising total control. Although standard dictionaries translate *ujeuri* (*jeuri* in some Swahili-speaking communities) as "violence, outrage, brutality, assault, injustice, oppression . . . tyranny," even this horrific litany does little to convey the character of those, such as Monica, whose power is not exercised through brute domination; nor can it tells us much about why *wajeuri* would be especially admired, particularly by those—like the unemployed, lumpen, restless, and eminently expendable young men who typically form *daladala* crews—who we might assume to be most likely to suffer under such tyranny.

To grasp the force of this admiration and the braggadocio with which minivans bearing the names of such brutal figures sally forth, we need to understand what it is that makes power both admirable and available to public interpretation. How does the power of the *mjeuri* present itself? How does it appear to others in the world? In what way do the conditions of this exercise of power speak to or exemplify the insecure conditions of Arusha's youth? There can be no doubt that Slobodan and Osama are widely known figures throughout Arusha in the present day. No one that I knew of would defend the actions of these men or praise the merits of the causes for which they committed their atrocities. Many of the young men I know in Arusha are Muslim, and Bosnian Muslims were a prin-cipal target of Serbian ethnic cleansing; all of these men and women are Tanzanian and certainly know that their own territory was subject to bin Laden's terror. The acts of these men (and the acts of Abacha, Carlos the Jackal, Pol Pot, and even, in their own ways, of Clinton and Lewinsky) were felt by all I knew to be unspeakably horrific; but there is something in this very unspeakability that neatly conveys the potency of their actions as well as the meaning of *ujeuri*. For as impossible as their actions may sound, these notorious figures were able to carry them out—indeed, to carry them out with relative impunity. The force of their celebrated exploits lies in the fact that they are transgressive, that they violate what can be said or done, and so gain notoriety in the saying and doing. As transgressive acts, the feats of these *wajeuri* may be terrifying (even tyrannical) or titillating, but they must be known to flout what is permissible if they are to be recognized as noteworthy.

Mere transgression, though, is not sufficient to qualify as *ujeuri*. To cite a related counterexample, Oprah Winfrey is widely known throughout East Africa (and undoubtedly the rest of Africa). Although she is renowned for her celebrity status and incomprehensible wealth as a black women in a white man's country, the majority of local (tabloid) press stories about Winfrey, to say nothing of the conversations in barbershops and salons that are sure to accompany the reception of media report about her, turn on questions of her sexuality—specifically, the strong suspicion that she is a lesbian. This is a popular rumor, pedestrian and unremarkable, perhaps even predictable in a global ecumen of celebrity images. I cite this instance simply to point out that although Winfrey is well known and suspected, even presumed, to be transgressive in a prominent fashion, these transgressions certainly do not make her a *mjeuri*. Her celebrity, and indeed her celebrated, if fabricated, trespasses, do not make her notorious and imposing in the style of Pol Pot, or even Monica Lewinsky—and I would venture to guess that she would never be enshrined in the pantheon of minivan stylings. To understand why some transgressions make for compelling sources of demonstrative expression while others make for endlessly fascinated stories in popular rumor mills, we have to position the subjects of these transgressions in a context of power. Oprah Winfrey, for all the speculation with which her persona circulates, is well known to be successful, beloved, and fabulously popular in the United States and elsewhere. Slobodan Milošević, it's fair to say, does not enjoy the same support and goodwill. He is a well-known figure of contempt, subject to international condemnation, indicted in the world court, and bombed by the most powerful armies in the world. And yet Milošević endures through intense hostility and confrontation. Even an all-out assault on his position and resources was unable, at least through the summer of 2000, to curtail his vicious aggressions. It is no paradox, therefore, that the most prominent international opponent of the Serbian tyrant, Bill Clinton, was equally embraced. He, too, survived the open confrontation of his tireless enemies and emerged unscathed, even as he fully confessed his transgressive actions. To pull the strands of this perspective together, the *ujeuri* exhibited by these notorious characters entails the continuous pursuit of transgressive acts when confronted with the aggressive antagonism of authoritative and dominant opponents. *Wajeuri* defy the very power they provoke. As Samuel suggested when he told me of their embrace of *ujeuri*, "Young people do not love Sani Abacha, but they know no one can 'force' him to do what they want." The *mjeuri* emerges as invincible: challenged by seemingly all-powerful antagonists, he carries out actions that anyone can recognize as worthy of outrage and contempt, yet nonetheless lives to fight another day.

Seen from this perspective, the discourse genre of the minivan nickname exemplifies the same characteristics that animate active participants in barbershop encounters. Like Pol Pot and Milošević, the subject positions of Ahmed, Staf, and Shabani as speakers benefit from their relative marginalization and suppression—a position that perhaps was made even more evident when I was their interlocutor. The vitality and validity of their assertions is, in effect, confirmed by the strength of the forces that impose this suppression. Young men's own transgressive personae as Street Niggas, and even more commonly as thugs (*wahuni*), in the face of such suppression is further evidence of both the depredations they endure and the fact of their endurance. Clearly these responses to power, even a power that establishes coercive and violent constraints, are never simply sanctifications of losses suffered or evidence that communal continuities can transcend brutal ruptures. Rather, these youth in Arusha are seizing stances of a legitimacy verified by the potency of the overarching domination to which they have been subjected.

The organization and production of *ujeuri* as a social value through which oppression and entitlement are dialectically elaborated is neatly encapsulated in these *daladala* slogans. We can further recognize that these mottoes are not mere ideas or representations of a shared public ethos. Rather, they are icons of the intensely competitive and grueling activities in which the minivans and their crews are constantly involved. Further, the slogans have a metapragmatic function (Silverstein 1993; Hanks 1995), offering explicit self-characterizations and further promoting the esteem of the *daladala* by shaping the way their practices are to be interpreted by the public. Indeed, insofar as such minivans proudly display names that incite scandal, even hostility, the transport crews demonstrate their own invincibility by their capacity to persist in their labors and overcome the contempt that these signatures invoke. The *ujeuri* of minivans is thus a dimension of their socioeconomic status and competition, of their fast-paced, dangerous driving and conducting, as well as of the signifying practices by which these actions are publicized and known.

Policing Performance

The poetics and performance of minivan transport provide an apt illustration of broader sociocultural processes in Arusha. Although confronted with a host of social, economic, and political constraints, *daladala* crews simultaneously concretize the specific meanings of these particular conditions by enacting their irrefutable truth. A tenuous world of conflict, marginality, and triumphant bravado is promulgated and lived in by means of these enactments. Taking these synthetic possibilities of a rather general process (that is, the daily life minivan traffic) as our cue, we can return to some more particular instances of performance as well as a different genre of performance. Again, my aim is to explore how the enactment of sociocultural values, like *ujeuri,* can create a frame of action in which participants feel their claims have validity—in short, a world to which they belong. It should come as no surprise to find that young people in Arusha often find themselves in situations where they feel that this sense of belonging and the authority of their views are not respected. There are routinized ways in which these aspirations are actively denied to them by a host of forces. The performative genre I want to consider in some depth emerges out of just such a context of refusal and obstruction, and it concerns commonplace encounters between young men, like those tenuously employed in barbershops, and members of Arusha's police force. For reasons that will be discussed (if they are not already obvious), youth like Ahmed, Staf, Shabani and their companions are especially vulnerable to intimidation and harassment by the police. However, it is not the mere condition of their relative incapacity that motivates the performances that record and recirculate reports of these encounters. The enactment of a lack of power, even by people of some means in town, in the face of capricious state authority is often essential to the production of the social values, such as competitiveness, provocation, or *ujeuri,* through which their world is organized. In the course of exchanging and participating in these performances, which explicitly invoke the possibility of violence, young men explicitly articulate and demonstrate the criteria of belonging that they hope to realize among themselves, and that they may equally use to identify those who do not belong.

One afternoon I heard a group of friends, coworkers on the staff of a private home in town, expressing their concern for one of their fellows, Robert, who had not arrived for work that day. Word had reached them that Robert had been picked up by the police the night before, and the group's employer had gone to bail him out. As it turned out, this proved to be an arduous undertaking, not just because of the typical bureaucratic delays of police procedure, but because the police had taken Robert all the way across town to detain him in a facility remote from the town center and from where he originally had been rousted. Robert's employers were concerned that he would be upset, even distraught, by his arrest, but when I spoke with Robert the next day, he was not unnerved by these events. Rather, as he said, he was really angry about the way he had been treated. The police, he told me, had picked him up because they were checking identity cards, and Robert's had expired a few years earlier. "Identity cards," scoffed Robert. "Who carries an identity card? You can't even get them renewed when you need them. This is just a lie!"[5] The police had been rounding up young men (many of them coming off *daladala* on their way to work in town), demanding to see their identity cards. Of course, Robert continued, the police knew full well that none of these young men would have identity cards, but these youth "don't have the ability to do anything about it." Given the lack of proper identification, the police gave them a choice: pay a fine of 3,000 shillings (roughly $4) on the spot, or "we'll put you inside" (*tutakuweka ndani*, a colloquialism for imprisonment). When they took Robert to the first point of incarceration, he told them he had no cash on him (3,000 shillings being three days' wages), and this lead the police "to swing [him] around" (*kumzungusha*) to the other side of town. "Thieves!" he cried. "They knew they could get money from me because I have a job. They have no right!" (*Hawana haki!*).

Over the next few days, I discovered that Robert's mishap was hardly unique. All over town, I found young men talking, in similar terms and with equal measures of outrage, about the injustices committed by a pernicious police force. It was all too easy to find groups of young men, cowed and restless, huddled together on street corners under the supervision of a baton-bearing police officer. Before detailing the formal qualities of this animated talk, let me provide a bit of contextualization for the police actions because crucial features of this broader context not only shape young men's response to police practice, but they are also referred to directly when young men discuss these ongoing activities. The events I am describing took place in mid-July in Arusha. The time and place are not simply fortuitous: they mark the onset of the height of the "season," as it is known to many young men around town. The high tourist season in Arusha is absolutely critical to the entire Tanzanian economy. Arusha is the epicenter of the tourist industry, poised as it is at the gateway to the Serengeti and Ngorongoro Crater, as well as a host of other national game parks. It is also a popular destination for those looking to find guides and porters to make the trek up Mount Kilimanjaro to the east. Tourists are warned to be wary of local tour operators and touts who offer to arrange safaris and treks on the streets—"flycatchers," as they are called in English—but usually just abscond with the tourists' down payments without providing any service. Partly in an effort to safeguard the flood of extraordinarily precious tourists arriving in town, Arusha's police come out in force to round up suspicious idlers and vagrants who, in the police's view at least, are not only likely to become involved in malicious schemes, but will also create an unattractive appearance that may keep tourists from promoting the town's refinements.

This, at least, is the official view of suspicious youth in town. The young men under suspicion see the arrival of tourist season rather differently. In their view, the arrival of tourists brings dollars, and the police see this as an opportunity to line their pockets. On the one hand, keeping idle youth off the streets might ease the competition for tourist dollars; many people I knew suspected that police had their own ties to tour guides and safari companies from whom they received kickbacks in exchange for their winnowing of the informal sector. More frequently, police were suspected of taking advantage of the arrival of tourist dollars by expanding the grasp of their corruption. High season means *rushwa*—bribery—because police assume they can extract revenue from young men who are likely to have a (very) little more disposable income during the tourist season. A few men and women also pointed out to me that this high season (in 1999) would be especially bad in terms of corruption because rumor had it that in light of stricter adherence to structural adjustment procedures, the Mkapa government was not paying full wages to the police. In the midst of a loud tirade among barbers and clients in Casino Hair Cutting about the threat of police harassment, Faisel pulled me aside to explain the nature of official extortion. For Faisel, this kind of bribery was the result of life in a city like Arusha, where a good deal of money circulates through unofficial circuits. Most specifically, he referred not to the tourist trade, but to Tanzanite mining in Mererani, the trading for which is centered in Arusha. A great deal of money moves in tiny sums, Faisel quite rightly observed, and this motivates *makops* (plural of *kops*, from the English "cops") to cast a wide net in the hopes of reeling in some of these covert funds. Moreover, there were suspicions that a large find at Mererani had just come in, and the police needed to get their cut. This sense that wealth is tied to a conspiracy of hidden forces (see also Comaroff and Comaroff 1999b), even in such public trades as tourism, contributes to the feelings of resentment and frustration that are routinely tapped into in discussions of police corruption—a corruption that is unconcealed and overt, an official, parasitic counterpart to the unofficial, erratic production of mining and tourist dollars.

The corruption that is routinely vilified as an impediment to development in nations like Tanzania is explicitly understood to be grounded in the way that global fluctuations in value, like tourism revenues and mining receipts, mesh with local instruments of authority, social policy, and employment opportunities. More importantly, this reflexive understanding of Tanzania's tenuous location in this encompassing context informs the standardized complaints levied by young men against the police. In effect, they marshal support for their claims of exclusion and mistreatment by reference to this global position and to their own standing within that global order in a way that lends even greater force to their assertions, moving their complaints, as it were, onto a far broader stage with much greater implications. In part, we might say that the terms of the dialectic of oppression and entitlement are exaggerated, crystallized, and so sharpened when seen through this translocal filter. The injustices suffered become more oppressive, and so their challenge becomes more valid, in this broader view. Thus, in the midst of a raucous denunciation of the cops at Seven-Eleven Haircut, another barber, Seifu, announced that what was happening to *vijana*—"youth"—in Arusha's streets was "just the same as what happened to Tupac in *Gridlock'd,*" a movie that had recently played to huge audiences at the Metropole Cinema in town whose denouement turned on a racist, corrupt police force setting up this hip hop hero. Tupac's undoing in this globally recognized forum not only parallels these young men's experience, but also compounds its significance and clarifies its truth. At the same time, in the views of Arusha's youth, the transparent nature of official corruption also suggests that the apparent power of the cops might be tied to their ultimate dependency on forces over which they have little control. As we shall see, complaints about police harassment are as likely to belittle the ultimate powerlessness of the police as they are to decry their wanton excesses.

Shortly after my discussion with Robert, I visited with a group of guys at Bad Boyz. This *kinyozi* caters to a younger, somewhat less respectable clientele. Here, I came on a couple of guys already engaged in a full-blown discussion about *makops*. One of the guys, Hussein, a tall, well-built man who worked as a barber at Bad Boyz, was describing what was clearly a quite recent encounter with the police. Hussein insisted he had been grabbed by the cops that morning on his way to work. Rather than showing restraint or deference in this difficult circumstance, Hussein assured us that he had simply refused to be subdued by the authorities. As evidence of his encounter and his total disdain for the cops, he pointed to the oxford cloth shirt he was wearing; all of us could plainly see the cluster pattern of wrinkles where the shirt had been firmly grabbed. "Tssk!" sneered Hussein. "You see what kind of fools these are! They don't have any intelligence, they have no respect!" Hussein also wore tightly twisted braids ("dreds" in vernacular Swahili), which he well knows are often taken as a sign of suspicion by the police. In general, he tucks his locks under a baseball hat, but in his dismissal of the police actions, he tore off his cap and said, "You see these dreds. Just look. I don't care [if they provoke the police]. I won't cut them!" These rebukes elicited vocal responses from the increasingly animated crowd: "*Watu namna gani?*" ("What kind of people are these?"), "*Balaa!*" ("Chaos!), "*Norma!*" ("Trouble!"). But this tangible evidence of a recent conflict also invited other men to (re)enact a range of related reports, all of which turned on harassing encounters. A few men simply described how they would handle things if they were ever treated this way, all confirming the refusal demonstrated by Hussein. "A cop could never take me," said one. "I'd just stand there and say, 'I'm not going.'" Much more common than these retorts to hypothetical clashes were dynamic retellings of similar previous experiences with the cops. Here, the emphasis was not simply on the story told, or even on the attitude of resiliency displayed. Instead, it was on the reenactment of the bodily postures that dramatized and demonstrated the thrust of these discourses. The way to forcefully yank your hand out of the feeble grip of a cop; how to look straight ahead as you walked down the street past a roundup, a way both to avoid looking suspicious and to show due contempt for the authorities; a method for recognizing a police officer skulking behind the corners of a building. All of these physical gestures were forcefully performed as recollections of injustice and tangible indications of the vigor with which these injustices were met.

In Casino Hair Cutting, during the same heated discussion in which Faisel had informed me of the dangers of Arusha, I noted a further critical feature of these performances, one typical of such performative recollections. This discussion took place as the police crackdown was coming into full swing, and a number of guys had either had run-ins with the cops or had observed an unusually heavy police presence on the streets in recent days. Casino is located in the heart of one of the most affluent African quarters of Arusha.[6] There was, to some degree, a debate over the role of police in this urban milieu. It was a one-sided debate because the sole person (a young barber, with higher aspirations than some of his coworkers) who defended the necessity of obeying the law was loudly shouted down by coworkers, patrons, and everyone else hanging out in the shop. What was especially noteworthy (but also standardized) about the criticisms of the police offered in this fracas was their didactic character. Each performer made a point of instructing others about the actions of the police and of demonstrating what they had learned about them. This didactic quality was especially evident in the phatic forms that framed these young men's account. Thus: "*Unajua, polisi, wakitaka kukamata watu . . .*" ("You know, the police, when they want to catch people . . ."); or "*Sikia, huwezi kukaa karibu na magari ya polisi . . .*" ("Listen, you cannot just stand near police cars . . ."); or "*Nitakuambia kitu, siku hizi hakuna makops mwenye haki*" ("I'm going to tell you something, these days there are no honest cops"). These frames clearly work in an instructive fashion: they establish the authenticity of the report (often the claims are generalizations that do not derive from direct experience but from broadly common knowledge), and they alert the assembled to the fact that the performance is meant to inform, to enlighten, to be shared. The discussion here is not idle conversation or even a highly contentious argument; it is a means to create the forms and knowledge through which the gathered participants may share in and act on the world so defined.

From Authority to Terror: Public Ambiguities

As my examples show, critical dimensions of performance are embedded in speech acts and embodied in gestures through which memories of conflict and a sense of the nature of reality itself are realized and reiterated. These features of performance reveal how such enacted violence serves to constitute the specific character of a public sphere inhabited by a host of youth, the citizens of Arusha's streets. This public is profoundly shaped by formal aspects of practice (mottoes, embodiments, speech forms) through which it recognizes its participants, all of which instantiate sociocultural values like competitiveness, resilience, *ujeuri*. In other words, the public sphere created by performance authorizes and entitles certain performers to act. Especially given the antagonistic nature of the values encoded in these performance, this is an authorization simultaneously grounded, as other recent examinations of such publics have also observed (Comaroff and Comaroff 1999a; Wilder 1999; Geschiere and Nyamnjoh 2000), in the necessary exclusion of others. What is ironic about this performative process in the youth practices I have described is the fact that the attempt to exclude the youth themselves, to undermine their legitimacy and call into question their presence in this context, is a challenge that is adhered to by youth as a source of their own validation, and in a reciprocal fashion, this becomes the foundation for their challenging the challenger. That is, police harassment becomes not evidence of youth's susceptibility and incapacity, but of the police's insubstantiality, a truth that is widely shared, openly reported, and endlessly elaborated on by these same young men. It is not surprising to find that youth in Arusha not only routinely assert their indignation and invincibility in the face of police hostilities (I never heard accounts of police successfully subduing and harming their detainees),[7] but they also further denounce the weakness of the police as sources of real power. The transparent corruption of police actions and their attempts to prey on the marginal residents of Arusha were taken as evidence of the police's inadequacy.

Thus, it was not at all unusual to hear the same young men, as a part of their same diatribes against police weakness, praising the virtues and authority of the army. Ahmed tells me how he has real "respect" for soldiers, men with "pistols and rifles," of whom the cops, who carry only feeble batons, are actually afraid. Showing support for the army is explicitly described as a means of resisting the police because the power and respect accorded to soldiers shows up the truth of police invalidity. The apparent power that marginalizes young men through its relentless surveillance is thereby ultimately shown to lack the capacity to pose a real threat. This embrace of military might over police authority reverses the positions of power regarding the powerless with respect to routine harassment, thus restoring the rightful position of youth in town. But more importantly, the threat that soldiers purportedly pose to police demonstrates that the police have only a facade of power that is not informed by the same values of invincibility, combativeness, and *ujeuri* through which these young men define their own actions. Youth and the military, from this (ideological) perspective, are thus aligned, as each group understands itself to embody the identical qualities of indomitable, even terrifying, power.

In fact, youth often do see their lives as akin to military campaigns. Ahmed would regularly draw laughs from the crew at Bad Boyz by aiming a pantomime pistol at Asians, performing his contempt for *Wahindi*, when they came past the shop, saying he was ready to go into "battle" (he used the English word). A number of young men, many working in barbershops, also told me they intended to join the army some day, often as a form of police defiance. At the same time, this aspiration, which counters the weakness of harassment with the power of excessive force, can become a poignant reminder of the tenuous coherence of this public sphere and worldview, and of the subject positions of these young men as actors in such social fields. Take Abdallah, who was a good friend of Hussein. In 1999 I hung out with both of them at Bad Boyz pretty regularly. Both Abdallah and Hussein were footballers and would work out with their teams several days a week. Like Hussein, Abdallah also wore tight dreds, but he did not conceal his under a cap. Rather, the twisted ends of the locks were adorned with brightly colored rubber bands, making his hairstyle into a plainly visible, highly public statement. Although Abdallah spoke of pursuing a career in football, he also said he expected to join the army some day; he had been especially adamant about the inability of the cops to stand up to soldiers. When I returned to Arusha in 2000, though, I met up with Abdallah, now passing time with Hussein in the barbershop to which he had relocated—yet another Bad Boyz Barbering. Abdallah, with few prospects in sight, and plainly lacking the sources of patronage needed to join the army, had entered police training. He was still playing football with Hussein on occasion, but his brilliant dreds had been shorn, and Abdallah sported a pedestrian close-cropped "low cut." Abdallah's life course trajectory is not only entirely predictable as employment opportunities have become increasingly restricted in Tanzania's restructured market economy, but his acute transformation from insurgency to acquiescence demonstrates the fragile nature of this antagonistic world. The simultaneous move of valorizing their own oppression and vilifying the weakness of their oppressors is clearly fraught with ambiguity. The transition from the resilient victim of intimidation by a feeble police force to one who perpetrates such acts of terror on those who are forced to obey is all too readily imaginable.

Making the Rounds: Belonging in Space

On one of my final days in Arusha, in summer 2000, Ahmed and Staf told me they wanted me to come with them. "Come on, let's go. We're going to make the rounds (*kupiga round*)," Staf told me. As we walked past the market, south of Mnazi Mmjoja Street, Staf began to narrate the events of a recent confrontation. His voice was low, his tone was entirely flat. This elimination of all inflection from his delivery (in a highly exaggerated, almost laughable way) was meant to highlight his own implacability in the face of this confrontation. It was as though his utter indifference to the danger and the mere facts of the encounter plainly demonstrated the strength of his position: "This is where I was talking about," Staf said to Ahmed, knowing I would overhear the report. "The cops were grabbing people here. And one saw me, and said, 'You, come here.' I said, 'What do you want?' and the cop said, 'Your ID, show it to me.' I said, 'No.' He said, 'You don't have an ID card?' I said, 'I do, but I don't like to show it to anyone.' The cop said, 'Where do you live?' I said, 'I live right here, just ask anyone. Everyone knows me.' Then I left him there. He couldn't say anything." We continued making the rounds, walking up Sokoine Avenue, until we arrived at the major landmark in town, the Cape-to-Cairo clock tower. We sat down on the low wall in front of the post office and waited a bit. Ahmed and Staf then got disgusted and told me that the guys we were looking for weren't coming. Ahmed had hoped to introduce me to "some Rastas" who regularly hang out downtown. He had let them know that he would be coming by with me to meet them, but they didn't make it. Ahmed and Staf both complained they knew what must have happened. The cops were cracking down on Rastas in town. The government did not want tourists coming to Arusha, only to see these guys right in the center of town. It was a clear sign that the season had begun.

This pathetic episode encapsulates the indignities that are regularly experienced by "thugs" like Staf and Ahmed, but also discloses the way in which the performed enactment of those indignities might generate a shared sense of truth and the entitlement to possess and articulate that truth. In his laconic reporting of this recent hassle, Staf concretized an entire order of action, framing the meaning of this harassment in an unmistakable fashion. "The cops were grabbing people *here* . . . I live *right here*." Staf constructed a veritable *paysage moralisé*, narrating the streets of Arusha as a field at his command, the very one through which the three of us purposefully but easily strolled, making the rounds. The impact of this encounter is lived in the ways it takes place, a mode of practice that authorizes those who belong in this place and who hold it as their own. This sense of belonging, performed in circuits and narratives like this one, is plainly essential to these young men's sense of their own power, and what is at stake in the exercise of that power. Saidi, a sign painter in town, invoked this sense of belonging as a form of control when he contrasted the commonplace praise for the army with disdain for the police. "Cops," he said, "will hassle you on every corner. But soldiers, even if they see you smoking *bhangi*, will just leave you alone." For Saidi, as for Ahmed and Staf, every corner is a site of struggle over defining who belongs here.

At the same time, the authorization to inhabit place enacted in these activities reveals the ambiguities inherent in the terms of this struggle. In casting themselves as thugs whose vigilance in the face of subjection justifies their claims, they must also see this landscape as one beset with threats and obstacles that compel their antagonism. By this performative entailment, the Rastas we were to have met became the victims of these nefarious forces. At the same time, the police are shown to be pawns themselves, following the dictates of the government, itself beholden to the cash receipts of tourists. The onset of the season thus both proves the dependence of the cops even as it ratchets up the intensity of their assaults. From the perspective of Arusha's youth, the police's show of force emerges most clearly at their moments of greatest weakness. This particular show of force confirmed the harsh realities that these young men feel themselves to be up against. Nonetheless, the rounds that we took that afternoon were interrupted and incomplete. The command of place envisioned by Staf and Ahmed in their efforts to introduce me to a world to which they had privileged access (a world exemplified by Rastas, the embodiments of transgressive contempt for suppression) was undone, according to Ahmed and Staf, by police intimidation. This attempt to inhabit a world whose grounds for participation is confrontation with oppressive force produces a form of belonging that is shared, performed, and palpable but ultimately highly vulnerable. This point was driven home to me in the winter of 2003, when I returned to Arusha to find that Ahmed had been in prison for the last ten months. He had been picked up for stealing a mobile phone, a charge he claimed had been trumped up by the police. He further claimed that he had been set up (in a scam whose workings I never fully understood) by Staf himself after the two had a falling out over a bad debt the year before. As this sad case makes clear, there is an ever-present risk, a kind of moral ambiguity, that haunts the persistent indignation and antagonism that suffuses a lived world so configured. When the world is held together by a conviction that the subjugated draw strength from their disenfranchisement, a sacrifice to one's oppressors becomes an ontological requirement.

In the fall of 2000, Tanzania faced the aftermath of the most brutal upheavals in its national history. Supporters of the Civic United Front (CUF) on Zanzibar and especially Pemba, already dismayed by electoral irregularities in 1995, planned a demonstration in January 2001 to protest similar problems with the elections held in October 2000. Before the rally even took place, security forces in Zanzibar began firing into crowds and beating demonstrators. On Pemba, roadblocks were set up, and systematic attacks on CUF supporters and suspects were carried out. At the center of these horrific events was the police force. Residents of Pemba especially decried the fact that police were "dragging people from their houses," even as the "president of Zanzibar, Amani Abeid Karume [of the ruling Chama cha Mapinduzi, or Party of the Revolution] spoke on television on January 28, congratulating the police for their efforts" (Human Rights Watch).[8] The police themselves rapidly became the target of demonstrators; among the four members of the security forces killed on Pemba, one policeman was beheaded. Youth in Arusha are not to my knowledge directly involved in these events, although they are fully aware of them. Many of them are sympathetic with Zanzibari complaints, even if they voice little support for CUF per se. I am certainly hesitant to suggest that the harassment that young men in Arusha routinely recall is tantamount to the attacks undertaken by Pemba authorities. Yet parallel sensibilities seem clear. Partisans of a front advocating civic mobilization feel themselves put on by police authorities dragging people from their houses. Whether residents of Pemba and Zanzibar (where the police station in Zanzibar Town is known as "Babylon"; Remes 1999) can transform these horrors into the foundation for the future legitimation of their claims remains an open question.

That violence and terror have the potential to foster generative and enduring social bonds should hardly be surprising. Evoking the injustice of such trespasses can be a potent political tool, a call to action, and a means of mobilization. As Cole (1998: 121) puts it, "If winners write history, losers dwell on it more." Like Cole (who follows Lambek 1998), I see the recollections of harassment and intimidation of the kind suggested in Arusha's young men's performative interaction as a form of moral practice. It is surely not violence itself, if such an entity exists, that is at issue in these interactions. Indeed, the transgressions and bravura of *ujeuri* generally take a violent expression. Of course, the same contempt felt toward the cops fuels an admiration of military power as well as terror itself. The young men I know in Arusha rarely refuse violence as a course of action; it should come as no surprise that they regularly feel the need to fight their adversaries—and one another, as shown by the ultimate plight of Ahmed and Staf. This embrace of violence plainly depends on occupying a specific position in the performance of that violence, a position that is compelled to action not by the effort to maintain order or impose its will, but by its subjugation. "It is precisely the situations of powerlessness," Mbembe

(1992) reminds us, "that are the situations of violence *par excellence.*" This powerless position gives violence its moral force, but we must recognize that it also lends the exercise of violence great moral ambiguity. For the oppressed, the triumphant obliteration of unjust authority can be both exhilarating (like the bombast among thugs swapping stories), or horrifying (like the beheading of a policeman). When we place the terms of subjugation felt by Arusha's youth at the hands of the cops in the context that Mbembe reminds us of—a global context in which youth, police, the state, and international tourists are all nesting levels—we find that the situation of powerlessness encompasses all parties to this violence. The risk and the tragedy that emerge from this far broader legacy of domination is that the moral imperative that justifies righteous retaliation often renders the oppressed indistinguishable from their oppressors.

Portraits 1

Bad Boyz Barbers

Hussein

I introduced some of the young men I know best from my time in Arusha in chapter 2, and I want to flesh out my description of a few of their lives here in order to provide an ethnographic backdrop to the kinds of activities that go on in the shops and streets of town that are described in greater detail later. These portraits[1] are drawn from the staff of the *kinyozi* that I am calling Bad Boyz.[2]

Hussein was in his late twenties and working at Bad Boyz when I met him in 1999; he had been there for the past year and a half. He was known around town for his dapper appearance, especially his carefully kept twists, or dreds, which he kept tucked under a baseball cap, except for the occasional Friday when he would dress in a flowing *kansu* and pristine white *kofia* to attend afternoon prayers at the central mosque. Hussein was especially well known by young men and women as a good footballer who played for one of the local amateur clubs.

Hussein had come to Arusha in the late 1990s from Tabora, a town in central Tanzania, south of Mwanza. When I inquired about it, he identified himself ethnically with the Nyamwezi, saying his father was Nyamwezi and his mother was Sukuma from Mwanza (there is some scholarly debate as two whether these are even distinct ethnic groups). However, he never made any other reference to these ethnic affiliations; nor, to my knowledge, did he speak KiSukuma or KiNyamwezi. He talked with me frequently about his moving from Tabora to Arusha, and his embrace of

Islam. I never asked Hussein about the source of whatever financial support he had at the time, but it was clear from his dress and the friends he associated with that he came from a family of some means—not elite, but certainly not destitute. It was extremely important, for example, for Hussein to talk with me about his beloved mother, who had recently passed away.[3] His mother had been a schoolteacher who gave him a profound love of learning, but she also made him feel a profound loss in the limitations of his education. For example, Hussein often expressed regret that he could not carry out our conversations in English, as his mother would have liked him to be able to do.

I knew little about Hussein's father, other than the fact that he had, like his wife, also died in the 1990s, and his death precipitated Hussein's move to Arusha. Because of quarrels over the inheritance of his father's estate, Hussein had had a falling out with his father's brother—who had also, in Hussein's view, shown great disrespect to his mother while she was alive ("*Akamdharau!*" "He despised her!"). This had led him to seek greener pastures in Arusha. "You never know what can happen tomorrow. You live in peace in your home, but another day you might find yourself without a means of support. Your condition has collapsed (*hali imeangaika*)." Again, I cannot say what Hussein's source of support in Arusha was, but clearly he had some financial resources, however meager, that allowed him to live in town on more than the paltry salary he might have made as a barber.

Hussein's younger brother, Shabani, came to live with him in Arusha in the summer of 1999. He, too, was experiencing difficulties from the pressures of his patrilineal relations, pressures compounded by being dependent on elders without having parents of his own in the lineage to advance his position. Shabani came to Arusha to seek a bit of money in the *kinyozi,* and he hoped to return to Tabora to continue his education the next year. Hussein was also pursuing more education in Arusha, taking classes in tourism from a small tour operator owned by an Asian family. These classes, which are offered everywhere around town, never amounted to any kind of employment in the tourist trade for Hussein, and many people I knew suspected that the classes were simply a racket for a financially insecure tour operator to make some easy cash.

The following year, when I returned to Arusha, I found that Hussein had left Bad Boyz, although he was still working as a barber at another *kinyozi* in the congested area of the bus stand. Hussein told me he had left Bad Boyz because of a falling out over *mkwanja,* cash, and the repeated failure of the operator of Bad Boyz to pay him what (Hussein thought) he was owed. At the new shop, where Hussein worked in the company of the only female barber in Arusha, I got a slightly better sense of how Hussein was able to survive financially. The barbershop he worked in, like most in town, was not just a place to get a haircut, but was also a place to negotiate informal business deals and sell cheap goods without having anyone ask questions about where they came from. The owner of the shop paid Hussein not only for his work as a barber, but also for his ability to facilitate meetings with potential buyers and sellers (of perhaps a small shipment of radios, a box of movie cassettes, a sack of used clothing) and to provide some muscle at the meetings where these deals were transacted. Hussein was especially good at keeping things peaceful in the crowded, sometimes chaotic environs of the bus stand. He knew when the authorities were likely to come around seeking taxes or licensing fees, and he could rapidly put an end to the occasional fights that broke out.

By this time, Hussein had abandoned his aspirations in the tourist trade, but he was also engaged to be married to a young woman who worked as a manager at a well-known tourist resort near Ngorongoro Crater that was also run by Asian entrepreneurs. Hi fiancée was regularly in the bush working at the resort, but Hussein told me they lived together in town when she was in Arusha. Their marriage was delayed, he told me, by difficulties with bridewealth payments (*mahari*), complicated by his fraught relationship with his agnates; but he did intend to get the funds together for marriage within the year. When next I returned to Arusha in 2003, I was told that Hussein had moved to Dar es Salaam, where he was working as an announcer for a football club. I do not know anything further about his whereabouts our fortunes, but the impression I received from the few people who had heard about his move suggested he had found some success.

Ahmed

Ahmed was approaching twenty when I met him while he was barbering at Bad Boyz in 1999. Ahmed was clearly the leader of the crew at Bad Boyz in terms of his stylistic aspirations. He was a trendsetter, and well known across town by men and women in different lines of work in the informal sector. Ahmed had been born in Arusha, and his family occupied a compound of rooms in the heart of the old Swahili quarter of town. I also got to know Ahmed's family very well during my time in Arusha.

Ahmed had taken up work as a barber at Bad Boyz through his friendship with Ali, who ran Bad Boyz. They were roughly the same age, had gone to school together as kids, and had lived within a block or two of each other. Ali and Ahmed were not great friends—I rarely saw them socialize together apart from work—but they had begun working together at a different *kinyozi* a year or two before opening Bad Boyz.

Although Ahmed was a minor celebrity among his peers in this milieu, he thought of himself largely in terms of his experiences as a student who had pursued secondary school in other parts of East Africa and as a member of a family with global ties across the Swahili diaspora. His grandfather—his mother's father—was Zanzibari and described himself (according to the surviving contemporary members of his clan) as Omani. He had come to Arusha in the early 1950s as a trader. His grandmother, known as Bibi to all in the compound, married his grandfather just after moving to Arusha from Tanga in the late 1950s. She presided over the family compound, which consisted of Ahmed's mother, his deceased father's younger brother, and this brother's wife and two young children. At various points, Ahmed's younger brother lived in the compound with their mother, as did another of his father's brothers and his wife and school-age kids. Ahmed's mother was a trader, who in 1999 was importing electronic appliances (mainly VCRs and TVs, but also other cheaper goods like fans and clocks) with the help of a sister-in-law (her husband's sister) who was living in Dubai, where she was married to an Arab. By 2003, she was no longer able to sustain this business and was struggling to make some income in the gemstone trade in town. The indices of her economic decline were concretely appreciable in her domestic arrangements. When I first met Ahmed's family, his mother's sitting room (perhaps eight feet by eight feet) in their compound had a large cupboard with a TV, a VCR, and a cassette deck. She also had a separate rack that held dishes and photos, along with fashionable images of Mecca during the period of the *haj*. The room also had a nice settee with antimacassars on the cushions, a coffee table where meals and snacks were consumed, and—unavoidably—an upright refrigerator stocked with fruit and occasionally commercial loaves of white bread. By the winter of 2003, the room was completely denuded; all that remained were a few woven prayer mats rolled up in a corner that guests might use for sitting on the floor.

Ahmed's father's younger brother was an interesting presence. Baba Razzak, as he was known, had come from Tanga, like many of Ahmed's paternal kin, to live with his older brother in Arusha. Baba Razzak was an active healer with a sizable clientele in town who sought his services—using mainly herbalist and astrological techniques—in order to secure blessings, primarily in their quests for employment or for success in business.

Ahmed himself spent most of his day in this compound, where he ate meals, carried out household chores, and occasionally relaxed with friends as they watched videos or listened to music. Yet he did not actually sleep in the compound. Instead, he slept with some agnatic cousins in a nearby compound. Moreover, Ahmed reportedly had a small child with a former girlfriend—although I never heard him talk about, nor did I meet, the child or the girlfriend, so I suspect this may have been as much a rumor as a fact. What was most important about Ahmed, in his own view, were the opportunities he had had in secondary school. Ahmed had attended two secondary schools, both in Kenya. Ahmed was unable to remain in either school and had left secondary school altogether by 2000. But he recalled the time he spent there, and he especially prided himself on his ability to speak very good English as a result of both his formal education and his travel. He also never failed to introduce me to friends and relatives as "a professor from America," while most others simply describe me as an American friend. Ahmed did work sporadically at a number of *vinyozi* in town, and he did not return to barbering once Bad Boyz closed in 2000. He could still consider himself a dependent on his senior relatives, and he relied on the members of his compound for some meager sources of support. Ahmed also took up bodybuilding—clearly an indulgence available to a young man with no (acknowledged) dependents. He became quite muscular and fit at the end of the 1990s, which certainly attracted attention from his male peers, and like Hussein's interest in football, these skills and bodily attributes fit nicely into the masculinist performance style of the *kinyozi*.

By 2003, Ahmed's economic fortunes, like those in the rest of his compounds, had greatly deteriorated. He was imprisoned for eleven months, then released after a process that, according to all involved, required substantial bribes to be paid to judicial officials. Even while in prison, Ahmed told me that he had maintained cosmopolitan aspirations. He said that he had passed himself off as an African American "from Brooklyn" who only spoke English. In this way, he hoped to avoid compromising entanglements (as he put it, "the guys and the guards who harass you all the time") with locals in prison. I last saw Ahmed in the summer of 2006. By then, his family's financial situation had deteriorated to the point that his grandmother had left the compound and moved out of town to a home with kin who could provide for her. Ahmed was living with her there and trying to attend classes in tourism in town, still hoping to make the best use of his education to work in that prevalent trade, which lures so many young men and women in Arusha, with its global attractions.

pied by *vinyozi* is crosscut by a host of other equally tenuous kinds of places, such as shoeshine stands, the open-air sewing machines of seamstresses and tailors, and fruit and vegetable sellers along the sidewalk. Processes of displacement are thus readily apparent throughout the town and are never far from the thoughts of those who occupy these places.

Considering these shops only as physical places in this way objectifies them as zones or maps that are characterized by a certain terrain. In this case, the imagery of popular global locations such as Brooklyn, Liverpool, and Kosovo establishes critical cardinal directions on this map, points of orientation that establish the position of the present in Arusha. The interconnectedness of these positions, as external places conflated on this urban scene, creates a certain image of the world, and of Tanzania's place in it (or outside of it, as the case may be). These points of orientation are important for indicating imagined boundaries and links in the world, and for suggesting forms of transposition and global interconnection. Understood in this way, Arusha's barbershops constitute what Lefebvre (1991: 33) calls *"Representational Spaces,* embodying complex symbolism, sometimes coded, sometimes not, linked to the underground side of social life."* Nonetheless, this way of approaching barbershops, as representational spaces or as a set (even system) of places, needs to be complemented by a consideration of popular practice in Arusha as a spatial field of action. The image of the world displayed by barbershop names and decor represents a particular locale in which activities take place. In my view, this objective representation or image is only the product of what Munn (1996: 451), following Lefebvre (1991), calls a "mobile spatial field." Within this framework, space, including places like barbershops, is not the "setting," or the "container" of activity; rather, it is an ongoing social activity that has, and thus concretizes, a spatial form. Social practice, in other words, defines a spatial world, its "boundaries and directions . . . lines of force, [and] perspectives" (Merleau-Ponty 1962: 112).

When we situate problems of imaginative practice within this model of spatiality, we can begin to ask different kinds of questions. My aim in this section is to ask: how does social practice in Arusha define the *kinyozi* as a frame of action that permits the articulation of the distanced places, persons, and things already described as a horizon for this present within a field of lived practice? How, in other words, do the popular practices that bring barbershops to life in social experience constitute the global as an aspect of the local, and thereby produce locality as an intrinsically global reality? When we consider how the space of the barbershop incorporates lived spatiality, including especially the lived spatiality of the body, we

Fantastic geographies, from Brooklyn to California

have a basis for grasping how barbers and their clients bring the world into the shop, and how they project the shops as distinctive features of this world.

The activity in and around a barbershop includes much more than getting a shave and a haircut. As I mentioned previously, barbershops in Arusha are hubs for the dissemination of a variety of media, including radio and television broadcasts, and for the circulation of daily and weekly papers and magazines. They are also central nodes in the public presentation of self. A wide range of activities dealing with personal grooming and appearance, such as selling used clothing door-to-door, shining shoes, and tailoring outfits, are brought to the barbershop. A barbershop is in part a venue where one can create a display and display one's self.[3] Here, the *kinyozi* inserts itself into the "street life" (*mtaani*, or *kitaani*) of Arusha and simultaneously enfolds the street into itself. Barbers and clients call out to passersby from the open interior or from the immediate front of the shop. When folks in the street enter the social field of the shop, they make their presence felt by shaking hands and greeting everyone assembled at the *kinyozi*, a gesture that must be repeated in reverse when anyone takes leave. In all these ways, the barbershop is a gathering place, a pivot for the mobile dispersal of persons and things, a social field created by an active coming together of forces, that also anticipates a continuous circulation outward from within. In this respect, the *kinyozi* is less like a house in which people reside, leaving and returning during the course of the day, than it is akin to the street itself: it is both a recognizable place and a medium of traffic and movement.

These social qualities are explicitly recognized and commented on by the denizens of the *vinyozi*. Indeed, it is common to hear a barbershop described as *kijiwe*, "the little stone." This diminutive term draws an immediate parallel to rural locales and connotes a fixed place—a stone—for gathering in conversation and greeting. It epitomizes a place at which bonds of intimacy are publicly forged and enacted, created and made known to others in the community. The recognition of the barbershop *kijiwe* as a dynamic place within a field of activity is also complemented by the way it organizes social bonds. Amid the coming and the going, with handshakes constituting and demonstrating the contours of the space, people will often greet those gathered at a barbershop, if only to say that they cannot stop to chat, or that they will return later. "*Nipo round*" ("I'm around"), they will tell their friends. This greeting has a locative form (*-po*) that connotes an immediate area that circumscribes the shop, and it further refers to the movement of the person that establishes this circumscribed area (which

Kijiwe: barbers and clients in conversation

includes the *kinyozi*) by their act of "making the rounds" (*kupiga round*). By these actions, in language and motion, the barbershop is created as the stone, the solid gathering place in the midst of (and so a part of) the dynamic circulations of social life.

These innocuous features of spatial practice in Arusha may seem unremarkable, although they are directly invoked whenever young men gather and greet or take leave of one another at a shop. If we put this practice in a broader context, we will see that this specific spatial field reveals a good deal about the sociality embedded in it. *Kijiwe,* for example, is not simply "the little stone," a metonymic extrapolation from a rural idyll. In fact, the term itself has multiple referents that reveal a great deal about the way the space of a public sphere is gendered in this urban locale. To begin with, the *kijiwe* in many Tanzanian villages is the grindstone, a place where social ties are forged in the course of often grueling physical labor. This concern with the demands of strenuous activity is directly linked to most young men's characterization of their own lives on Arusha's streets. The grindstone, moreover, is characterized by central qualisigns of social interaction for many of these young men. The *kijiwe* is solid and enduring; it is a form that "survives" (a vernacular term that denotes persevering through struggle). By its very nature, a *kijiwe* is "hard" (*gumu*), a quality much admired—and absolutely necessary—in this milieu. The grinding activity of the stone is likened to the conflict that needs to be confronted and worked through in daily life. Calling a barbershop *kijiwe* suggests that it is a place of work, and so a site of struggling and striving. This struggle is further in evidence in the terms that a great many young men in Arusha use to describe themselves: *wahuni* and (in English) *thugs*, a term that has been widely adopted in global hip hop expression. These are both terms that carry enormous negative implications (see Setel 2000 and Stambach 2000a for extensive discussion of the way that *muhuni* has become a central term in contemporary Northern Tanzanian moral discourses about reprehensible character and behavior), and the self-designation as a *muhuni* ("thug," in Tanzania and elsewhere) is plainly a way of inviting scorn and thus showing one's toughness in a world of confrontation. These practical understandings indicate that the fantasy space of *kijiwe* is not a convivial respite *from* hardship, but that even the pleasures of conversation are framed *by* hardship.

As a "hard" place of hard work, *kijiwe* captures central aspects of a social world imagined and admired by many young men in Arusha. Equally central to the fantasies of struggle and endurance sustained by allusions to the grindstone is what is (purposefully) occluded by this transposition of the rural *kijiwe* to the urban *kinyozi*: and that is, quite simply, women. For wherever there are grindstones in rural Tanzania, it is women who carry out the grinding there, turning grain into flour in preparation for porridge or beer. Even young unmarried men such as those who hang out in barbershops would not be expected to carry out this kind of food provisioning activity. How might we account for this gendering of the barbershop? To begin with, we might note that such appropriations of cross-gender practice, for both men and women, have long been characteristic of rites of passage that are essential to the formation of gendered persons across East and Southern Africa (Turner 1967; Comaroff 1985; Beidelman 1997). In this way, initiation often proceeds by conflating gender identities, defining a liminal being whose ambiguity must then be reworked in the embodiment of mature gendered personhood. But what is especially pronounced in men's rites are the ways that the embodiment of mature masculinity is held to depend on the appropriation of femininity in order to dominate a powerful creative force that otherwise escapes masculine control (see, for example, the Ndembu tale of the origins of circumcision; Turner 1967: 152–53). I am not arguing that the barbershop as a social institution is simply a direct urban translation of rural or regional initiation rites, although neither would I dismiss this association. Rather, I argue that the gender dynamic of appropriation as a means of domination, often at work in initiation, is relevant to the social world of these young men in this urban context. It is surely no accident that Arusha's barbershops, which take their colloquial name from rural sites of female work, are urban places and places of work where women never work.[4] Identifying the urban shop with the signifiers of the rural grindstone asserts a parallel between these locales, and through this parallel, it draws explicit attention to the fact that barbershops are places from which women's work is excluded. In effect, this gendering of the barbershop makes reference to rural women's sociality in a way that draws attention to the gender asymmetry characteristic of this urban space.

At the same time, an additional rural referent for *kijiwe* is also pertinent in this context. In the Meru and Chagga villages densely settled across Mount Kilimanjaro and Mount Meru, *kijiwe* can also refer to the hard stone altars where clan sacrifices are offered.[5] Like grindstones, these sites are also points of gathering and conversation, but unlike grindstones, these altars are especially associated with masculine actions. Bloodshed and violence are harnessed by senior men for collective ends at sacrificial altars. In this way, these *kijiwe* are characterized by distinct temporal rhythms; on a daily basis, these stones are the site of conversation and sociality, a sociality iconically represented by the punctuated acts of sacrifice. The sacrificial *kijiwe* is thus constituted by hierarchical relations, in which the ebb and flow of daily conversation is embedded in place that is intrinsically bound up with the masculine authority of clan elders and the danger of bloodshed.

When we situate these rural gendered meanings and practices in the context of urban life, a further dynamic in sociality can be explored. Barbershops are not only metaphorically grindstones and altars; they are also described by those who frequent them as *baraza*, a term used to describe any sitting area provided for meeting and conversation. Stereotypically, a *baraza* is a narrow, backless wooden bench set against an outside wall, often under an awning or on a veranda. In most cases, the seats provided are portable and can be shifted around to accommodate additional interlocutors. Just as frequently, any stoop or low wall can serve as a place to sit, in which case the motility of the speakers' bodies, and not their chairs, creates the *baraza* in the act of sitting down for conversation. Occasionally *baraza* are fixed places, with permanent seats made of stone or cement, but even the most fixed *baraza* accommodates whoever comes for conversation. Indeed, a widely spoken proverb recognizes the sociocentric character of these spaces: *Baraza ni watu, na watu ndiyo sisi,* "The *baraza* is people, and the people are us" (that is, those who are gathered here, uttering this proverb). Conversation at the *baraza* thus reflexively constructs the space as well as the participants in the conversation as a *baraza*. In the course of social practice in Arusha, the *baraza* to which people commonly refer, and to which barbers and clients refer when they characterize these shops as *baraza*, are the shaded benches set up in front of the open verandas in most of the city's mosques. These are sites where senior men—and only men—gather before and after prayers, often sitting for hours at a time; they may finish midmorning prayers and stay until midday prayers. These are almost always elder men (certainly they were described as places for elders to me) who have the time to sit in extended conversation, to say nothing of bodies that appreciate the rest.

The performative features of this shifting yet grounded place reveal important aspects of the barbershop, a place that can also be said to be or to make a *baraza*. This generational contrast and the religious identification add an important dimension to the gender asymmetry already described. By drawing parallels between a rural site of women's activity and a rural and urban site for male elders, the *kinyozi* thickens the gender symbolism already discussed. As a point of generational contrast, the senior *baraza*, as opposed to the junior *kijiwe*, emphasizes on the one hand the young men's aspirations to propriety and social standing of the kind epitomized by men's talk at the mosque and by male elders' sacrifical authority; and on the other hand as the way that male elders' dominance over juniors incorporates an element of gender hierarchy. In effect, the *baraza* of junior men is the *kijiwe* of women. Again, the dynamic of inclusion and exclusion characteristic of these young men's efforts at belonging is thrown into relief. Moreover, comparing the barbershop to the *baraza* as well as *kijiwe* not only feminizes young men (which simultaneously demonstrates the authority of elders and bespeaks young men's sense of their own displacement), but it also further compounds the ways in which the construction of masculine personhood is predicated on the exclusion of women. The urban *kijiwe* as a space occupied and enacted exclusively by men highlights, I have suggested, the absence of women from this place of work. The transposition of this rural domain into an urban one as a gendered, hierarchical process is also confirmed in vernacular speech, in which *kijiwe* is rendered as *kiSTONE*. This double voicing of Swahili and English (with the Swahili diminutive prefix) serves to situate the semantic value of the term in the urban community of speech where English is used and understood, despite wide disparities in competence. Again, this highlights the transformation of the rural women's zone into a fundamentally new kind of place when it is urbanized. I can only add that the emphatic utterance "*kiSTONE!*" has a way of sounding aggressive and creates an exclusive community of speakers who can grasp the nuances of the metaphoric grindstone, urbanized, Anglicized, and inherently male-centered. What is more, if this masculinist appropriation of the *kijiwe* is also likened to the *baraza*, a characteristically Muslim and quintessentially urban (to say nothing of masculine) place, the implication to be drawn is that the urbanization of a female locale as a male enclave is tantamount to the expulsion of women from urban sociality itself. My argument, then, is that by means of a spatial practice understood and performed at the intersection of "the little stone" and the *baraza*, young men in Arusha, or at least barbers and their clients, come to inhabit the experience of their own displacement (that is, as junior men, subordinate to elders, scrambling to find a life in a tenuous informal economy) through their assertive erasure of women from their social field.

Let me immediately qualify this assertion. As I will discuss in greater detail below, these spatial practices do not consist solely in metaphorical aggrandizements about sitting around a barbershop. Rather, they are ramified through a host of related practices and discourses that constitute the sociality of the shops. Second, I hasten to point out that this removal of women from urban sociality is plainly a fantasy, one that imaginatively enacts a central tenet of this hyperaggressive masculinist reverie. For Arusha is a city where women have long been active in exactly the kinds of commercial activities in which these young men are now struggling. As an enterprise, women's salons have a longer history than do men's barbershops; salon employees are older and on average have more experience than barbers; and salon clients tend to have relatively greater means, as more young women move into service industry and office positions that expect (and provide the income to procure) good grooming.[6] Further, the social interaction surrounding women's hair as opposed to men's has significantly deeper and more complex roots (forgive the pun). Women routinely care for one another's hair at home and at work, parents and older siblings tend to younger children's hair, and friends plait and comb each others' hair, often several times a week. Beyond these hair-related endeavors, my (relatively incomplete) exploration of social organization in town suggests that households, especially those in the predominantly Muslim city center, are increasingly matrifocal. Many of the young men whom I know well in Arusha live in homes under the authority of a mother or mother's sister; and many household are composed of persons related by matrilateral ties.[7] This pattern is as true for relatively elite families, in which fathers and senior men regularly travel to Dar es Salaam, the coast, Kenya, or even the Arabian Peninsula on business (and in many cases rarely return) as it is for poorer families in which men hope to find work as waiters or porters in the safari industry, or, increasingly, seek out work in the wildcat tanzanite mines in the region. Under these conditions, which are illustrative of the widely lamented contemporary "crisis of masculinity" the world over (Comaroff and Comaroff 2000: 307), the barbershop dream of women's subordination has to be seen as a form of symbolic violence that both denies women's legitimacy even as it bespeaks these young men's own subjugation.

This masculinist fantasy is enacted and demonstrated in the most banal and self-evident ways every day in virtually every *kinyozi* in Arusha. It is not only that young unemployed (almost exclusively) men spend a great deal of time in these shops; it is also the case that much of the focus of their interaction turns on the boastful denigration of women. There is certainly nothing surprising about the kinds of encounters with women and antagonisms between men and women that these young men's conversations describe. What is noteworthy are some of the ways that this gender exclusivism has begun to be organized and articulated in terms of a wider imagined world. In effect, the performance of masculinity becomes a switch point in Arusha for articulating local social worlds as intrinsically grounded in a global context. As one example of this articulation, let me recount a conversation I once had about local clubs in Arusha. One especially popular club was dismissed by my *kinyozi* friends as one they would never go into because the men who frequented this club were said to be only interested in attracting women. The patrons at this club, I was told, "would buy a beer for a girl before they would even buy one of their male friends a soda!" Wasn't this OK? I asked. Not at all! Even if a woman begged him, said one guy, he would only spend his money on his male friends. A woman, he continued, did not deserve the respect of your "boys," your "niggas" (both words he used in English), because *"tupo mitaani, sisi, tuna SURVIVE!"* ("we're in the streets, us, we SURVIVE!").

This forceful rebuke of my suggestion is noteworthy in a number of respects. Note that the social world defended is not only "tough" and "hard," demanding endurance and struggle, embodied and temporal qualities already discussed; it is also firmly rooted in spatial practice: "we're in the streets." This place, a moving hub amid a mobile world, is one, like a *baraza*, in which the gathering together of people simultaneously constitutes the social relations in and as the locale they inhabit. The street, and the *kinyozi* that enfolds the street into itself and extends itself into the street, is not just a place where people live; it is also a way of living. Note further that this characterization is implicitly a claim that derives force from its global underpinnings. "We SURVIVE" is an affirmation that is uttered in English; it is also a quotation derived from the verses of gangsta rappers. Indeed, many of the self-avowed "thugs" I know in Arusha have also described themselves to me as "street niggas" as a point of prideful independence derived, again, from the explicit ideological claims of African American hip hop artists. Quite clearly, locating this contentious independence in spatial practice is also gendered: survival in the streets is not a viable attribute of women, at least in these young men's views. Further, these young men not only affirm their commitments to one another by their exclusion of women, but they also evaluate the quality of those commitments in terms of relationships to women. That is, men measure their masculinity relative to their attachments to women, casting praise and blame on those who demonstrate greater or lesser disdain for women.

Embodied Fantasy

This way of grounding masculinity as a local imagining of a global real-ism may also be deriving some of its force from what can be described as a renewed interest in Islam in Arusha. The same young men who listen to gangsta rap, tune in to Channel O (a South African music video cable network), read pornographic tabloids, and watch Jackie Chan movies are also "returning to Islam," as many of them put it. Most of the young men I knew in 1999 claimed to be Muslim, and although they professed belief in Almighty God, they rarely if ever went to prayers. In June 2000, many of these same young men were praying five times a day, reading Islamic literature imported from Kuwait, and engaging in conversations about the importance of faith in their lives. I have only begun to explore the meanings and implications of this movement, if it can even be so char-acterized. I do think, however, that there are certain standardized claims that a wide array of men, young and old, offered to me that contribute to this return to Islam. For every Muslim with whom I spoke, the force of Islam as a religion was not the strength of its "faith" (*imani*); even men I knew who prayed regularly told me that "faith was hard" and a source of much struggle. Rather, they claimed, Islam was critical to their lives (and should be to mine, a great many insisted) because Islam is "true" (*kweli*). The Koran, in their view, is not just a guide for living; it is a source of empirically verifiable knowledge—indeed, the Koran is a guide for proper scientific investigation, its foreknown truths awaiting demonstration by research.[8] A great many men further held that the surest "truth" of Islam, and the clearest "proof" of Koranic validity, was our own bodies. A male body is different from a female body, a fact reported in the Koran and self-evident to all. The superiority of the male body, and its similarity to the body of Muhammad in particular, is confirmed in the Koran, and our own bodies thereby confirm Koranic truth. These kind of bodily discourses inform a good deal of discussion of Islam. At the turn of the millennium, a number of young men I spoke with insisted that the signs of the end of the world were already apparent. Foremost among these signs, and a claim known and asserted even by those who were skeptical of apocalyptic pronouncements, was the fact that women are said to "exceed" (*kuzidi*) men. To "exceed" is taken to mean everything from women being more powerful than men, to women wearing pants, to wives simply being older than their husbands.

In keeping with this embodied sexism, it is worth noting that one of the signs of male superiority is men's hair, or more specifically men's beards. Beards, a topic of conversation quite relevant to passing time in a barbershop, were taken by many men who spoke with me to be a strong sign of divine preference for men. A man's beard showed his similarities to the prophet, and Muhammad himself was endowed with a substantial beard as a sign of his election. The many hairs that make up a man's beard are each *jinni*, a tremendous blessing, but also a potential danger that only masculine strength can control.

This fascination with matters hirsute is telling. It also provides an entry into some central practices through which masculinist ideals, with its conjunction of local and global imaginings, are directly enacted, in barbershops and elsewhere in Arusha, which is to say, haircuts. My interests here touch on questions of what Mercer (1994) productively labels "Black Hair/Style Politics," although the racial dimensions of this style/politics are substantially different than the largely African American practices Mercer addresses, and can also be set against the broader anthropological question, "Why hair?" (Berg 1951; Leach 1958; Derrett 1973; Obeyesekere 1981; Synnott 1993; Mageo 1994; Stambach 1999; Turner 1980). What I offer here is an illustration of the ways that current hair fashions, men's as well as women's, embody and display the broader dynamics of fantasy as a lived practice. I was first attracted to the study of barbershops by the fabulous iconic artwork that graces these shops. These images are usually immediately recognizable for the celebrities they depict, many, though not all, of whom have distinctive haircuts. Some of the most distinctive and

pervasively illustrated haircuts (if I can call them that) are the renowned
bald heads of Michael Jordan and Tupac Shakur. There is nothing intrinsically surprising about this, of course; even bald heads need to be shaved.
In fact, this point (discussed below) is more relevant than it might seem.
What is at least a bit surprising is the fact that few, if any, of the spectacular celebrity hairstyles painted on Arusha's *kinyozi* facades are actually
selected as hairstyles by the men of Arusha. In fact, few men shave their
heads completely, although they do prefer closely cropped hair. Even fewer
men choose to have designs, words, or patterns shaved into their hair,
although every shop lists "design" (*mtindo*) and a complete head shaving
(often listed as "R. Kelly" after the R&B performer) in its display of prices.
Men in Arusha, it seems, recognize the spectacular and the fashionable
as created and effected among African American men, but they do not in
any simple way imitate or even directly appropriate these styles.

How might we account for this paradox? I asked many men and
women whether head shaving was still a practice of mourners in and
around Arusha, and to a person, everyone held that this was an antiquated
practice, one that was not only irrelevant to city life, but hardly ever prac-
ticed anymore, even in rural areas. In any case, this sacralization would
hardly account for the celebration of other peoples' bald pates. When I

Shaved heads and barbering styles

asked why so few men chose to shave their heads or "design" their hair, I was offered a few standardized explanations. First, some men told me that people in Arusha—or "we Africans"—do not like to depart too much from tradition. People's hairstyles "follow custom" (*fuata mila*), even as they "keep up with the times" (*endelea na wakati*). This tension is quite interesting, and conforms, I would argue, to the broader sociocultural emphasis on distancing already described. Just as Arusha's *vinyozi* publicize a landscape that marginalizes Arusha itself, so to do the bodies of those who occupy this landscape remain excluded bodies. In my view, this distancing expresses both the displacement of those who spectacularize images that cannot reflect themselves, and a reflexive understanding of the necessity of this distance. For in order to show that one is fully in the know and grasps the profound significance of these ultimately most real of places, persons, and styles, one needs to recognize a contrast between what is here and now and what provides the encompassing, overarching context that organizes the meaning of this present. Conflating the distance, simply copying the ideal, would reduce its magnificence and render it simply one place among many other, some possible lives no different from any other possibilities. Moreover, it would make the subjects' appreciation of these fantasy worlds indistinct from any other kind of knowledge or insight. Aspiring to participation in this imagined horizon apprehended as a truly fantastical reality is thus fundamentally predicated on one's absence and exclusion from that world.[9]

While some men did express a tension in the relationship between "customary" and "timely" hair fashions, others offered a related but different view of current hairstyles in Arusha. For many, wearing hairstyles associated with global hip hop (bald heads and dreadlocks in particular) is simply dangerous. In fact, the dangers of hair are a regular topic of conversation in many barbershops. People told me, and more regularly told one another, stories of how guys who shaved their heads faced punishment from principals if they were still in school, or were likely to be seen as threatening and suspicious in the eyes of the police. Similarly, the daily paper, *Nipashe*, carried a story about a teacher in Tanga who, in keeping with his understanding of Islam, refused to shave his beard and so was denied his pay for several months because he failed to "set a good example for his students" (Nipashe, December 27, 2000). On the day before I left Arusha, three or four different friends told me the story of how a friend of theirs, widely known for his fabulous dreadlocks (in fact, carefully cleaned and braided lengths of hair) had been misidentified as a mugging suspect by the police, taken in for interrogation, and had all of his hair cut off. Indeed,

Rastas, as they are known, are said to be regularly rousted by the police, who worry that they project a bad image of the town to the Euro-American tourists (a topic I discuss in chapter 2). Again, local bodies are evaluated (and imagined) with respect to the place of Arusha as it is positioned in global terms. In each of these cases, hair, and especially men's hair, is a means of provocation as well as a medium of discipline. In these regards, it confirms the wider sociality of confrontation and survival that pervades life on the streets and in its barbershops, and so it further provides a means of participating in the broader fantasy that motivates this sociality. To cut your hair in a way that demonstrates your command of this extremely desirable fantasy demands a highly public submission to discipline. This form of desire imposes a clear burden on its subjects, requiring that they face danger and then endure in the face of these potential threats. Again, the global fantasy of participation in a deterritorialized order of strife and expulsion is lived in concrete ways through which it is embodied and inhabited. Turmoil is never simply chaotic and incomprehensible. Rather, it acquires its sense as being something unsettling and tangible through the ways it is and must be enacted.

Even at a much more mundane and less discursively elaborated level, hairstyles are performances (in the technical sense that this term is used in much of cultural studies) that encapsulate these processes of embodying a "thug"-like persona. Although most men in Arusha do not directly invoke particular celebrity images when describing their haircuts or think much about why they do not cut their hair in one way or another, all of the young men I spoke with could give some reason as for why they cut their hair as they did. I was interested in the popularity of closely cropped hair (a style that some, but only a few, actually labeled with respect to the fantastic as a "marine" cut, or more frequently, a "Tyson cut"), and almost to a person young men told me that they cut their hair short because it was simple: "I am too busy; I don't have time to comb out (*kuchanua*) my hair"; " I travel often and with a short haircut I can just pour water on my head and I am clean." These are entirely commonplace explanations offered by men about their hair, which appear as matter-of-fact as can be. For men in Arusha, hair is simply a pragmatic concern, and it is cut in order to devote as little attention to it as possible. Even Rasta braids are said to be easy because they do not require daily care once they are grown. This pragmatic attitude exemplifies the qualities of the global fantasy that predominate in Arusha. Such close cropping is a way of reducing the body to unadorned simplicity, refusing all indulgences and pleasures, and showing indifference to appearance. Men who keep their hair cut short are avowedly treating their bodies as mere instruments of utility, and so they abide by the logic of the realism they project (see also Wacquant 1998: 333 on the prizefighters' *"instrumentalist conception* of, and relation to, the body"). These short, practical haircuts display the qualities of toughness and hardness essential to struggling and surviving, thereby demonstrating one's commitment to this world. In making such displays, these men also concretely show that the world is grueling and exhausting, and permits of no extravagance. In effect, the most pragmatic and unremarkable of haircutting practices (emblematic of an unspoken habitus) offers a performative confirmation of the truth that reality as imagined and engaged holds in urban Arusha.

Of course, the extreme irony of this pragmatic attitude—and further proof that this "pragmatism" is as symbolic as it is instrumental—is the fact that it takes a good deal of time, effort, and money to maintain this indifferent appearance. A great many men in Arusha get their hair cut at least once a week; literally every customer I spoke with said they got their hair cut at least every other week, which, even if an exaggeration, shows an ideological allegiance to the value of short hair. Haircuts are cheap, and barbering wages are completely inadequate to maintain the multitude of *vinyozi* in town. Even so, a hair cut once a week is an expense that only a select few in Arusha can actually afford; even a cheap haircut amounts to half a day's pay for most. I would add that the concern with using hair as an instrument of saving time can be seen as plainly symbolic when we contrast men's haircuts with women's hairstyles. Women's salons and styles are topics that demand perhaps even more consideration than I have devoted to barbershops (see Stambach 1999 for a rich discussion). Here, I only want to highlight some central points of comparison. If men are concerned with time-saving hair, then women are more interested in what we might call the timeliness of their hair. A great many women get their hair styled in Arusha for the purpose of a specific event: a job interview, a wedding celebration, a return to one's natal home. Indeed, the form of their hairstyles demands this temporal specificity, as the most popular styles are ephemeral. On one occasion, I remarked to a woman who owned a successful salon that the carefully teased and curled style that a customer had just received couldn't possibly last more than two or three days. "Ha!" she said, "that hair won't last until tomorrow!" Perhaps the most popular contemporary style in Arusha, and one that demands professional treatment, is a teased-up, massive curl. The curl is produced by relaxing the hair with a petroleum gel, setting it in curlers for a quarter of an hour, then teasing the hair and pinning it back in a curl that sweeps

A range of women's hairstyles

up high on the crown of the head. Occasionally it is teased to the back in a curl pinned to run from the crown to the neck. The resulting style is called a *bomba*, "pipe," so known for the size of the curl produced. This teased-up curl is thus evanescent, in contrast to the closely cropped hair of modern men's fashion; the form of the hair itself is massive and voluminous, again a direct counter to the neatly shorn, simple men's cut. A successful woman creates an appearance of timely and fleeting elegance, while a man projects a time-saving indifference with minimal adornment. Each is an embodied performance that sustains, in both its own form and its gendered contrast, an alluring fantasy.

Inhabiting Fantasy

These barbershop poses are evidence that imaginative practice is an increasingly dynamic and expansive feature of social life in much of the world. How can we account for this expansion? Is this a new phenomena, one ushered in by innovative structures of globalization? Have fantasy and the imagination seized social purchase through a process of rupture—of disjuncture, dispersal, (perhaps even distortion), and most especially deterritorialization, described by Appadurai (1991: 193) as "The loosening of bonds between people, wealth, and territories," a rupture now compensated for by the genesis of imaginative forms of "realism"? In my view, linking the imagination to processes of rupture and deterritorialization under conditions of neoliberal reform obscures the ways that imaginative acts are just that: activities. The forms of fantasy considered here should instead be understood as evidence of the many ways that Arusha's young men have found to inhabit the processes of their own displacement, to live through rupture, not simply react to it. Displacement and rupture are all too apparent in Arusha today. They are ever-present anxieties in each area of town, the constant topic of conversation, even, or especially, in barbershops and salons. Barbershops seemed vital and boisterous, if constantly on the verge of collapse, in the summer of 1999. By the following year, although still thick on the ground, they had lost more than a little of their luster. Many young men whom I spoke to in Arusha in 2000 seemed to be hardening themselves to the limited prospects they faced, preparing to embark on some perilous course of action to "look for a life." The appeal—and dread—of tanzanite mining was much more apparent; others said they knew someone who knew someone who could get them a green card in the mythological African lottery for American work permits.

These relatively new fantasies speak to the "millennial" reduction of value production to sheer speculation (Comaroff and Comaroff 2000: 295ff.). In a world where tomorrow is only a dim prospect, striking it rich is hardly more fantastic than scraping by. As unmistakable as these processes are, we are not well served by analytical attention to the imagination as something that only comes into existence under such conditions. Fantasies are real, and they are poised, in Arusha at least, at precisely that intersection of global possibility and local limitation. The thug realism of Arusha's many young barbers is a richly detailed fantasy that depends on marginality and exclusion, as well as intimacy and incorporation. The locality they make and inhabit is configured through its relationship to what is recognized and treated as a potent, forceful world. It is only by inhabiting these imagined worlds in the intimacy and concreteness of specific social frameworks that locality is produced, global forms are constituted, and fantasy is brought to life.

Portraits 2

Aspiration

The informal economic enterprises that I have described thus far are motivated primarily by a concern with aspiration. The barbershop milieu, in particular, is oriented toward neoliberal processes of value production that focus on the expansion of possibilities for consumption and the proliferation of highly diverse forms of self-fashioning. These processes demonstrate the difficulty of distinguishing between such ontological categories as production and consumption, locality and globalism, displacement and dwelling, for they reveal that each of these positions is a necessary ground from which to evaluate the other. Thus, for example, the sense of oppression and marginalization that saturates many young men's experience of the state is a critical dimension of their attachment to one another and their sense of belonging to a particular sociospatial world: a corner, a *kijiwe*, a round. I have focused on the way in which popular sociocultural practices in Arusha attempt to resolve the contradictions of belonging as lived in neoliberal Africa today, the simultaneous sense of exclusion and inclusion, through forms of opposition, antagonism, and confrontation. I do not mean to suggest these are the only ways that such contradictions are resolved, or even addressed. Indeed, although the unpredictability and intractability of the future is a widespread felt quality in Arusha and across the globe today (Weiss 2004), those who aspire through the participation in a range of popular practices across Arusha *do* envision a future, and they attempt to enact it. How these futures are formulated and realized (or fragment and collapse) is something I learned a great deal about from the men and women whose lives I describe here.

Elizabeth

One of the first women I met in Arusha, and the one I got to know best, was a young seamstress named Elizabeth. I met Elizabeth in 1999 when I walked past her sewing machine on a bustling street in central Arusha, near the zone where gemstone deals are made. I saw a *khanga* with a provocative proverb (*methali*) printed on the margin (see Linnebuhr 1997, and chapter 5 here for more detailed discussion). *Usiwe Na Macho Kilicho Ndani Si Chako*—"Don't Look at Me, What I Have Inside Isn't Yours," it said. What might it mean? I asked Elizabeth. "Buy the *khanga* and I'll tell you," she said. So began a long series of discussions with Elizabeth, with whom I visited, if only briefly, almost every day that I spent in Arusha. In fact, this turned out to be almost the only curt remark she ever made to me—or virtually anyone else she met with at work or at home. Elizabeth was just twenty when I met her at her seamstress's station that day. She had arrived the previous year from Moshi, where she had been born and where much of her family still lived. Elizabeth learned to sew on a machine through *ufundi* (vocational) classes at her home Lutheran church there, and soon after, she decided to follow her older sister to Arusha to look for work. In Arusha, Elizabeth lived with her sister, her sister's husband, and their children in the cramped residential neighborhood near the Unga Ltd. factory. Here, she helped her sister out with child care responsibilities and worked as an apprentice to a seamstress. As an apprentice, she acquired the skills needed not only to sew, but also to cultivate a clientele and manage her funds. In less than a year, she had saved up the equivalent of the $40 or so she needed to set up her own business as a seamstress.

In order to work as a seamstress, Elizabeth needed not only her own machine, but also a secure location where she could work and where customers could contact her. Like most seamstresses and tailors, Elizabeth ran her sewing machine on the sidewalk (only a few tailors had shop space), and she offered a small bench for her customers and friends to sit and chat. This kind of open-air business sustained a great deal of interaction among the many similar businesses that operated in her vicinity: a shoemaker, other seamstresses, delivery boys working for Asian-owned shops. Elizabeth also regularly trained apprentices, who learned their trade from her, made a few shillings sewing, and generally held down the business when she was away for short periods of time. Elizabeth rented space for only a few dollars a month in the hallway of the shop in front of which she placed her sewing machine so that she could securely store her machine at night.

The bulk of Elizabeth's work consisted of simple repair jobs on used and weathered clothing. She also did many alterations, sewing hems on *khanga* to keep them from fraying, taking in skirts and pants, restitching old zippers and fasteners. Occasionally Elizabeth had the opportunity to create original designs using cloth, either lengths of commercially procured fabric, or printed *kitenge*, to fashion skirts, blouses, and jackets. She kept small notebooks to record her clients' measurements, record her accounts, and sketch simple designs for the clothes she would produce. If business was especially slow, Elizabeth might work on outfits of her own design as a kind of advertisement for herself, and indeed, clients often evaluated the quality of a seamstress's work samples before asking her to make them something.

In an intensely competitive field like this, where rates for services are more or less set by overt, publicly visible competition, it will come as no surprise that it was awfully difficult for Elizabeth to make much money in her chosen line of work. But she kept with it, has built up a regular clientele, and continues, according to her recent e-mails, to work as a seamstress today. Over the course of the eight years that I've known her, Elizabeth's family life has changed considerably. She no longer lives with her sister. She married, and she had a son in 2002. Elizabeth's husband, Edison, dealt in clothing. He traveled extensively across eastern Tanzania, as many petty traders do, looking for cheap bales of used clothing and taking them to markets where there are prospects of higher prices. Elizabeth met Edison through their Lutheran church, where they both sang in the choir. Between the two of them, Elizabeth and Edison were only able to afford a small single-room flat that the family of three shares. The room was made of packed mud lined with a plastic tarp—not cement, as are many slightly finer similar dwellings found across town—and has a tin roof. The single room was packed with all their furniture and possessions, a full-size bed on a wooden frame, a comfortable couch, a smaller love seat, two small wooden chairs, a low coffee table for serving food, and a cupboard loaded with utensils and drawers of clothing. Their shoes were racked on small sticks wedged into the dry mud walls. Edison kept an old, nearly unplayable guitar. All of their cooking was done on a small kerosene burner in the area in front of their room. The front door was covered by a simple length of cloth that served as a curtain when the door was open. Their room was at the end of a row of five similar rooms rented by other families amid a warren of perhaps three or four comparable complexes. The common area shared by the renters was a place for sitting and chatting with neighbors, and for exchanging small snacks. It was carefully landscaped, with a few well-tended plants adjacent to each doorway. The entire complex was only steps from the main road, where *daladala* transport took Elizabeth on the twenty-minute ride into the city center each day.

Elizabeth and Edison rented their room at the cost of 10,000 shillings per month (in 2006, just over $7) from a landlord who owned a group of similar buildings in their neighborhood. But Elizabeth told me that she and Edison had also made plans to build a home of their own, and they began the process by purchasing a small plot of land from the same landlord. The small plot—less than fifty by fifty feet square—was uninhabited, and they will have to clear it of growth before they can begin to build. Like young families across the town, Elizabeth and Edison had not begun to build or clear the land, but they did try to purchase building materials—mostly bricks and bags of cement—when they had a bit of cash to spare. According to Elizabeth, she and Edison wanted to build a home for the reasons that many others offered: "We want some peace and security (*usalaama*)." In addition to the material limits of a small, cramped room, which would be alleviated by a single-family house (*"tunataka kupanua, kidogo,"* "we want to spread out," is how she and many others in similar straits put it), Elizabeth also thought of her social world as constraining. Although she clearly enjoyed the company of the other renters in her complex—most of these households were headed by the mothers of young children—she also worried about the *fujo*, the wrangling of deceitful, malicious, perhaps even criminal neighbors in a densely settled location. In recent years, our discussions frequently turned to problems relating to *uchawi*, "witchcraft," or simply *nguvu za giza*, "the powers of darkness," that motivated many of her neighbors. She told stories of her husband's struggles to overcome nefarious efforts to deny him of a small inheritance he had received. She also mentioned the countless get-rich-quick schemes involving the use of malicious *jinni* spirits that attacked victims to enrich their owners. Possessors of these spirits inevitably (and stereotypically; see Smith 2001) all end up undone by the unconstrained demands of the greedy *jinni* themselves. In an effort to protect herself from such dangerous forces, Elizabeth told me that she had carefully chosen Edison as her husband. She respected not only his Christian practice, but also his parsimony: "I don't want us to spend more money to live in a more expensive room. Better we should live in an average room (*chumba cha kawaida*), and save our money for building our own house. Edison knows how to keep our money. We don't want a 'quick' fortune (*hera za haraka*)." The "security" she sought is thus a complex whole. Elizabeth used independent private assets to disentangle herself from cosmologically fraught social relations.

Saidi

Saidi was a sign painter who operates out of the city center in Arusha. I first met Saidi at the small kiosk that served as his main office in 1999. His kiosk was a place of work, a form of advertising, and a modus operandi, as he was constantly painting it and repainting it, trying new techniques, honing his craft, and updating the portraits on the windows and sides to reflect the changing cultural and political fortunes of East African and other international figures. Saidi, who was in his early twenties at the time, operates under the *nom de stylo* Nevada Art, a term that signals his cosmopolitan consciousness of a fantastic geography and reflects his own biography as a craftsman. Nevada was also the name of Saidi's first teacher, with whom he apprenticed in the mid-1990s. His close friends called him Saidi, but the clientele and acquaintances on the street simply called him Nevada.

Saidi, a nonpracticing Muslim, was born and raised in Tanga—as were a great many people living in Arusha today—where he lived with a large family until the late 1990s. His father had been in the Tanzanian military and had traveled extensively throughout the country, but Saidi had only lived in Tanga, Dar es Salaam, and Arusha. He arrived in Arusha to follow his older brother, who was also in the military and who was stationed in Arusha. When he first arrived in town, Saidi lived in a wattle-and-daub room in a less congested part of town up Mount Meru, near the Mount Meru Hotel. Again, the rent was cheap (about $10 a month), and the location was not too far from the Nairobi road, where transport by *daladala* into the town center was readily accessible. In 1998, he moved onto the compound of the military base where his brother lived, building a poorly constructed, if more spacious, small house consisting of two rooms: a living room where he cooked and ate, and a much smaller room that (barely) held a foam mattress. The advantages of living here were strictly financial because he could regularly take meals with his brother's family, and he lived essentially rent free in exchange for occasional child care duties.

Over the years that I knew him, Saidi had proven himself to be a successful entrepreneur. He always worked with an apprentice, had a steady flow of customers, and regularly expanded his clientele. Saidi's work consisted almost exclusively of painting in what I've called the industrial arts: he painted advertising signage for shopkeepers and small businesses, as well as items in bureaucratic genres such as license plates and identification tags on vehicles. Saidi only occasionally painted portraits (some of which I commissioned for myself and friends) and some bits of

Nevada Art from 1999 to 2000

tourist art. He was also an aficionado of electronic technology. He always had the latest mobile phone, and even in 1999, he had a small television prominently displayed in his living room cupboard. In 2006, he decided to considerably expand his business. He had always been friendly with a Swahili family in front of whose compound he rented the small space for his kiosk, and in the summer of 2006, he rented a small storage area on their property that he converted into a storefront. Saidi went into business with two other partners, also painters—in the tourist trade, not the commercial variety for which Saidi was known—in this shop (which was not yet up and running in 2006), where they hoped to sell their art and cheap imported electronic appliances.

In 2003, during the Christmas season, Saidi made plans to marry. He knew a woman a few years younger than himself and also from Tanga whom he met through mutual friends from home. She worked in a small textile factory in town and lived in a neighborhood Saidi called Uswahili ("the Place of the Swahili"), which simply meant it was packed with people, as indeed it was. I met with Saidi as he made plans with his fiancée for their wedding, which involved returning to her father's home in Tanga for a wedding ceremony. She seemed exceedingly quiet and demure during these discussions, which I took to be the expected demeanor of a prospective Muslim bride, but at times I sensed a more ambiguous reluctance on her part. In any event, the two were married that December in what Saidi said was a successful wedding. "I was able to take care of each little thing," Saidi told me proudly. "Her father was very impressed and pleased." When I saw him in 2006, I asked Saidi about married life, and he told me that he had a two-year-old daughter who was his real delight. Only a few days later, when I asked him when I could come see his family, thoroughly dismayed, he told me that his daughter was living in Tanga because her mother had taken her and returned to live with her natal family over a year ago. I was devastated for him: he seemed honestly unable to figure out what had happened. "Her family was always inciting trouble," he told me, "and when she went to stay with them, they only made it worse. They have all turned her against me! Now he whispered, "They even say I have used *nguvu za giza* (powers of darkness) against her. How would I know about such things! They are just telling her lies."

To my knowledge, Saidi's marital dilemmas remained unresolved. In truth, Saidi's experience remained as much an enigma to me as his marriage seemed to him. He was certainly dedicated to his work, and he had a useful skill to offer—although his artistic skills were not much better than any number of other painters who ply their trade in kiosks across the city. He had some financial support from his family, but again, this was not substantially different from many other young people in similar social and economic circumstances. Saidi seemed to be enjoying the kind of financial success that would allow him to marry in a way that demonstrated his maturity as a man, his independence, and his ability to provide as a husband and father. Of course, I am reluctant to make his personal tragedy stand as evidence of larger social processes, but it does demonstrate how daunting it can be, even in the face of modest economic achievements such as those that Saidi undoubtedly experienced, for young people in Arusha today to secure viable social futures for themselves.

4   **The Barber in Pain**

Consciousness, Affliction, and Alterity

In February 1996, Tupac Shakur released his double album, *All Eyez on Me*. Recorded while he was out on bail on a sexual assault charge, *All Eyez on Me* was the first album Tupac recorded for the Death Row Records label, with which he would become indelibly identified. Although it was uniformly panned by the mainstream American press, including *Rolling Stone* (April 4, 1996), *Entertainment Weekly* (March 8, 1996), *Time* (March 4, 1996), *Newsweek* (February 26, 1996), and *New York Times* (February 13, 1996), *All Eyez on Me* became the first hard-core rap album to reach number one in the Billboard charts after Tupac's still-mysterious murder in September of that same year. Now hailed by his fans and critics alike as a pathbreaking work, much imitated but never matched by the likes of Ja Rule and DMX, this more-than-twenty-track CD was also a crucial medium for the globalization of hip hop, and of Tupac himself. The fact that Tupac's death followed so closely on the heels of the release of *All Eyez on Me* undoubtedly contributed to the tremendous popularity of this product. Just as important as the music, the iconography of hip hop that this album disseminated had a major effect on visual culture worldwide. The image of Tupac on *All Eyez on Me* and in the album's artwork has become a kind of standardized representation, infinitely reproducible on any number of goods and surfaces. Arusha barbershops displayed these iconographic images of Tupac, wearing a studded leather vest that exposed his heavily tattooed torso, but they were also available on T-shirts and plastic shopping bags throughout Tanzania. *All Eyez on Me* has become a highly visible im-

Images of Tupac: All Eyez on Him

age and a polysemous claim, at once an insistent assertion with a pressing immediacy and a spectral evocation of a still-troubling enigma.

There are a set of complex visual qualities embedded in this imagery that are ramified in popular practice in Tanzania, and in Arusha in particular. What is explicit in this iconography is a claim about visibility as a field of social power. This relationship is dynamic and multifaceted. On one level, to be able to see something, to render it visible, is to acquire a kind of mastery over the thing. Thus, to subject something—or more to the point, someone—to scrutiny is to subject it to the authority of the viewer. This understanding seems patently evident in Tupac's declaration that all "eyez" are on him. Recently released from prison, signing with a new record label, making his affiliation with the West Coast unambiguous, both through Death Row Records and throwing the "W" hand gesture on the album cover, Tupac recognized that he was being closely examined by the state, the music industry, fellow rappers, and hip hop–dom more broadly. As he raps in both "Picture Me Rollin'" (a further visual provocation) and "All Eyez on Me," "Y'all got me under surveillance." At the same time this iconography produces a subject scrutinized by antagonistic and threatening powers epitomized by this inspection, the simultaneous recognition and excoriation of those powers embedded in the imagery work to transform that hostile scrutiny into a kind of potency for its object. If all of these powerful eyez are on him, then there must be something extremely powerful about Tupac himself. Tupac deploys the power of this surveillance, using it as a ground on which to confront authority directly, and so to demonstrate his capacity to endure this examination and to overcome it.

To go further, Tupac not only signals his awareness of this visual attempt to control him, but he also actively invites, even incites, it. Again, the imagery of *All Eyez on Me* has multiple visual implications. In the photos on the album's insert, Tupac adopts a pose that has now become de rigueur in gangsta hip hop: his torso bared in a pair of shorts, taken front and back, in what can only be called reverential lighting, displaying a panoply of sinew and tattoos. What is striking about this now commonplace stance is the way that it explicitly articulates with the wider concerns about the power of being watched. Tupac not only acknowledges this field of vision, he also puts himself on display. The domination of surveillance is matched by and dialectically entailed in the power of the spectacle that Tupac makes of himself. If all eyes are on Tupac, it's likely because we can't take our eyes off him. Tupac's iconography performs the dynamic potential of the claim *All Eyez on Me,* demonstrating with bodily force the ambiguity of this insistent contention, offered now as a lament, now as an allegation, now as a command.

Clearly the notion that the gaze is a formidable episteme in modern state technologies of subjectification (Foucault 1977), that vision is a privileged, modern mode of knowing and controlling the object in view, is both confirmed and complicated by Tupac's images. The uses of these images in places like urban Tanzania further compound the complication. What this image and its appeal in Arusha indicate is that both seeing and being seen need to be examined as reflexive processes. Each constitutes the possibilities and delimits the constraints of the other. These possibilities are not mere abstract capacities of human perception or historically emergent only under modernity, for the shape of this tension is culturally constituted in ways that are significantly enacted under conditions of neoliberalism but not reducible to its demands. "[T]he great epistemological—and therefore social—break," Mbembe (1997: 152) writes of the oral culture of southern Cameroon, was "between what is seen (*the visible*) and what is not seen (*the invisible*)." Yet this is a break in which "the reverse of the world (the invisible) was supposed to be part and parcel of what there was to see as its obverse (the visible)." This insight resonates with Perry's observation about the trope of invisibility in African American hip hop: "Lines about invisibility are prevalent in hip hop. They assert the power of the unknown, the mystical forces of the Invisible Man, as well as an intellectual depth that eludes challengers" (2004: 123). What is hidden from view also makes an appearance in the visible world. The fact of concealment must itself be displayed in order for the fact and the force of enclosure to be effective. This is not a quintessentially African model of perception that underlies diasporic epistemologies, but it is a useful heuristic for thinking through certain problems of appearance, bodies, and the powers these exemplify in contemporary social practice. I have discussed this dynamic elsewhere (Weiss 2003: 26–32) with reference to a far different part of Tanzania, and in a far different time. Turner (1967) describes a kind of pragmatics that informs ritual processes designed to reveal—literally to make visible—the hidden powers of objects and relationships in order to activate them. From this perspective, Tupac renders himself visible, simultaneously acting as one who discloses the powers of the invisible world and partakes of that same power.

This excursus on the visual field of Tupac serves as a prelude to a discussion on the dynamics of domination, its material embodiment, and, most particularly, the lived experience of oppressive power. These dynamics recall the accounts of *ujeuri*, the transgressive invincibility embraced in much of Arusha's popular, informal economic practices. The felt qualities of confrontation and subjugation as these are reported and explored in everyday discourse among the denizens of Arusha's *vinyozi* complement and reveal important differences from the celebration that attends to images of invincible *wajeuri*. The dynamics of domination and their concrete effects in everyday life are, of course, an immensely important theme in scholarship. There can be little doubt, for example, that emerging understandings of the postcolony as a mode of "illicit cohabitation" (Mbembe 1992: 4) have generated some of the most provocative and productive assessments of the nature of power relations in contemporary African culture and society. In their rejection of standard, oppositional dichotomies, scholars of Africa and elsewhere (Brown 1996; De Boeck 1996; Kaplan and Kelly 1994) have turned their attention to the ways that dominant regimes and their dominated subjects collude in the production of spectacular, dramatic, and grotesque performances of power. Mbembe, in particular, emphasizes the postcolonial subject's ludic potential, the playful capacity for ridicule and ribaldry through which subjects affirm the majesty of the *commandement* and remake themselves, splintering, to use Mbembe's word, into myriad mutant personae (Mbembe 1992). Most importantly, these subjects, the target populations (the *cibles*) of officialdom, are not merely the mercurial witnesses and audiences for an absolutist authority. The conviviality of domination demands that the preferences and values of the common man are always already embedded in the banal performance of the *commandement*. We might ask what forms these common and popular values take. "[T]he official world," writes Mbembe (1992: 10), "mimics popular vulgarity, inserting it at the very core of the procedures by which it takes on grandeur." This critique directly confronts the fetishism of postcolonial hegemonies and plainly demonstrates that even the most abstract authority fully realizes its efficacy in and through embodied representations and practices. Is the popular body of necessity banal and unbounded? Might popular consciousness be grasped in terms more compelling and complex than vulgarity and down-to-earth realism? Or are postcolonial subjects bound by their regime to be likened to nineteenth-century French peasants, in Marx's celebrated phrase (Marx [1852] 1978: 608), "potatoes in a sackful of potatoes" glorified by Bonapartist splendor?

The elaboration of ever more disturbing, compelling, horrific, and uproarious exhibitions of command has clearly proliferated across the African continent (Ciekawy and Geschiere 1998; Comaroff and Comaroff 1999b) and in our own backyard (Geschiere 2003). It is the subjects', and the subjective, participation in such spectacles of power that is the particular theoretical concern of this chapter. Without disentangling the palpable entanglements of command, it's possible to shift the analytical focus from performances of statecraft that tend to take for granted the subjectivity of the state's subjects—more often a target population subjected to authority than a people possessed of subjective intentions—and investigate more closely the forms of consciousness that both motivate and are motivated by the spectacular. In particular, the processes of subjectification—the formulation, creation, and concretization of local and specific varieties of subjectivity (understood as lived experience and capacities for action)—that may be realized in the course of social life need to be detailed. The genera-tion of subjectivity is a crucial dimension of domination, for domination is itself a relationship between subjects endowed through their relations with different potentials for action.

The problematic possibilities of postcolonial subjects are only amplified when those subjects are postcolonial youth. The contradictory character of young peoples' lives, not only but perhaps especially in Africa, has been widely described. Simultaneously soldiers in the vanguard of social transformation, dangerous deviants, or social problems par excellence, youth are often represented as, and even feel themselves to be, external to social totalities. This may either be because they are held in some ways to be unique and thus able to transcend cultural and political forms (Malkki 1997); or because they sense their own exclusion from sources of social value and power (Durham 2000). Central to this contradiction is the fact that although cultural forms of popular practice often represent youth as marginal and excluded, a theme that clearly resonates with many young men in Arusha today, youth culture is absolutely central to the contemporary global production of culture. The implications of this contradiction are especially striking with respect to the forms found in the world of African American hip hop and rap, and the compelling allure these have for young men in Arusha. In the musical and wider stylistic forms of hip hop and gangsta rap that are a central focus of Arusha's own youth culture, the counterhegemonic and oppositional possibilities of young people are hegemonically celebrated—indeed, sold!—as icons of power and value of the highest order. Such ambiguities are central to the dynamic that characterizes the agency and experience of Arusha's youth. Their sense of themselves as submerged by power is also a means to engage power, perhaps one especially available to youth among all the disenfranchised.

The profusion of globally mediated images and expanding possibilities for mass consumption has altered the frameworks for social participation, fostering new alliances and modes of patronage, and generating novel and contested voices. All of these processes and institutions of interaction inform the new constructions of identity widely lionized in so much contemporary work. Not only identity—the forms of representation through which social beings come to know (that is, to identify) themselves and others—but personhood—the relative ability to participate in, and so define oneself through, processes of social construction (including identity formation)—can be usefully examined.[1] Exploring personhood further entails addressing the shifting terms in which personhood can be recognized by means of new relations between persons and objects, engendering of new motivations and desires, and creating the dynamics of characterizing and enacting persons that resonate with more enduring patterns of sociality.

Urban Scenes and Suffering

Arusha is a thoroughly global cosmopolis and a burgeoning, socially complex, interethnic town. Commercial enterprise is still largely dominated by a prosperous Asian community; a rift between Pentecostal and Lutheran dioceses has torn Christian communities apart in recent years (Baroin 1996). Although WaArusha and WaMeru are the predominant peoples who reside on the farms ascending Mount Meru, Arusha itself is a town of relative newcomers from virtually every region in Tanzania, with especially large communities that retain ties to the coast (from Dar es Salaam to Tanga), Tabora to the southwest, and Kilimanjaro and the Pare Mountains to the east.

Terms like *local* and *global* do exceedingly rough justice to the ways the totality of these relationships can be articulated in Arusha. Nonetheless, these social threads are articulated, even in such mundane venues as the aforementioned barbershops. Indeed, barbershops are explicitly and self-consciously about creating and demonstrating these connections as well as these disjunctures. In many establishments, one can watch satellite television broadcasts from the United Kingdom, South Africa, India, and the United States. Contemporary popular styles in much of Africa are never simply an appropriation of Western fashion (Ferguson 1999). Popular culture in Arusha includes an interest in Congolese *bolingo* (aka Rhumba; Remes 1999) as well as (or, for some, in opposition to) gangsta rap music, Nigerian and West Indian footballers alongside American basketball stars, soap operas from South Africa and the United States, and religious education programs infused with Saudi capital, or German, Canadian, and American evangelists. In barbershops, the ubiquitous posters that display a range of hairstyles for clients are an apt icon of this polygenesis. Each poster is a pastiche of head shots, cutouts from glossies like *Vibe* and *Word Up!*, extracted from advertising copy for Dark and Lovely hair care products, or simply snipped from past years' barbering posters, then compiled, printed, and reproduced, as was every such poster I saw in Arusha, in Nigeria.

Just as the imagery and iconography of marginalization is characteristic of this social milieu, so too the commodity form provides a means of articulating similar processes. There has been a true proliferation in the array of commodity forms widely available in Tanzania during the last decade. The structural adjustment that liberalized a one-party socialist state led to a meager influx of corporate capital, and it also permitted wealthy Tanzanians to display accumulated fortunes without sequestering assets in offshore accounts. Predictably, the boom of investment in the first years of this neoliberal transition has given way to a massive bust as inflationary pressures and unemployment today escalate to levels as perilous as any in the socialist era. Under these conditions, many residents of Arusha are acutely aware of a radical rupture, not simply in their standard of living, but in their shattered expectations. Such senses of rupture are increasingly standardized in Africa's neoliberal era (Comaroff and Comaroff 1999a; Ferguson 1999; White 2004). The growth of foreign and domestic media, the introduction of new goods, and the veil that has been lifted from what was once hidden wealth result in a clear recognition of the complex and compelling forms that value can take under globalization. These forces also result in a pressing frustration that such values are only available to a small portion of the globalized world Tanzania finds itself a part of. There is an ongoing commentary on the decline of resources, particularly jobs, throughout Tanzania, as well as a devastating understanding for many Tanzanians that the allure and promise held by the early 1990s may never be achieved again in their lifetimes.

Barbershops proliferated apace with the expansion of consumerism, and their always tenuous existences as business enterprises in a highly competitive environment make them locations where clients and workers typically confront the hardships that their own social practice and position exemplify. Analysis of sites like barbershops, where consumption is grasped as a practice with a productive potential, often focuses on the creative, dynamic, playful forms that consumption can take (Miller 1994;

Friedman 1990a; Hansen 1999). The fabrication and bricolage of consumerist practice has been seized on by much of social science as perhaps the most central contemporary arena for mounting exhibitions of hybridity and creolization (Hannerz 1996). In consuming, marginalized subjects are able to rework disparate signs, forms, and materials for the conveyance of powerful countermessages, subaltern identities, and disruptive mimicry, all of which demonstrate positive, assertive, and perhaps authentic voices. Youth are some of the most important and complex subjects in this process. Again, the contradictions are to the fore: youth are targeted as audiences and so are made complicit cohorts in a global spectacle of popular domination; yet they are also authorized by popular culture, presented with possibilities for creative assertion (Cole and Durham 2006). Much of the activity in Arusha's barbershops could well be characterized in these terms as young men, and more than a few young women, combine a diverse and, to a Western observer, at least, unanticipated array of popular styles (country music *and* hip hop clothing *and* devotion to Islam, for example) in ways that incisively participate in what are often fractious local political tournaments of identity. Studies of a vibrant popular cultural scene insurgent in the face of global downsizing, as compelling and necessary as these studies remain, have become something of a commonplace. In contrast, the sociocultural (and not simply political economic) significance of subjugation is frequently approached simply as an absence of assertive capacity. Talk about subjugation often threatens to shatter the agency of those who endure it. If there are weapons of the weak, weakness per se is not often counted among them. Discussions of social misery all too easily reduce the experience and expression of oppression to mere evidence of dependency, if not deprivation; but the concrete forms in which such suffering is felt and lived are rarely explored in themselves as meaningful sociocultural phenomena. Indeed, the forms of decline and anomie widespread in Arusha today are often taken as the antithesis of meaningfulness. Ferguson (1999: 19), for example, holds that this pervasive misery can

> confound one of the most basic anthropological expectations of fieldwork—
> the idea that by immersing oneself in the way of life of "others," one gradually
> comes to understand and make sense of their social world. What happens to
> anthropological understanding in a situation where "the natives" as well as the
> ethnographer lack a good understanding of what is going on around them?
> What if "the local people," like the anthropologist, feel out of place, alienated,
> and unconnected with much of what they see?

Ferguson's puzzlement neglects the fact that anthropology, for as long as there have been anthropologists, and nowhere more than in Africa, has made attempts to comprehend the experience of rupture, discontinuity, and alienation of precisely the sort that Ferguson describes on the Copperbelt. We may certainly debate the merits of different approaches to the study of affliction and ask whether theories of suffering and alienation, and the host of practices through which communities attempt to manage them, amount to anything more than functionalist explanations premised on social reproduction. Still, it is at least worth recognizing that not all anthropology proceeds from the same assumptions, and that questions like these may have been asked before.

There are further grounds for asserting that hardship and dis-ease deserve to be explored as cultural—which is to say meaningful—forms of experience. Confusion and disarray are no less capable of being articulated, interpreted, and engaged with than order and stability. Indeed, they seem to demand concerted attention. Both the characterization of chaos and the sustained efforts to remedy it can be communicated to others and so form the grounds for active intervention. There are ineffable and inchoate features to suffering, but cultural understanding need not require that all those who express their frustration have identical experiences. Moreover, distress is never simply an abstract or generalizable emotion and condition, but is always realized with respect to concrete circumstances. Surely Baudelaire's ennui, as vague and indeterminate as it may have felt, is distinctly different from the fear and humiliation of losing a job, or the grief and disbelief of a lost pregnancy. The meaningful differences between these qualities of torment derive from the ways that affliction is inextricably grounded in a wider world. These grievances speak to the subjective perception that certain specific contours of a sensible world of well-being have been rendered senseless. Affliction is a phenomenon whose attributes are themselves significant and so can be understood and acted on in specific ways; and it further reveals, by negation, the lineaments of the taken-for-granted order called into question by affliction. An understanding of affliction and its management, perhaps especially in the context of Africa, may help us grasp the contemporary experience of rupture and distress in Arusha. There are ways that the forms of subjectivity organized by spectacular modes of domination, and the conviviality afforded by consuming these spectacles, resonates with the constitution and transformation of subjectivities often brought about in cults of affliction, and possession cults in particular. Participation in the practices of popular culture, like participation in cults of possession, provides a means of both defining and confronting powerful sources of oppression, and of defining one's self in relation to such masterful powers. This parallel builds on the indispensable observation that misfortune is always a potent index of an encompassing cultural reality—not a static system, rule governed and uniform, but a world of meanings and values, broadly and unevenly shared, that makes sociality possible.

Kinyozi: A Place to Work, a Place to Think

In order to explore these processes of subjectification and sociality in Arusha's barbershops, I want to return from a different vantage point and ask: what kind of space is a barbershop? To begin with, there are two interrelated aspects of barbershops: they are places of work and public spaces. As sites of businesses, the barbershop milieu bespeaks the social crises of neoliberal transition in Tanzania, as well as the meanings of these institutional shifts and the kinds of consciousness embedded in them, that are the pervasive sense of rupture, and especially of unrealized expectations. Although anyone with a pair of scissors and a stool can establish himself as a barber in the city's market, and not a few attempt to do so, maintaining a moderately successful barbershop requires some sources of investment as well as cultural competence in the popular forms of barbering. Rents must be paid, infrastructural maintenance is required to assure an adequate supply of electricity, tools like electric razors for the barbers and aprons for clients must be purchased, and hair care products must be provided. All of this is independent of the cost of generating the sounds and scenes that make a barbershop attractive: the newspaper, radios and cassettes, even satellite TV, all of which the clients expect. What this means is that barbers and their clients tend to be formally educated young men, and barbershop owners have access to investors with small amounts of capital sufficient only to maintain an informal, tenuous operation. There is an intensely felt juxtaposition of a wider familiarity with the images and material forms of success, as well as some—albeit limited—connection to persons who enjoy such success, in contrast to the declining real opportunities to enjoy these values and fully participate in the world they embody. Not surprisingly, this juxtaposition meant that all the young barbers I spoke with saw their jobs as a compromise. For some, it was the best they could do until something better came along. For a great many, the tremendous promise of life in the city, especially for young men from more provincial parts of Tanzania who had completed secondary school, was abruptly confronted with the reality of working in a barbershop. This juxtaposition of expansive potential and declining opportunities, perhaps the one unifying feature of African youth (Cruise O'Brien 1996), is a central dimension of these young men's biographies and of the forms of social life they create.

At the same time, it must be noted that barbershops, as sites within a regional political economy, afford a degree of opportunity and a sense of entitlement that is otherwise unavailable to an expanding disenfranchised population. For some barbers, a *kinyozi* is a place where one can be independent, where you didn't need to work for some boss. Although there are infrastructural expenses required to open a barbershop, these costs are significantly less than those associated with other businesses. Opening a retail shop or bar requires substantial capital to manage inventories and to pay the license fees (which barbers are notorious for avoiding). Even the smallest hair salons require much more expensive machinery than the *kinyozi* (for example, dryers, steamers, electric kettles for boiling water), and they make far more extensive use of hair care products: virtually every customer at a salon will be treated with some commercial product, be it relaxer, cholesterol, or petroleum-based gels. Further, barbering is treated as a kind of profession by young men with virtually no formal training in hair cutting. And it is not uncommon for barbershops to close for lack of business, or because a patron suddenly withdrew support. Under such circumstances, young men who had initially taken up barbering simply because they could find no other work will generally continue to look for work as barbers, rather than seek some other kind of work. Many of these barbers indicated to me that they saw their work as a set of skills that they had learned, and they hoped to use this *elimu*, "education," to get ahead in town. Moreover, these skills and the work of barbering were embraced as signs of a certain sophistication, and at a minimum, of a competence and mastery over the forms of urban living. Barbershops, as virtually all barbers told me, are never found in villages, where people have neither the electricity required for electrical razors nor the education to appreciate a stylish cut. One barber told me, as he gracefully shaved a client's hair, "My hands cannot even use a razor blade any longer." Barbering, as this statement eloquently reveals, can be a testament to the skillful mastery of an urban lifestyle under conditions of material constraint.[2]

These political economic features of the barbershop—as a place of work, as a site of hardship and marginality, and as a place of urban distinction and entitlement—are directly relevant to the *kinyozi* as a public space. The term *public* is ideologically fraught, immediately suggesting an opposition to a private domain, but the public quality of the barbershop really transcends this opposition. Barbershops are private enterprises, but their existence depends on their ability to participate in and to make a public. The display (and performance) of a barbershop is intended to publicize the shop in a dual sense: to promote it as an attractive, contemporary establishment, but also to demonstrate that the shop and its denizens are of the public, that they are hooked into a reality outside of the shop, beyond even the here and now of Arusha and Tanzania. It is surely no accident that the bus stand and the Nairobi road, places of perpetual movement and connection, are the most visibly, densely concentrated sites of *vinyozi*. An important part of the public character of barbershops is therefore their permeability, the ways in which they are ever oriented beyond themselves. This is made evident through the shops' representations, the images, sounds, and styles that explicitly reference faraway places like Brooklyn, California, Liverpool, Kinshasa, and Kosovo. It is equally true of the sociospatial form that the shops take. A *kinyozi* is an exposed arena, its front door always open during business hours, and the social flow of staff, clients, and visitors perpetually traverse a series of thresholds that encompass the shop. Clients getting haircuts joke with friends within earshot outside the door; next to the *kinyozi* door is a small sitting area, lined with small benches, perhaps a chair or two. Clients wait; idle barbers chat among themselves with customers, neighboring shopkeepers, and passing friends in a continuous movement from barber chairs to waiting area, outside the shop, into the street, and back again. Shoeshine stands are frequently adjacent to a shop, providing a service that contributes to the stylistic accomplishment of a good haircut, but also adding a venue for conversation, a spot to wait, to watch, to talk. *Vinyozi* actively insert themselves *mtaani* ("into the street"), with barbers and clients calling out to passersby, leaving their seats to accompany girlfriends and *fanya biashara* ("do business") down the block before returning to the shop. Lest this public character be construed in functional terms as simply good for business, it is important to point out that this public style is a specific feature of barbershops. This expansiveness unmistakably contrasts with both women's hair salons, which are closed off from the street, typically behind a curtain, if not a closed door. Nor were there any salons at the bus stand in 1999 and 2000. The contrast is also clear in comparison with barbershops frequented and owned by Asians on the high street of Arusha: they have closed doors, and no visible publicizing of their establishment, other than a simple barber pole, is evident.

As an aspect of its public character, the barbershop also enfolds the street into itself. As noted in chapter 3, passersby and clients do not enter into the social field of the shop indifferently; all must make their presence felt by shaking hands (always a performance that demonstrates semiotic virtuosity) when entering and leaving. These gestures are crucial to the spatiality of the barbershop because they establish that a shop that is open and accessible in its attachments to the world is also framed and circumscribed as a social field, never simply a motley array of people. In all of these modes of constructing space, the social practices of barbershops confirm its character as a distinctive place.

The stylistic performances of a *kinyozi* are complex and changing, but every shop, like every *kijiwe,* is indispensably a place of conversation and companionship. They are places to be among other people.[3] From the point of view of lived experience and the felt qualities of subjectification, it is important to note that this kind of social interaction is explicitly described as important to one's sense of belonging and well-being. The barbershop is a place to *punguza mawazo,* "ease your worries." *Mawazo,* a semantically complex term, are a central concern of the barbershop and of everyday life in Arusha. In the context just described, *mawazo* can be translated as "worries" or "troubles." But in most contexts, *mawazo* are "thoughts," and "worries/troubles" are precisely one particular variety of thought.[4] As Fabian has perceptively noted for speakers of Swahili in Shaba, equally consumed by *mawazo* (1978: 323), "thought . . . is not neutral ratiocination; it is active imagination." Although speakers of Swahili in Arusha do not, to my knowledge, describe themselves as "thinking" or use the verb *kuwaza* (in the Arusha vernacular, "to think" is *kufikiri*) as they do in Shaba, men and women in Arusha do describe themselves as "having thoughts," *kuwa na mawazo.* This understanding of "having thoughts" also moves "thoughts" beyond conceptualization and points to a condition of activity; indeed, as I will argue, it is a condition of bodily activity. What is further clear from commonplace discussion in Arusha about "having thoughts [troubles/worries]" and "easing thoughts [troubles/worries]" is that—paradoxically, perhaps, from the perspective of Western forms of personhood—thinking is not only an active process; it is also quintessentially a felt one.

As active processes, thinking or having thoughts are never just thinking about things, a detached contemplation of reality; rather, what is emphasized is a thinking toward some anticipated (or dreaded) possibility. Tshibumba persistently describes his practice of painting as a form of thinking, Fabian (1996) tells us, and sees his paintings as realizations of *mawazo yangu,* "my thoughts." Similarly, in Jamaa practice,[5] dreams, which are synonymous with thoughts, are sources of prophecy, revelations of things to come (Fabian 1998: 323). In all these ways, thoughts are ways of working through life's circumstances, forms of creative practice that imaginatively select, organize, and communicate what is ultimately significant. In Arusha, and in barbershops especially, having thoughts is not only about creatively working through present conditions so as to realize a meaningful future; it is also about confronting the present as an obstacle to that realization. In having thoughts, one encounters an unknowable range of possibilities. For one who has thoughts, the future is an open prospect, and for that reason, thinking is demanded in order to generate the future as a knowable, viable certainty. For young men in Arusha today who are in positions of such tenuous employment as barbershops, the depths of this uncertainty, the profound gap between one's severely limited or intractable present conditions and the limitless prospects of the future, confront the thinking subject as a formidable obstacle—so formidable that subjects, the young men gathered in the *kinyozi,* are less the agents of their own thinking than they are overwhelmed by thoughts that act on them.

This formulation of subjectivity and personhood is a critical feature of barbershop sociality. This characterization of having thoughts means that thinking is an imaginative and creative process; to think in these ways is also to suffer, to be in pain. This pain is characteristically premised on an absence, a void. The chasm between now and later, the unknown prospect of the future, is one such absence, and it is one to which thoughts incessantly return. One young man I met with daily talked a good deal about his mother, who had recently died. She had been a teacher, and before her death, she had not only helped to educate five of her children, but also instilled in them a desire for education and an expectation that education would provide for them in the future. This value was put into practice each day as my friend spoke to me in English, demonstrating how well he had learned, and how much he hoped still to learn. He also commented frequently on the fact that his mother had died leaving him, as her eldest child, to care for his siblings, all of whom were still at home in central Tanzania. But the education his mother provided had not assured any of them the opportunities that she—and he—anticipated. One day, as I sat silently with him in the empty barbershop, he revealed to me that he had dreamed that night of his dead mother. Without mentioning all of the responsibilities he shouldered or plans he was pursuing, which were typical topics of discussion every other day, he simply told me, *"Kichwa kinajaa na mawazo"* ("My head is full of thoughts"). The dreams that Jamaa depend on for prophecy, itself predicated on an unknown future, are here dreams of loss, distance, separation, and unrealized possibilities, all of which are manifest absences. This absence seems inevitably to be flooded with thoughts. Moreover, the felt qualities of thought, the painful process of being overcome by worries, are plainly embodied experiences. Thinking is not just experienced as the active doing of thought; it is also perceived as the accumulation of *mawazo mengi,* "many thoughts"—thoughts that take on weight and mass. The volume of thoughts makes your "head feel jumbled," *kichwa kinachangayika.* Indeed, thoughts of this kind are *gumu,* "hard," and they are *uchungu,* "pain/bitterness," itself. Productive social interaction thus works to *punguza,* "decrease" or "lighten," one's thoughts. I once asked Saidi to paint some portraits for me. Saidi, who almost invariably smiled and joked with me, suddenly looked remarkably dour. Are you ill? I asked him. "No," he said, "when you get a job like this, your head starts to hurt" (*kichwa kinaumwa*). I soon found that he and other painters I met through him across town talked about their work as "thought-provoking" (*inakupa mawazo*) and headache-inducing (*inuma kichwa*) labor. Thus, even the creative process of working through the present and prospectively imagining the future is a source of bodily pain.

The Power of Pain

Such suffering and bodily pain often seem irreducibly personal, individuating, and isolating. Yet it is important to recognize that they are also subjective conditions of encountering the world, and in this regard they are active practices. Pain, moreover, is a social mode of consciousness. It is about "others" in a variety of ways. There is pain in sharing the injustices that characterize social life, in readying oneself with others for the hardships one has had to endure. Pain also involves caring for others. The young men gathered in barbershops are familiar with one another's stories, know of the struggles they face every day, not only because they face the same struggles themselves but because the *kinyozi,* as I have indicated, is a place where conversation works to ease your worries. But suffering is social, not only because it is set in a collective context and shared, but also in the sense that it is itself a manner of relating to others and the world. As Asad (1983: 313ff.) notes in his discussion of pain in medieval Christianity, the monastic's body is made to testify to the truth of Christian virtues by means of social relationships. The monastic's pain is truth as revealed to those who observe, authorize, and discipline him. Pain is the medium through which monastic brothers, and in a radically different context Arusha's youth, enact sociality. Suffering, never simply an internalized, silent condition, a mere impediment to pleasure, or the repression of pain-free self, is a dimension of engaging with reality as it presents itself to the active subject. Pain, then, is being-in-the-world.

There are ways in which the phenomenology, or what we might call the generativity, of pain are realized and acted on in young men's social world. Pain can be grasped as both a defining feature of personhood and the grounds for sustained sociality. In a conversation about local clubs in Arusha, I asked a young barbershop crowd about a place I knew to be especially popular. I was surprised to hear them dismiss the place as one they would never go to, and especially to show disdain for the typical clientele of the club. The men who frequented these places saw themselves as *special*, an English word in everyday use, used especially to describe a manner of flashy and ostentatious dress. The term also betokens the singularity of one who sees himself as special, different, and distinct from others. These club patrons were further characterized as *msenge*, current slang for "fags," who, somewhat paradoxically, are only interested in attracting women. In contrast, the streets and survival are paramount features of a social world; they are icons of a world that is rife with pain and thus values survival. Most importantly, the capacity to survive—to endure through struggle, to never give in to weakness, especially a weakness for women—is a central attribute of the person. Survival is something that can only be achieved through this social world on the streets, and it further qualifies the person to participate in this world. Without a capacity to confront pain, one is less than fully human. Indeed, one man described the indignity of slavery by saying, "When the master says 'I have an ache,' the slave answers, 'Boss, I'm in pain.'" If I am subject to the pain of others in ways that strictly dictate my ability to face my own pains, then my very existence as a person is denied.

Thus, pain is a form of consciousness that can be grasped as a generative, productive, and perhaps even positive attribute of persons and their social relations. If we approach the affliction of pain in this way, it may be possible to see how the subjugation of pain, the subject's sense of being acted on by thoughts, of struggling to survive, may provide a means to its own resolution, if not absolute transcendence. Because pain is an attribute of the person that bespeaks one's subjugation, without which one would not be in pain, pain can become a means of access to the source of that subjugation. In other words, the pain that subjects endure makes them available to some subjugating force and may therefore provide a means of dealing with, if not overcoming, that force. Let me offer a comparative example, worlds away from Arusha's urban barbershops, if not all that far from Tanzania's borders, that illustrates how this process of managing subjugation might work. Lienhardt describes the role of what he calls "Powers" in Dinka experience, which are held to be "the grounds of a particular human condition," which is to say responsible for human misery (1961: 148). To counter these deleterious effects, a Dinka will not only try to identify the Power that has attacked him, but he will further, and quite literally, identify with the threatening force. Thus, the (relatively) celebrated case of the man who, "having been imprisoned in Khartoum named one of his children 'Khartoum' in memory of the place, but also to turn aside any harmful influence of that place upon him in later life" (Lienhardt 1961: 149–50). Here, the former prisoner engages in what Lienhardt would call symbolic action, creating a model or image that captures an existential condition in order to act on that model and thereby transform the lived condition. In creating an image of Khartoum, this man produces an identification with the source of his enduring subjugation, and through that identification, he establishes a means to exert control over this oppressive force. Note, moreover, that the man does not attempt to eradicate the presence of Khartoum in his life, which will ideally endure long after him through his own children. Rather, he makes of Khartoum an image of self-identification (as a Dinka man's children are inexorably aspects of himself) so as to participate in the power that Khartoum has to oppress him. In this way, the man becomes more like Khartoum, and his own recognition of subjugation to this threatening Power provides a means of becoming more Power-ful himself.

From a certain perspective, the dynamics of pain and survival can be understood in similar terms. It is pain itself that certifies one's standing as a person, a *mdumu* (lit., "tough/hard person"), a *muhuni*, "thug," "street nigga." Embracing this oppressive power as a means of self-identification thus provides a direct means of countering that oppression, as the recurrent discussion of pain, bitterness, and especially thoughts enables the barbers in pain to engage more fully in a world that permits them to confront that pain through survival and, at moments, the easing of worries. To experience and self-consciously identify oneself as one who suffers is simultaneously an act of diminution and an assertion of entitlement. Pain for the young male urbanites in Arusha is the bodily trace of injustice and oppression, but it also presents an affirmation of one's ongoing confrontation with obstacles, a process of grappling with life's troubles that defines existence itself. To have pain is to demonstrate oneself to be one who endures through adversity. By identifying themselves with pain, these young men thereby articulate and index the larger purposes, even the transcendent reality for which they tolerate such hardship: for life in the street, the respect of one's thugs, the care of one's kin. In this they are akin to the Chicago boxers that Wacquant describes, who "have at their disposal a rich occupational vocabulary that enables them to confront pain . . . not with silent denial but with personal valorization and collective solemnization" (1998: 337). Pain is not so much overcome as it is seized on as a means of identification with the wider reality that is painful, and for which one faces pain.

Possessed by Pain

The predominant features of personhood, action, and sociality that are iconically expressed as pain go a long way toward elucidating the lived experience of everyday encounters for a great many urban youth in Arusha. Pain is an embodied quality that is both produced by and generative of a kind of micropolitics of social life. This is a micropolitics found not only in barbershops but also on the bus stand; in the breakneck competition of *daladala* (minivan transport) crews; among the working staff of bars and *nyama choma* (lit., "roast meat") joints; and the peddlers of *mitumba* (used clothing), all of whom scramble for a living, striving *kutafuta maisha*, "to find a life," in town. Pain is the generative principle of the habitus of Arusha's informal sector. Although this immediate, face-to-face lived reality is dynamic and even cohesive (if never systematically so), this micro-level order of practice is only incompletely understood when considered exclusively at this level of social action. Pain is a public discourse, and the barbershops have to be seen as one especially lively node in a wider public in which they participate. This broader public projects the significance of pain in mediated signs and images that have a far-flung—indeed, global—circulation. For Arusha's young men, perhaps the most compelling global signs and images of personhood, and especially of a public persona, are embedded in the world of rap and hip hop music and style. Barbershops throughout town are painted with icons of the most celebrated performers, like Tupac, and shops repaint and repaper their interiors with new and different icons as fashions and reputations shift. Even shops that do not blare gangsta rap music from their radios and tape decks, or that cater to a clientele who prefers *bolingo* or R&B sounds are still bedecked with images that derive from African American gangsta iconography. The potency of these images, and the modes of personhood they exhibit, can and should be tied to the ongoing concerns with pain and suffering that characterize lived experience on Arusha's streets. To fully grasp the import of pain, and to see how it motivates and formulates subjectivity and domination—to return to the spectacular—we need to situate the sociocultural practices of thugs in barbershops in this context of global fantasy, which is to say, within a wider cosmology.

Anyone with a passing familiarity with the sights and sounds, the lore and life of hip hop in the United States, will recognize that pain is a widely proclaimed motif of this popular cultural scene. The violent deaths of Biggie Smalls (Notorious B.I.G.), Freaky Tah, Big L, and paradigmatically Tupac Shakur are not only evidence of the suffering characteristic of the rap and hip hop world. They are also comprehensible as inevitable, even predictable, outcomes of a life dominated by an intensely competitive struggle in a world of pain. Tupac is often described in the American press as having a messiah complex. This is borne out by tracks like "Only God Can Judge Me," "How Long Will They Mourn Me?," "No More Pain," and "Check Out Time," by his crucified appearance on the album cover of *The Don Killuminati: The 7 Day Theory*, which he released under the name Makaveli; the crucifix tattooed across his back; and his series of posthumous albums, including *Still I Rise* (or Notorious B.I.G.'s new release, *Born Again*). The suffering directly addressed in gangsta rap is never simply a way of decrying the social conditions of racial and economic struggle in the United States, although this should not be overlooked. Rather, pain is a focal point for constructing a social persona, for creating, enhancing, and demonstrating the viability of one's reputation. The reputation for pain—*Me Against the World*, "So Many Tears"—that Tupac promoted, and that disciples like DMX profess in "Ready to Meet Him," challenges it by working through it and identifying with it. Respect and reputation accrue not to those who project an invincible self-image, but those who live with pain and thereby show that they have the strength to endure and withstand it. Again, such a world, and the kinds of persons who inhabit it, are dependent on the ongoing experience of pain.

It is clear that these models of subjectivity promoted and disseminated in the global commodification of hip hop have profoundly shaped the specific consciousness of pain in Arusha. Young men in town routinely describe and avow the hardships that they face by means of forms that derive directly from the world of hip hop, such as slogans on *daladala* such as "100% Pure Pain" and "Suffer and Survive," and names of barbershops like "Death Row Barberhouse," which not only evinces an image of oppression but is an homage to Death Row Records, the label founded by Tupac and his producer, Suge Knight. Moreover, I often heard young men describe their own hardships as being just like those endured by the rappers they admired, or discussing how Tanzanians were "the same as 'Black Americans'" in their pain. The influence of these cultural forms is

Death Row in Arusha

palpable, but how, exactly, can we account for this influence? Is gangsta rap, in spite of its revolutionary, outlaw promotion of struggle and strife, just one more version of cultural imperialism? Is the barbershop set in urban Arusha simply emulating American celebrity as emblematic of a self-evidently more powerful and irresistibly more desirable world? Certainly there are powerful interests that mine the commercial potential of hip hop and rap, but need this mean that the interests and motives of youth in Arusha are ultimately irrelevant?

There are a number of ways that studies of globalization have addressed precisely such issues. It is possible, for example, to argue that Tupac, Snoop Dogg, Dr. Dre, and others provide concrete material and meaningful forms through which the social experiences of those in places like Arusha can be imaginatively articulated. Suffering and pain enacted in the rhythms and rhymes of rappers could be said to provide a means of expression for the feelings of alienation and oppressions that pervade this urban East African scene. The signifiers may be global, but the signified remains resolutely local by this logic. The problem with this perspective is that it retains a fundamental and insupportable distinction between the cultural form and the social experience, as though the pain of urban life were ever present and simply waiting to be expressed in a powerful new language. This perspective fails to consider the ways that subjective forms of pain and survival do not merely represent social life but actively constitute it. This means, at the same time, that the constitution of the world of persons and objects, and the relations between them as it is lived in the barbershops and street life of Arusha cannot simply be an imitation of some other reality. The local is not merely expressed in global terms; nor are global images defining local experience in Arusha. What is needed in order to articulate these dimensions of total sociocultural process is a recognition of the fact that as these particular Tanzanian young men consume popular global media, from gangsta rap to South African satellite TV, they are actively aiming to remake a world that they can fully inhabit.

As a form of consciousness, pain is not overcome but seized on as a means of identification through which Arusha's youth could qualify or authorize themselves to participate in their social world. In this regard, pain becomes a generative form of subjectification, that is, a constructive means of generating a subjectivity (inherently embedded in sociality) with which to confront a world of suffering. From this perspective, the identification with the themes, signs, and images of global hip hop, especially in the form of figures like Tupac, who publicly insisted on his own suffering, becomes a way of asserting the positive value of pain as a means of access to a wider world—indeed, a worldwide community of affliction. In other words, pain becomes more than just the negative feeling of oppression, more, even, than the foundation for a micropolitics of everyday encounters. Under these circumstances, the felt experience of pain becomes a way of situating the subject of pain in a powerful global order of meanings and relations. Popular cultural practices in a wide array of urban contexts serve to organize and realize what Foster (2002: 15) describes as an "imagined cosmopolitanism," in which media consumers understand themselves to be participants in a worldwide scene. This imagined and imaginative reality is a potent, spectacular form of fantasy, and so it is a cosmopolitanism laden with subjective potential and imposing sources of domination. The possibilities of this situation, as in feeling one's self a subject in an overarching cosmos, are profound. For the barbershop crowd in Arusha, imaginative participation in this cosmos can be daunting enough to confirm their felt sense of suffering, but also powerful enough to transform that condition of suffering.

The theme of participation through exclusion is a central dynamic in popular cultural practices across Arusha. As I mention in chapter 3, it shapes the fantastical geographies of Arusha's *vinyozi,* where Brooklyn Barber's Shops and Liverpool Haircuts, more than a dozen California Kinyozi, and even a Cosovo Cuts can be found, but no Kilimanjaro, no Serengeti, no Dar, not even a Nairobi is in sight. This dialectical theme also shapes the ethos of economic enterprise more broadly in town. Virtually every person I met in Arusha was consumed with pursuing business, but none was consistently able to get access to the jack, benjamins, and cash money that was part of the dollarized tourist and mineral economy. Instead, they hustled to get *mkwanja,* a euphemism taken from the piles of hacked-off grass created by landscaping road crews armed with hand machetes, a plainly grueling and debasing occupation. Such examples illustrate that the dynamism and force of the global world constructed by these urban actors are clearly felt to lie elsewhere, and the crucial structuring principles and media of value that organize that world are inaccessible, even irrelevant, to life in Arusha.

Nonetheless, the palpable distancing from these potent sources is essential to the productivity of the fantastical and spectacular processes of popular culture. In part, this distancing contributes in direct and substantial ways to the feelings of pain that shape subjectivity in Arusha. Many young men in town, for example, voiced their complaints about urban life to me in terms of the poor and uneven quality of the consumer goods that they desired, a complaint expressed by contrasting the radios, cassette recorders, and even hair clippers that they could get in Arusha and the "real" (*kwa kweli,* "true," or *haki,* "honest") goods that were available in some imagined *kwenu,* "your place" (that is, America or Europe). This distrust of local goods articulates a sense of dissatisfaction that has a local focus, with charges laid against the honesty of local retailers, as well as a more global bewilderment at the plight of "we Tanzanians," who, in a high-tech conspiracy of the first rank, receive only lesser-quality goods while the best of things are reserved for First World consumers. It is not simply that Tanzanians have an acute, if largely imagined, sense of the contrast between "we Tanzanians" and "your place" as mediated by consumption. In addition, this contrast is felt as part of the pain that comes increasingly to characterize social interaction in Arusha. This sense of the contrast between "here" in Tanzania and "there" in America, Europe, or elsewhere makes these highly valued and desirable consumer goods, as well as the multiply mediated images and practices of consumerism more generally, into powerful forces of domination. The intense desire for those things that are desirable explicitly because of their unattainability (for the desirable "true/real/honest" goods are always projected to lie elsewhere) allows these highly valued products to subjugate the consumer in Arusha. That is, consumers can experience their desire as a source of constraint and limit (Gell 1988). In Mbembe's terms, the domination of command is achieved by means of its thoroughgoing fetishization.

Here is a potent and creative paradox embedded in the fantasies of popular culture and the subjectivities of the youth who participate in it. In Arusha, these young men perceive themselves to be marginal to, and so subjugated by, the global order of signs and values they intensely desire. Yet this subjugation is experienced as pain, which, as a way of qualifying personhood and constituting sociality, can greatly contribute to the subjective sense of connection to that worldwide community. How might we resolve this paradox? More importantly, how might this paradox permit of a kind of resolution for those whose lives are defined by it? The dynamics of this dialectic in consciousness suggest that the lived feeling of subjugation, the pervasive and routinized awareness that vital sources of value, meaning, and power, are always distant and seemingly inaccessible, which makes these cultural forms and forces seem simultaneously (if paradoxically) uniquely real. If this is so, then one's own existence must, by definition, be formed through its relation to this ontological order. From this perspective, pain becomes not only an expression of the subject's relationship to that unique reality, forming a conduit to this wider truth; pain also becomes a way of seeing one's own subjugation as itself an aspect of this fundamental, ontological pain. To use Lienhardt's language of symbolic action, for the denizens of Arusha's shops and streets, their own pain is a model of their existential condition of marginality, a model through which they can act on that subjugation so as to transform it. The trick is recognizing that these practitioners of popular culture make themselves (that is, their consciousness of themselves as being in pain, having thoughts) models for their own action, in effect turning themselves into exemplars of an imagined transcendent, ontological realm. Identifying yourself as a person acted on by overarching and unique forces that are themselves characterized by pain and oppression (as the themes, images, sights, and sounds of the global gangsta make unambiguously clear) is to assert that you are commanded by an all-powerful reality—and that is a potent claim to agency and self-construction.

If we trace the implications of this language for the making of subjectivity to the specific field of affliction as a paramount sociopolitical concern—and a long-standing domain of symbolic action—another way of describing these dynamics of consciousness, already alluded to in the earlier discussion, suggests itself: the barbershop crowd become hosts for the Powers who, in their own obsessions with pain, come to possess their alters. Arusha's youth routinely make themselves over in the form of the exquisite suffering of some peerless "others" (that is, celebrity rappers). Their own suffering—the thoughts that fill, hurt, and jumble their heads—is thus performed simultaneously as a core feature of themselves as suffering thugs, and of themselves in the guise of even more legitimate, real, and certainly powerful others (see Boddy 1989 for an apposite perspective on the performative qualities of *zar* possession). An apt comparison are the Sakalava tromba spirits described by Lambek (1998), who return to possess their hosts during festivals held at ancestral reliquaries. These spirits are royal persons, real historical figures, who inevitably appear in trance as they were at the moment of their own deaths. These most powerful of figures are available to their human alters in a condition of unsurpassed suffering, as death becomes the "foundational moment" for these spirits' performances (Lambek 1998: 118). The (often traumatic) death of the tromba not only permeates their presence as spirits, qualifying them as powers, much as pain qualifies persons in Arusha; but the remembered death of the spirit also provides a substantial, corporeal connection between tromba and host. Hosts will prepare to receive their spirits "by applying white clay to the parts of the body whose traumata lead to death" (Lambek 1998: 118). The embodiment of tromba is further elaborated in the ways that mediums make themselves the objects acted on by these most powerful of spirits: Sakalava hosts "suffer when they speak the secrets of their spirits" (Lambek 1998: 123). Suffering is both the embodied grounds of dominant social relations, iconic of the presence of the tromba in the bodies of their hosts, and a poetic trope of Sakalava history. Transposed into the practices of popular culture in Arusha, pain, too, is the presence of celebrated, fantastical global persons incarnated in urban youth, their heads filled with too many thoughts.

To suggest that participation in global popular culture in the specific context of urban Arusha can be likened to a modality of spirit possession might raise the objection that none of these activities ever entails trance or dissociation. Although that is true, these practices do entail embodied forms of alterity, which is to say a bodily consciousness of one's self as another. Although this consciousness may not be explicitly—that is, self-consciously—expressed as that "other" (*wahuni* in barbershops may quote the rhymes of many a rapper, but to my knowledge, they never claim to actually be those superstars), nonetheless, the subjectivity that they do present is closely attuned to the consciousness of these powerful figures. Because so much of contemporary social and cultural theory has gone to great lengths to demonstrate that consciousness cannot be contained in overt self-awareness or in constructs of the mind but is equally dispersed in embodied, implicit, and collective practices, it makes little sense to say that possession is a form of consciousness that depends on the explicit self-awareness announced by possessing spirits.

Global hip hop in Arusha is plainly not the manifestation of some survival cult of possession, the old wine of an authentic African practice in new skins. There are any number of possession practices, both historical and contemporary, that have been associated with current residents of this region of Tanzania, from upepo spirits from the Swahili coast, to Waswezi spirits from Tabora and Mwanza, to modern-day Majini that afflict the town. The link between popular culture and possession is less at the level of historical forms and more at the level of social action. Both possession and popular culture itself are ways of formulating subjectivity under conditions of domination in ways that use the subjects' position of subjugation as a vehicle to articulate and identify with the force of subjugating powers. A focus on the actional nexus of these relations of domination may therefore permit us to transcend the unproductive dichotomy between appropriation and emulation, a view of popular cultural practices as quintessentially African or slavishly imitative of the West. Moreover, the terms of both possession and popular culture as modes of domination recall Mbembe's insights into the efficacy of conviviality. Yet this view does not reduce such forms of subjectification to mere vulgarity. Instead, it sees them as productive forms of pragmatic action.

Possession as a potent way of expressing and fantasizing about social relations that are at once intimately meaningful and overwhelmingly powerful is an equally cogent illustration of the way that globalization can be imagined and lived. Popular cultural practice performed by Arusha's youth, conceived of along the same lines, is therefore not the local expression of a global set of forces and institutions. Popular culture, like possession, is about the connection and copresence of specific times, places, and persons, with encompassing powers, images, and relations. This copresence is a lived reality, felt and worked through in the experience of pain, pain that is simultaneously your own and another's, embodied and objectified, specific and transcendent. It is pain as an organizing theme of consciousness and a mode of being—pain as a central criterion of persons that enables them to participate in the social world of Arusha's turbulent streets—that gives the practices of popular culture many of the definitive attributes of a cult of affliction. Urban youth, who simultaneously embody the social crisis of postsocialist Tanzania, the radical contrast of aspiration and opportunity, and the superlative power of global spectacle, are this cult's most proficient adepts. Amid the contemporary upheavals of this neoliberal moment in Africa (and elsewhere), where once unimaginable wealth and well-being are now all too easily imagined and instantaneously mediated, and therefore all the more painfully unattainable, we should not be surprised to find that cults of affliction (re)emerge as a persuasive means of illicit cohabitation shared by those enraptured by these fantasies.

Portraits 3

Uncertain Prospects

Over the course of the many years that I've been engaged in research in Arusha, beginning with my first trip in 1999 and culminating in my most recent visit in 2006, and as my thinking about the dynamics of exclusion and inclusion developed, I became concerned with trying to understand what kind of future the young men and women I know might find for themselves. How, for example, could marriage and kinship relations—those foundational themes in the ethnographic description and anthropological analyses of African community—even endure in a neoliberal context? Not only are projects of value production in such contexts stripped down to a focus on narrowly imagined units—consumer citizens, each independently bearing their individual rights—but the resources, material and otherwise, for envisioning a future in the face of tremendous ambiguity and fluctuation seemed strikingly limited. Moreover, the antagonism between genders (to say nothing of the anxieties surrounding HIV, which is scarcely discussed openly in Arusha) seemed to make the link between social and biological reproduction much more tenuous. Women might value the prospect of having children, but they rarely thought of husbands as necessary to that ambition or as reliable partners in long-term relationships. Meanwhile, men often expressed their hostility toward the putatively materialist motives of most women. In the face of such pervasive distrust and overt hostility, who would get married, and why? As I discussed these matters with my friends and followed them through the trajectory of their lives, in many cases into (and in some cases out of) marriage, I was struck by the difficulty of predicting marital prospects and outcomes. Amy Stambach (personal communication), who works with many well-educated Chagga in Moshi and Arusha, tells me that most Tanzanians she knows think that an educated women is unlikely to get married; she is not thought of as a "good wife" by young men, and most of these women do not think that a husband can contribute anything to their social prospects. I have found that many far less privileged women in the milieu in which I work in Arusha are also suspicious of marriage. Ultimately, these portraits offer a glimpse into the lives of men and women in Arusha, not to make an analytical understanding of kinship more systematic, but to suggest some of the range of possibilities of family life so that the many meanings of marriage, kinship, and family (and thus belonging, inclusion, and the future) might be illuminated.

Miriamu and Julietta

I offer here a twinned portrait of two women I got to know over the summer of 2000, the only year I was able to find them in Arusha. Miriamu and Julietta both worked in the Fashion Beauty Salon near the city center of Arusha. These two women, both in their late twenties, had regularly worked at salons, they told me, leaving one after another in search of more reliable pay—not that salaries ever improved, but salon owners were notorious for irregular payment to their employees, who were, after all, said Julietta "just women" and so easily taken advantage of (recall, though, that Hussein told me much the same thing about his previous employer at Bad Boyz). Julietta and Miriamu had always worked together and had arrived at Fashion Beauty nine months before I met them in May 2000. They were already suspicious of the salon owner, a Chagga woman, they told me, whose rich husband had set her up in business as an investment.

I met Julietta and Miriamu in typical (for me) fashion: I walked into their salon and asked them how long they had worked there, and how long the salon had been in town. The two were engaging in their responses to me, Miriamu vivacious and chatty, Julietta more laconic, but witty and ironic. They were immediately curious—and critical—about a man on his own visiting salons in Africa. Didn't I have a wife? They could only imagine what people must be saying about me. But they seemed to enjoy my presence in their salon, and they always got a kick out of encouraging their friends and clients to gossip about me in my presence, only to have me respond in Swahili and give them a humorous frisson. "Hmm," said Miriamu's friend, as she walked into the salon from the street. "I see you've found a sugar daddy!" (*umaeanza kuchuna 'buzi*—lit., "you've decided to butcher a goat," that is, to strip a carcass of its tasty meat). "Hey," I said, "do I look like a goat to you? And what kind of a *kidenti* ["small student," a term used for young girls out to entice older men] are you?" Howls of laughter. Miriamu and Julietta thoroughly enjoyed the agonistic patter of the street, mocking the friends I told them about who worked in barber-shops as posers and petty criminals, offering up lots of gossip about the sexual proclivities of the women of Arusha, including their own clients. Both of them enjoyed a beer after work. I noted Julietta's penchant for stout mixed with cola and asked her why she liked such a concoction. "It strengthens your blood" (*inaongeza damu*), she said—too tempting a com-ment, of course for the symbolic anthropologist. Julietta dismissed all of my niggling questions about blood, beer, and sugar, but thereafter, she'd invite me to buy her a drink by saying, "Let's go strengthen our blood!"

I visited Miriamu and Julietta in their homes only once. They lived in Mianzini, a notorious district just across the Nairobi road from the city center; they didn't even need to take a *daladala* to work, a nice daily savings for them. But Mianzini was a tough neighborhood, feared for its crime rate, and it was especially densely settled. Julietta lived in two rooms along a string of similar units. It was only when I arrived at her home that I discovered that she had two children under ten, who were cared for by a neighbor girl scarcely older than the children she was minding. Julietta's home was clean but spartan. Her furnishing in the family room consisted of only a bed, which also served as a couch, and a wooden stool where I sat while I met her family. On the wall above the bed, she had tacked up a large poster advertising Dark and Lovely, the American hair care prod-uct used in every salon in Arusha. There was something desperately sad yet poised and sensitive about the careful way in which this well-tended poster hung over the bare surroundings of the tidy room. Miriamu lived nearby, but in a much smaller, cramped room. Lined with tarpaulin, one wall had a bunk bed elevated above two chairs, which faced, only four or five feet away, an adjacent wall lined with a dresser that had all manner of items—radio, cassette player, pots and pans, dishes—stacked on top of it. Miriamu, too, did what she could to decorate the room, covering the dresser with shiny polyester cloth and draping a curtain under her bed, which she pulled aside so guests could use her chairs.

In discussions with Julietta after my visit, I found out that her husband had left her with her children because—well, she said, because that's what husbands do. He hadn't been able to secure work as a mechanic, and after a few years of marriage, he sent her back to Arusha from Karatu (a town to the west), where he thought she'd stay with her parents. Instead, Julietta ended up on her own—her parents were displeased by Julietta's failure to accommodate her husband—and had been trying her best to raise her children alone. She told me that Miriamu also had a child, but because she was a Muslim, the father had kept the child and had sent his wife back to live with her parents in Dodoma. Again, Miriamu was not welcome in her natal home, so she struck out for Arusha *kutafuta maisha*—in hopes of "finding a life." Miriamu rarely returned to Dodoma, and she only occasionally corresponded with her family about her young child.

As I say, I only knew Miriamu and Julietta in 2000. I was not able to keep in touch with them, and when I returned to Arusha in 2003, they were no longer working at Fashion Beauty, nor could I find them in Mianzini.

Robert

My final portrait is probably the most hopeful, but it is not without its contradictions and ambiguity. Robert was a young man of twenty-three when I met him in 1999. Lean and well dressed but in no way flashy, he had begun working in the informal sector as a restaurant cook and had made his way in the world working first as a *nyama choma* (roast meat) chef in an upscale bar. He eventually found work as a cook and waiter in a guesthouse that catered almost exclusively to European and American safari-going tourists. Robert was born on Mount Kilimanjaro, the youngest in a family of seven children. His father was a mechanic who was only able to educate Robert and most of his siblings through primary school, and the limits of his formal education were one of the great regrets in Robert's life.

Working in a high-end guesthouse proved to be advantageous to Robert in a number of ways. He developed useful skills as a cook and improved his English through his interaction with tourists. He also learned to drive a car, both to escort tourists around town and occasionally into the bush, and to do the weekly shopping for provisioning the household. Through the numerous contacts he made in this work, he was able to get to know some well-placed purveyors of household goods, and so he was usually able to get a good deal on beer and soda, and often other staples, for his own use.

In 1999, Robert had begun a live-in relationship with a woman he met through work. Christina had been briefly employed as a house girl in the guesthouse but soon set out on her own—but not before she had begun a relationship with Robert. The two of them lived together in standard housing for a young couple in a style I have already described: a single room in a complex of similar rooms, with a tin roof, mud walls, and all of their furnishings, including a large wardrobe, some shelves holding appliances, pots and pans, and a pair of beds wedged into a back corner. The beds were hidden from view behind a light cloth that hung from the ceiling as a curtain. The curtain bespoke the respectability to which the couple aspired, and their housing, although modest, was more comfortable than many in their circumstance. Their housing unit was set very near Saidi's, the sign painter's, first housing in Arusha, a relatively peaceful, less congested area of town, up Mount Meru. A quiet courtyard, nicely tended by the neighbors, had a spigot for running water. Here, Christina worked out of her room preparing fried crisps of all manner of vegetables as snack food, which were sold in town, an enterprise facilitated by Robert's connections to grocers in town who were willing to sell these snacks for a small commission. The couple was able to generate an additional income and also reduce their expenses because Christina did not have to travel to town for work. Not selling these foods on the street—as most women engaged in this service would—also allowed the two of them to sustain the respectability that they both described to me as vital to their aspirations. "You can't ever advance" (or "develop," *Huwezi kuendelaea*), Robert told me, "if you're mixed up in that *norma* (mischief/trouble/strife) like those *machizi* (fools) you visit in town. You need some work that has some respect (*heshimu*)."

With the regular income the couple earned, they were able to demonstrate this respect in their appearance and reputations. They were not financially successful by any means, but they were secure. In 2001, Christina had a son, who was a source of great delight for Robert. The three continued to live in the one-room unit, where they still live today. But Robert also made plans for their future by buying a *sehemu*, a small plot of land, where he intends to build a home. This land is not far from where the three currently live and was formerly the site of an abandoned, half-built house. But as with most such arrangements, the house was removed, leaving only the land. Robert worked out a good deal on some of the leftover building materials. And although it isn't clear when he will find the time or resources to build the house, he has cleared most of the land and planted some vegetables to supplement his family's provisions.[1]

Amid all of these material, social, and cultural forms of respectability, what has been palpably absent in Robert and Christina's lives is that formerly sine qua non of respect: marriage. Robert and Christina were both Catholic, and although neither framed his or her outlook on life (at least in the many conversations we had) in terms of religion, both of them acknowledged being Catholic and retained a commitment to their religious backgrounds. And both remained close to their natal families, neither of which—according to the couple—expressed any disgruntlement at their reluctance to marry, even after their son was born. Robert did intend to marry Christina, someday, he told me after their son's birth. But it was so complicated today, he suggested. Finding a time for everyone in their families to agree to a wedding date, making all the arrangements, getting the groom's family to agree to meet with the bride's family. And of course, the bridewealth payments had to be agreed to, and it was not easy to make these payments without becoming embroiled in relationships with others whom you might borrow money from. Robert insisted it was vital that he provide the bridewealth from his own funds and not his father's or extended family—too many complications and possible conflicts might otherwise ensue. The expense was an issue, but less as a simple material constraint and more as a source of loaded entanglements—precisely the sorts of entanglements, I couldn't help thinking, that Africanist social anthropology had long insisted that marriage was all about!

As it happens, Robert and Christina did get married at Christmas—the wedding season in Arusha—in 2006. They sent me some wonderful photos of the large, well-attended reception, with well-dressed bridesmaids and groomsmen in matching outfits. Robert was proud of his ability to pay for the event, and to feed and entertain everyone such a large gathering. It would be plausible, in some respects, to see this wedding as a kind of consumerist achievement and, indeed, to see the marriage itself as simply one more choice Robert and Christina had made to produce a certain lifestyle. Living together, pooling their economic resources, planning a home, having a child—all of these might be seen as discrete options complemented, but only in the end, by marriage, and configured together to create a social position in the world. Indeed, there were times when Robert spoke to me of his family life in these terms: as a series of choices, as a set of options, each of which had its costs. And yet their marriage still gave consideration to extended family ties, brought together relatives from Kilimanjaro to the east and Karatu to the west, and followed closely on the heels of their acquiring land on which to build a home, an independent place for asserting the respectability and viability of their relationship. Neither an obsolete relationship nor a traditional requirement for creating a social unit, not simply a formal opportunity for demonstrating financial success nor a strategic relationship whose costs and benefits needed to be weighed against one another, and yet all these things at once: the marriage of Robert and Christina provides a rich example of the range of processes through which enduring social lives are forged in a neoliberal context.

Gender (In)Visible

Contests of Style

Hanging from the lintel of almost every salon (or *saloon*, in the vernacular) in Arusha is a simple white lace curtain. Typically made of polyester, sometimes of finer cloth, the curtain is a simple decorative touch that fills the doorway. When the doors to a salon are shut and locked for the night, the curtains are still often visible from the street, lining the windows and doorway of the storefront. When the shop is open, the door to the business will be opened, but the curtain remains pulled across the doorway, billowing gently in the breeze. The presence of this curtain creates a field of transition, separating the respite and beauty of the salon from the tension and uproar of the urban streets. The ubiquitous curtain produces a certain respectability—*heshima*—to which many men and women in Arusha aspire in their domestic arrangements. The space of the salon recalls the intimacy and refinement of the home much more than businesses that operate on the street.

The curtain produces a certain visual field, and the nature of the perspectival possibilities it creates recalls the tensions embodied by the dynamic spectacle created by Tupac and his visual provocations. Tupac generates a sense of hidden power by asserting his capacity to take the power of the gaze that obsessively and oppressively seeks to capture Tupac's force by placing him under intense scrutiny, while simultaneously seizing on and subverting that power to examine by placing himself on display. In effect, Tupac strikingly reveals himself in order to supersede the authority that attempts to master him through surveillance.

The ubiquitous salon curtain

This particular resolution to the problem of seeing and being seen, of concealing potential while activating it in display, represents an especially masculinist practice. In effect, the defiant stance of Tupac Shakur on the cover of his album, *All Eyez on Me*, embraces the very kind of power it holds in contempt. Tupac treats intense scrutiny as a challenge to be overcome, thereby asserting greater control over those who would control him. This corresponds almost exactly to *ujeuri,* which Tanzanians described—and which young men in particular celebrate—as the ability to elude subordination through transgressive defiance. Not surprisingly, Tupac is perhaps the most obvious example of a *mjeuri* that young men in Arusha identified to me, and his *ujeuri* was always one of the main terms they used to describe him. His presence all over barbershops and minivans, and in the music blaring throughout the bus stand bespeaks that embrace of *ujeuri.*

But plainly this is not the only way of organizing such visual relationships, and not just confrontations, between the seen and the unseen, the hidden and revealed, those who make an appearance and those who view it. It is probably not even a particularly effective one (if Tupac's fate is any measure of such things), for it ratchets up the stakes of this dynamic and transforms them into direct, absolutist conflict. One is either vanquished or endures, but there is little possibility for accommodation or engagement between parties to a relationship understood in this antagonistic fashion. What of the host of other ways in which performative problems of appearance and concealment are articulated and negotiated in popular practice in Arusha? These problems are especially relevant to the study of popular cultural activities surrounding the cultivation of style and fashion through the consumption of novel commodity forms. This is true on the one hand because so much of contemporary cultural performance in places like Arusha is attuned to questions of appearance, to the extent that questions of what constitutes style, and to the material forms that Tanzanians think demonstrate innovative cultural practice can virtually be equated with new forms of self-presentation—new ways of looking. On the other hand, the neoliberal reorganization of Tanzanian political economy has made commodity forms that relate to personal appearance at once more available and more exclusive (Meyer and Geschiere 1999; Comaroff and Comaroff 2000; Weiss 2004). Under current conditions, style becomes a potent medium for evaluating the interpenetration of cultural forms, social processes, and the distribution of economic resources. Moreover, this is so not only for the analyst of Arusha's sociocultural world; it is also especially true for the residents of Arusha who are active participants in the production of urban life. In Arusha, stylistic innovation embodies profound sociocultural shifts, new possibilities for appearance—distinct ways of organizing visual fields, the relationship between seeing and being seen—that constitute a privileged site for debating and negotiating the significance and value of these shifts. The organization of appearances in Arusha illuminates the themes of conflict and fantasy that are to the fore in the town's popular culture.

The terms of these debates about style are inevitably expressed in the register of gender. Understandings of the moral dilemmas posed by the excesses of consumption or by specific innovations made possible by new commodity forms are grasped and evaluated through gendered ways of being. Assertions of style always, and often explicitly, make claims about gender. Particular styles and the significance of style more generally are almost always evaluated with respect to the ways that they formulate qualities of femininity and masculinity. Gender is a kind of habitus of popular cultural practice (Bourdieu 1977); it is a structuring structure that both motivates and orients the consumption activities and desires of young men and women in Arusha, even as gender is itself produced through and demonstrated by consumption. In many ways, gender is the central metapragmatic dimension of contemporary social practice. More than being modern, being cool, or being desirable, to be stylish in Arusha is about embodying gender.

It should be clear that much of this book has been focused on expressions of masculinity and the understandings of men that are plainly concerned with gendered personhood. Many young men in Arusha comprehend themselves and their relationships with one another in terms of women: what they imagine women and femininity to be like. Here we can turn to women's practices in order to show how the cultural processes of perception and embodiment alluded to in the iconography of Tupac, the evaluation of social transformation, and the implications of neoliberal reorganization are synthesized and grounded in the production of gender in Arusha. What, we might ask, is the value of style? What makes it a central point of tension in Arusha today? Why is gender at the core of that tension?

Looking at Dress

One of the most celebrated examples of women's clothing practices in Tanzania is the use of *khanga* (pl. *makhanga*). These broad cotton cloths are sold in pairs, and although they are not accessible to everyone, they are among the more affordable of women's garments, often selling for as little as $4 or $5 per pair. Further, as Linnebuhr (1997: 138) describes them, *khanga* are "message bearing cloths worn by women in many parts of East Africa." The messages these cloths bear are, as Parkin puts it, "riddle-proverbs" (Parkin 1995: 209), *methali* in Swahili. Sometimes they are simply biting phrases printed on cheap cotton cloth. The patterns of *makhanga* are generally a field defined by a repeated motif in highly contrasting colors, often with a single visual form (for example, a flower, a pineapple, a cell phone, a soda bottle) in the center of the field. The field is framed by one or two borders that complement the field pattern and motifs in color and form. The Swahili inscription is usually printed in large blocks letters across the top and bottom of the horizontal edge of the field. Parkin's Zanzibari informants noted that the phrases on the *khanga* are more important than the color or visual design of the cloth when women are deciding which one to purchase (Parkin 1995, 210; Linnebuhr 1997: 138). According to women and men in town, the messages are especially important to women at the coast, who many in Arusha would identify as real Swahili people, but up country, in places like Arusha and Moshi, people don't care about these saying as much. This is in keeping with a much wider set of understandings of the relationship between the coast and the interior, which provide interesting points of contrast through which to think about a host of sociocultural transformations. In any event, there is some consistency in the recognition that there are some who purchase and wear *khanga* on the basis of the text printed on the textile.

Figuring out the significance of Swahili *khanga* messages—for anthropologists, *khanga* wearers, and their audiences—is a vexing problem. It is certainly much more than a matter of decoding the text. Linnebuhr emphasizes what she calls "age and context" as critical interpretive categories for *khanga* messages (1997: 138). In effect, the meanings of *makhanga* are contextualized by the life cycle, so that the message can be interpreted according to the major life experiences (courtship, marriage, birth of a child) that the woman who is wearing them is undergoing. This model of *khanga* meanings is complicated by the fact, as Linnebuhr herself recognizes, that the riddle-proverbs are almost always ambiguous; they never simply refer to a context but are always deployed to constitute a range of contexts. That is, *makhanga* are active attempts to intervene in the possible meanings of the circumstances that a woman may participate in. As Parkin notes, "There is always something incomplete about the *khanga* riddle-proverb, always more meaning that can be extracted from it" (1995: 211). This is a quality *khanga* share with other kinds of performance, especially performances associated with women's practices, that "draw on a long tradition of subtlety in language" (Askew 2002: 76) in East Africa. *Khanga,* therefore, lend themselves to a kind of generative process of meaning production, where circumstances are characterized, interpreted, challenged, and reinterpreted, a process that not only creates new meanings but also changes circumstances themselves.[1] It is this generative potential for producing change and commenting on it that has made *khanga* not simply endure but flourish as a form of dress across contemporary East Africa.

The patterns of *khanga* and the phrases printed on them regularly change. Every few weeks in towns across Tanzania, new *khanga* will be introduced in the market and will soon be seen on women around town. Although this form permits ongoing innovation, the broad themes of the *methali* have remained constant for several generations (Parkin 1995: 210). Perhaps the most common theme has to do with sexual relations; but more specifically, these proverbs tend to comment on relations not just between men and women, but between women with respect to men. That is, as many women and men in Arusha suggested to me, and as most who have written about *khanga* confirm (Parkin 1995; Linnebuhr 1997), those who purchase and those who wear *khanga* often intend to convey a message to some other presumed, often unspecified person who has some (usually inappropriate) interest in the relationships of the woman wearing the *khanga*. The simplest way to describe this complex set of relationships—and the way that most men and women in Arusha explicitly described it to me—is to say that *khanga* wearing is about "jealousy," *wivu* in Swahili. More broadly, we can say that people recognize that gossip circulates all around them, and *khanga* riddle-proverbs are attempts to recognize and transform that gossip. *Khanga* performance is a way of commenting on commentary. It is an intrinsically social act, not only because it always has an audience but also because the (often imagined) claims of others actively motivate the choice of *khanga*.

Furthermore, most of the young women I talked to about *khanga* insisted that they never purchased a *khanga* for themselves. Rather, they are purchased on behalf of friends who need support. Linnebuhr's (1997: 138–39) work supports this: she found that *khanga* were generally, although not always, purchased by others, often boyfriends, spouses, or children.[2] The collective dimensions of *khanga* dress are demonstrated by this practice. Moreover, the performative dimensions of dress are further highlighted. Wearing cloth purchased by others on your behalf ramifies the set of contexts and meanings that can be produced by dress. A boyfriend may use his girlfriend as a medium through which to communicate his intentions toward her to her parents or, more frequently, to other suitors. A friend may choose to distance herself from the wicked talk of her peers, conveying a message to them through the *khanga* she purchases for the friend who is the object of that wicked talk. And the woman who wears a *khanga* may align herself in a whirl of gossip not only by the text on her cloth, but by the choices she makes among the friends and relations who have given her different *khanga*. All of these are contingent actions that produce highly ambiguous possible meanings, and so perpetuate the open-ended, performative process of dress. Wearing *khanga*, then, does not simply communicate by a speaker sending a message to an audience. To use Goffman's (1981) language of performance, the communicative action of dress has multiple motivators, authors, vehicles, and audiences, some of whom are prefiguratively imagined, some direct observers, and others simply bystanders who overhear the message and in that way (perhaps only indirectly) shape its meaning and its effects. To dress in this fashion is necessarily to be enmeshed in a proliferating array of social relationships that are anticipated, imagined, commented on, and enacted.

It is certainly not the case that the persons involved in *khanga* dress— buyers, wearers, allies, enemies, and audiences—are merely occupying a range of roles that can be decomposed and reassembled to suit any occasion. But the dynamic of *khanga* performance is akin to the organization of visual processes exemplified by Tupac. The way *khanga* are worn and purchased always presumes not just an audience, but some other(s) who powerfully shape(s) the identities of those participating in this performance. When women wear *khanga*, their actions presume that others have some notion about them, something like a reputation that circulates in gossip, glances, and gestures. In turn, these notions become incorporated into the identities of those who give and wear these cloths. This means that the significance of the message conveyed in the *khanga* can never be grasped just as a form of self-expression or commentary meant to influence an audience, even if it is cutting, poignant, or incisive. The self that is expressed when wearing a *khanga*, even if collectively understood as the buyer, the wearer, and so on, is always motivated by the presumption of some external force, some other whose claims on the wearer are formulating her sense of self.

Consider the following blatant example of a *khanga* proverb. I asked a young woman, who soon became one of my informants, working as a seamstress on a prominent street in town to tell me about the *khanga* that was being sold by the neighboring shop. Elizabeth made a good part of her income by cutting the doubled cloth into separate *khanga* and hemming each piece to keep it from unraveling, so she was eager to have me buy them. The phrase printed on the *khanga* I bought was *Usiwe Na Macho Kilicho Ndani Si Chako* ("Don't Look at Me, What I Have Inside Isn't Yours"). When I asked Elizabeth to explain the meaning of the proverb, she said simply, "*Wivu*" ("jealousy"). She went on to explain that friends would buy one another a *khanga* like this to prevent jealousy. Everyone I asked about the proverb agreed that its meaning related to jealousy. Exactly what made the wearer or the buyer the object of jealousy was open to the particular context. Many women I spoke with suggested that the woman who wore this *khanga* was warning other women not to interfere in her love life; she had her lover "inside," and this relationship was not for public scrutiny. Others thought that the warning was directed to men and was a way of saying that the women wearing the *khanga* was spoken for, so other men would know that what was literally inside the *khanga* wasn't theirs. In this context, the man who buys his lover this *khanga* is preventing the jealousy of other men, even as he provokes it. Another interesting interpretation suggested that the wearer of this *khanga* might be pregnant and wanted to extol the value of what she had inside. At the same time, the audience for this tart message might be other women, jealous of the wearer's ability to get pregnant, in which case the message implies witchcraft prevention. Or it could imply that leering men shouldn't speculate about the father of the wearer's child. At a rudimentary level, most who interpreted this *khanga* felt that it condemned the unwanted interest of others—"people shouldn't be so nosy!" (*watu wanatazama sana!*), one said—and so anyone could wear such a *khanga* simply because it was increasingly difficult in the world today for people "to keep to themselves" (*kila kwao*).

All of these interpretations are examples of jealousy, and they certainly show the potency of "incompleteness," as Parkin (2000) aptly describes the innuendo of *khanga* proverbs. Moreover, the force of jealousy and the surreptitious potential of proverbial speech are tangibly embodied in clothing practice, and this process of embodiment shapes the wider field of popular cultural practice. Jealousy is both configured and countered in the form of appearances. The *khanga* wearer knows that she makes an appearance, and she recognizes the negative possibilities of others examining her, which defines jealousy itself. At the same time, she reflexively, and necessarily, makes use of that observed position, using, we might say, the power of the vision of the other to transform her own appearance (by the cloth she wears) and—crucially—to alter the perception of the other. If the other looks at me, they will see "Don't Look at Me." *Khanga* proverbs, says Parkin (2000: 179), "are written not spoken." From an embodied perspective, we can add they are seen, but not heard.

This entangled relationship is exactly parallel to the one set up in the iconography of Tupac, where the "eyez" of others provide the impetus and the opportunity for Tupac to assert himself and to assert his subjugation. The rap title "Picture Me Rollin'" neatly captures this complex encounter with the implicit other. It suggests that what directs Tupac's actions is the way he is perceived, but it further suggests that his actions are aimed at creating an image and thereby shaping the perceptions of those who observe him. It is not enough, in other words, simply to act in a way that defies the expectations of others, or even to act as one chooses. The other must be made to confirm the force of the self's actions by seeing them from this observer's perspective. Again, the scrutiny of others becomes the strength of the self, and in order for me to show that strength, you have to picture me.[3]

Another way to describe this relationship is to note that the other simultaneously demonstrates the subjective force of the self even as it objectifies the self. This is a highly productive tension, one that persistently reproduces a circuit of images and actions, appearances and reputations. At the same time, the force of the observing other, although recognized as absolutely necessary to the assertive creation of personhood, is usually experienced as intrusive and excessively forceful. This is why jealousy is most frequently cited as the meaning of particular proverbial expressions, and why wearing *khanga* is so often said to prevent jealousy. The implication here is that people's gossip is always at risk of being overly invasive, and women in particular must always struggle to prevent that invasion. The way to deal with the risks of jealousy and gossip, however, is not to maintain a tidy boundary between the self and the other. It is rather to control the interpenetration of these forces so that one is neither completely imposed on by external forces nor (in what would amount to the same thing) completely exposed as a demonstrative spectacle. When it comes to wearing *khanga*, this means securing a position that separates you from the intrusive gaze of others while simultaneously demonstrating that security in a way that asserts an image of viability. In concrete terms, this is precisely what a *khanga* does: it covers a woman's body while also creating an attractive appearance that draws attention, creating a verbal, visual, performative image for others. There is a fine balance to be maintained between protecting social value by concealing it, and confirming social value by displaying it.

This dynamic goes a long ways toward illuminating not just the complexities of *khanga* performances, but the moral, aesthetic, and political dimensions of style more broadly in Arusha. One *khanga*, of course, does not an argument make. It is not typical (but nor is it rare) for a *khanga* to make so explicit a claim about vision and appearances as "Don't Look at Me, What I Have Inside Isn't Yours," although Swahili proverbial speech is replete with claims about the power of vision (for example, *Macho hayana pazia*, "Eyes have no screens," [they're sure to see everything], *Mwenye macho haambiwi tazama*, "One who has eyes is not told to look" [some truths are self-evident]). Themes of visibility are prominent in popular stylistic practices in Arusha, and the value of popular practice is often determined with respect to the kind of appearance that a person makes, and what we might call the visual field they inhabit. One young man shining shoes near the center of town had written, in English, on the side of his shine box, "Don't Spy My Life," a slogan he had selected, he told me (if you can't already guess), "to prevent jealousy." Yet he provided a service that was aimed at creating a pleasing appearance, always working in the vicinity of barbershops and used clothing hawkers (and generally serving the same clientele) that appealed to similar desires. At another extreme, when I began to work with a healer in town, he informed me that I was sick and in need of his services because "people had been watching me" because I was a "rich stranger," and he would help me "prevent" those with the "evil eye" (*jicho*) from harming me. Both the destitute and the well heeled, then, have reason to repel the intrusive scrutiny of the jealous.

The power of vision is one way in which the presence of the other—at times intrusive, at times solicited—is invoked in popular cultural practice in Arusha. This perceptual force instantiates a more general tension between what is enclosed and what is revealed. This tension structures a wide array of practices and relationships. Considerations of concealment and exposure organize spatial practices and embodiment in ways that are closely aligned with gendered understandings of personhood and sociality. Furthermore, because this tension is relevant to the social production and demonstration of value, it can also be used as a gauge to evaluate the practice of others. This makes the relative control over appearances a central feature of popular cultural processes, and certainly a highly contentious question. It is also increasingly problematic, given the pressing political economic transformations that Tanzanians are currently experiencing.

Innuendo in *Taarab* Performance

As an indication of the ways that popular culture and gender are implicated by this dynamic, we can briefly consider the important genre of Swahili sung poetry, *taarab*. As both Parkin (2000) and Askew (2002) have noted, there is a close correspondence between the performative qualities of *taarab* and *khanga*. The poetic speech of *taarab* is parallel to the proverbial messages printed on *khanga;* indeed, popular *taarab* lyrics often end up printed on the borders of *khanga,* just as fashionable *khanga* proverbs are likely to be incorporated into *taarab*. In each kind of performance, it is almost exclusively women who deploy the deceptively simple words of proverbial wisdom to articulate highly complex, usually ambiguous claims to unspecified audiences. Further, as Askew's analysis makes clear, the performative power of *taarab* lies with members of the audience who communicate with other members of the audience conveying "messages that local protocol prohibits otherwise; it thus constitutes a very potent and highly gendered mode of communication" (2002: 126–27). As members of the *taarab* audience, individual women will respond to those phrases that move them by tipping (*kutunza*) the performer (Askew 2002: 139ff.). This tipping is usually a highly stylized performance: the tippers openly create a powerful appearance, often designed as much to reveal their luxurious outfits as express their feelings for the song as they dance to the stage to present their offerings. Tippers will generally signal the significance of the passage to which they is responding, casting a glance or gesturing toward other women who are meant to receive the message conveyed by the lyrics. This is an even more direct provocation than *khanga* dressing (where the intended audience for the *methali* is less clearly identified) can achieve, and not surprisingly, *taarab* tipping often becomes highly competitive as rivals attempt to outdo one another, and perhaps win the support of the assembled crowd through their performance.

In *taarab* performance, like *khanga* performance, a surreptitious form of speech is deployed to communicate in a way that requires an open display of intentions and relationships. It is not simply the case that *taarab* or *khanga* performances permit the disclosure of what must otherwise remain concealed. It is rather that both forms of indirection require that a form of expression that is intrinsically covert (the proverbial claim, sung or imprinted, is never a transparent assertion) be openly enacted as a hidden truth. The value of the woman, touched by the *taarab* lyrics or incited by the gossip of her peers, can be established when it is openly presented as something that remains secure and undetected by the intrusive speculation of others. The point of such practice is not to distinguish the seen from the unseen, but to reveal that what is valued remains concealed.

Taarab, like *khanga* performance, is a form of contemporary popular culture closely associated with women that demonstrates the ways that gendered modes of practices are organized in terms of the dynamics of enclosure and revelation. What is more, these forms exemplify a promi-nent structure of contestation and negotiation, where the oppressive intrusions of others are both recognized and countered through forms of innuendo and indirection. As Parkin (1995: 211) notes, both practices constitute "a very powerful field of communication whose strength and efficacy, however, depend paradoxically on people not knowing precisely who is rival to who, and who desires who." This dynamic is not simply a prominent feature of a wide array of popular practices in Aursha; it also serves to organize debates about the meaning of popular cultural practice itself. For example, Askew notes that many older *taarab* musicians and composers thought, as did many of my own informants in Arusha, that *taarab* performers today make greater use of the *mipasho*, "hidden mes-sages," that incite conflict and "that are paradoxically less and less hidden in the text" (2002: 134), and make less use of metaphors that offer more subtle challenges and critiques. In the words of one man I spoke with, the resurgence of *taarab's* popularity was especially unpleasant because the excessive use of what he thought of as "deep Swahili" (*Kiswahili cha ndani*) in *taarab* was, as he put it, "ruining Swahili!" (*kinaaribu kiswahili!*). In these examples, we see both that the relationship between enclosure and revelation is not simply an aesthetic feature of these performances; it is also part of the way that the performances are evaluated in historical terms. A concern with enclosure taken to extremes—the use of hidden forms of deep poetics—readily becomes too obvious and too overt, and thus destructive.

These kinds of claims are precisely the kinds of concerns that fuel debates across Arusha. They are not just contestations about popular culture; they constitute cultural practice in this contemporary, urban milieu. Further, such negotiations entail an understanding of gender and its reshaping in terms of these concerns with exposure and enclosure. It is important to note, for example, that it was a man who remarked with disdain on the ruinous implications of *taarab*, for *taarab* has become em-blematic of women's music in recent years. For a great many men—and many women as well—the tricky negotiation of discretion and assertive-ness that *taarab* promotes has made women too openly competitive; it simultaneous promotes secrecy and aggression. Many fans of rap music in particular say *taarab* is about love but not about reality. Indeed, the perfomative contrasts of *taarab* and rap are instructive. *Taarab* perfects the performance of indirection, with poetic utterances ideally couched in metaphors, permitting the audience members to express their social situation without ever speaking for themselves. Rap celebrates direct, unadorned expression. Rap fans say this music provides a voice that describes life "just as it is" (*jinsi ilivyo*). Indeed, rap audiences are more likely to form a crew and begin to "bust" (*vunja*) their own verses than they are to shower praise on other skillful rappers. Of course, these direct qualities are exactly what make rap seem utterly graceless and antisocial to those, especially women, who reject it. It is loud and full of "conflict" (*fujo*), a characterization that self-proclaimed thugs eagerly embrace. The point is that the tension between the concealed and the revealed provides a powerful dynamic through which central features of gender are constituted, and in terms of which transformations in gender relations and practices are evaluated. Moreover, the fact that this tension is markedly embodied and enacted in everyday life in the organization of gender (and so people most directly experience the meaning of exposure or enclosure in the contrasting ways in which men and women present themselves) means that gender becomes a central focus for evaluating the moral and political significance of sociocultural transformation more generally.

Keeping Up with the Times

The complex relationships between appearances, the spatial and temporal organization of perception, and the gendered constitution of sociality demonstrate that style is an especially contentious dimension of value production in Arusha today. What kinds of people and things can (and cannot) now be seen, and by whom, in this fluid urban context? What are the stakes of stylistic innovation and presentation? What, most specifically, are the risks entailed in engagement with the contemporary world of things whose value is so plainly tied to their public visual attributes? These questions are dealt with directly and indirectly in contemporary Arusha. They further provide a way of linking political economic transformations with changes in specific practices and concrete modes of embodiment and perception.

Men's attitudes in much of Arusha toward the presence and appearance of women in an urban context are complex and contradictory. Locales like barbershops where young men hang out cultivate a sense of public space that not only excludes women, but also defines associations with women as antithetical to urban social life more generally.[4] This is so even as these young men work in an informal sector where women hold a dominant position (Tripp 1996), and an increasing number of these men live in households headed by senior women, or depend on the support of senior women more generally. In talking with many of these young men about their perceptions of women who (quite obviously) did live in Arusha, they often raised questions of a woman's *tabia*, or character. Setel has noted that this is a central term in discussions of morality and personhood in neighboring Kilimanjaro. It refers to much more than mere internal dispositions of a person. It is something that is actively cultivated in children, that develops over time, and that is expressed relative to particular social contexts. In short, *tabia* is less a discreet property of persons than a way of relating persons, places, and social relationships (Setel 2000: 130ff.).

This question was explicitly cited in my discussions with some tailors about women's fashion preferences in contemporary Arusha. Juma and Seifu, tailors who ran a small but successful tailoring shop near the stadium at the center of Arusha, made their living catering to women's fashion tastes. Both tailors sewed outfits, sometimes from patterns, sometimes in imitation of the photos in *catalogi* that women would regularly bring them. Their outfits were from material cut from large bolts of synthetic cloth, usually imported from Southeast Asia. Juma showed me a drawer full of Gloria Vanderbilt labels (other designers were available at different times) that he would carefully sew into the waistbands and collars of the outfits he completed. These labels were important, he insisted, because women, especially in Arusha, even more than Dar, like to "keep up with the times" (*kwenda na wakati*). The labels—like the catalogs, the latest materials, and his own skills as a tailor, sensitive to the desires of his clientele—were eagerly sought out by young women, he said, because they were necessary if women were to show that they understood what was in fashion. "Keeping up with the times," he claimed, was part of the *tabia* of women in the city; it kept him in business, but it could also be an extremely dangerous quality. Women in Arusha, Juma insisted, were especially "fierce" (*kali*), a fact made evident by their aggressive competition with one another. "Keeping up with the times" has an intrinsically social and competitive form. Women, he said, know how to follow the times by trying to compete with one another. What about men, I asked? Didn't men care about their appearances too? Didn't they "copy" (*kuiga*) the trends from *catalogi* and commercials? Not like women, he said: "A man will wear what he can afford from the used clothing (*mitumba*), and if it fits him, *basi*, it will suit him. Yes, men are competitive, but their competition is in their hearts (*kwa roho*), it is not on display (*hayaonekani*) for everyone to see."

Here again, the moral risk is one of exposure, which Arusha as a place exacerbates. Social relations, place, and time all figure in the characterization of *tabia*. Needless to say, this quality is distinctively gendered, perhaps more explicitly so in the view of young men in town.

A tailor's shop

These links of *tabia* with gender, place, and economy were also expressed to me in discussions with young men and women about marriage. When I asked young men whether they preferred to marry women from Arusha or from elsewhere, I received a range of answers. Most young men said that they would prefer to marry a women from "the village," especially if they had some connections to more rural areas. Those who expressed this preference most often insisted that women in the city had *tabia ya mjini*, "city attitudes," which meant that they were only interested in money. As one young man put it, "A woman puts on those jeans, and then she needs the shirt and socks and shoes. It all has a price." Women "at home" (that is, from rural areas, for those who made such associations) had more *heshima*, "respect"; but city life, many agreed, demands money, and the pursuit of money makes women's character suspect.

There were those, however, that preferred to marry women from the city. Often this was because of a general mistrust of rural relations, who often *omba hera*, "ask for money," from urban kin presumed to have more cash. Others also suggested that they preferred to marry a woman from the city because women from the city were "already accustomed" (*wameshazoea maisha*) to city life and so had more realistic expectations of marriage. As one man put it, a woman from the village will develop *tabia mbaya* (a "bad character") when she comes to town: *Anajifunza ujanja* ("She learns to be too clever"), comes to town with unrealistic expectations and will not remain faithful to the man who brought her to town. In spite of their different perspectives on rural and urban marital prospects, all of these men's claims were grounded in essentially the same concerns and understandings. The city is a moralized landscape, and that morality articulates character, commerce, and competition.

Women's views of men were not entirely different from those just described. Although few women expected or desired to move to a rural area to marry (only a few young women who claimed they would "follow their parents" [*fuata wazazi*] in marital matters even admitted such a possibility), all women expressed a concern about finding a man who was "trustworthy" (*waminifu*). In particular, women were concerned about finding men who would demonstrate their trustworthiness by accepting responsibility for children. One inflammatory example of the discourse surrounding male trustworthiness is demonstrated by women's comments about a widely discussed crisis concerning abandoned infants. This problem of abandoned infants, often abandoned—or aborted—in public latrines (harkening back to an urban legend found across East Africa [White 1997]) was the subject of numerous newspaper accounts, and was the topic of discussion in a nationally televised episode of *Malumbano ya Hoja* (Debating the Issue), which I could not see. Women of all ages whom I talked to on this topic were adamant that this problem was due to the failure of men to be trustworthy. Infants ended up abandoned when pregnant women discovered that their boyfriends were unreliable and refused to acknowledge their obligations to their girlfriends and children. At a more mundane level, women frequently contrasted the *tabia* of men and women in terms of responsibility for children. Julieta, a salon worker, said she would keep at her job, and not follow some unpredictable opportunities elsewhere, for exactly these reasons. Women need to think of their children first, she told me, while men only think about how to spend what they've got immediately: "*wanamini 'kesho' sana*," "they have a lot of faith in 'tomorrow,'" is how she described the unreliability of men.

Screening the Salon

Such accounts of character with respect to marital expectations relate to the contemporary cultivation of style in Arusha. The moralized claims about brazen competition and reliability are often critiqued, but in many ways, they are confirmed by the actual practices of young men and women—practices in which young men and women not only aspire to command a particular sense of style, but also seek to make a living under conditions of serious economic limitations. Many young men in Arusha do aim to develop trustworthiness, to create a powerful sense of obligation founded on their sense of invincibility in the face of a pervasive global marginalization. The stylistic pursuits of these men, from hip hop performance to utilitarian haircuts, to street-corner Islam, all confirm these values. Their thuggery demonstrates their commitments to the struggle of enduring under such conditions, and their pain is an embodied qualification to attest to these struggles. At the same time, these commitments work to exclude women from this masculinist understanding of fidelity. Indeed, men who accommodate the interests of women, especially in preference to the requirements of masculine friendship, often have their masculinity called into question, a point I touched on in chapter 3.

Women's practices in Arusha certainly challenge the views of those men who see a female presence as anathema to the sociality of urban life. And yet at the same time, the ways that their practices—social, economic, and stylistic—are organized suggest that moral concerns about overt exposure and the need to manage the relationship between the seen and the unseen are especially important to women. Efforts to control this relationship, a struggle in bodily, perceptual, and material terms, are integral to gender politics in Arusha. They place gender squarely at the center of cultural practice in town, and they demonstrate how aesthetic problems about appearance and embodiment are pressing political matters.

The spatial and temporal organization of men's barbershops (*vinyozi*) is, in effect, an extension of the street and of street life more generally. The young men who frequent these shops regularly come and go, checking in each day, sometimes several times a day, shaking hands with those assembled. This is all part of the process of making the rounds, which creates a connection between the shops and the town, and which situates each shop as a distinct place and as a point of interconnection with the wider world. The interior aesthetic of the *kinyozi*, too, confirms its worldly character. Most shops are plastered with a collage of images taken from barbering posters, hip hop magazines, and other commercial items from the popular press. The effect suggests a kind of kaleidoscopic coherence between the *kinyozi* and these mass media images that extends even to the appearance of the barbers; each image works to form part of an overall pattern that articulates linkages between the barbershop and the world.

Salons also insist on their connection to the wider world. These connections are established in multiple dimensions: from the names of salons (for example, New Modern Hair Salon, Eleganza Hair Salon), which reveal a concern with contemporary styles and trends, to the artwork on salon store fronts that frequently mirrors images drawn from the packaging for locally sold (mostly American) hair care products; to hairstyles that frequently imitate the photo display posters printed in Nigeria; and the ongoing discussions in the salons among workers and clientele, many of which make explicit connections between hairstyle, appearance, and the place of Tanzanian woman in the world. As Stambach's (1999) analysis demonstrates, changing women's hairstyles in Tanzania were seized on by men and women as an icon of wider economic and political reforms. Her work shows how new hairstyles, especially women's hairstyles,[5] provide a privileged vehicle for debates, carried out in the press (and, of course, in the salons themselves), about citizenship, culture, and consumption, about the inabilities of Tanzanians to resist the cultural imperialism of the West, and the resiliency of enterprising, modern Tanzanian women. There are, in short, self-conscious understandings among Tanzanian men and women of the way that salons are grounded in a wider order of political economic transformations, and that hairstyles articulate the diverse implications of those changes.

These largely discursive links between salons and the world are configured in material practice in a distinctive fashion and in a way that is,
for example, radically different from the configuration of barbershops.
For although barbershops open themselves up to public interaction, even
inserting themselves into the flow of street activity, salons must use much
more discretion in defining themselves as simultaneously public and private places. The fact that open debate about the merits of hairstyling—and
about the virtue of women who style their hair—takes place in Tanzania
should alert us to the potential risks that are entailed in a profession and
place of business that would beautify female bodies. As with *khanga* and
taarab performance, the presence of the observant other is prefigured in
many formal features of the salon: in its spatial design, the techniques
of hair care carried out within them, and the interactions among salon
workers and their clients.

To begin with, salons actively distinguish the space of the salon from
the street. Although barbershops always have a small bench or a few chairs
outside the shop where clients and barbers spend a good deal of time,
salons do not extend out into the space beyond its doors. Barbershops
are often sites where other small businesses that cater to the same clientele (shoeshine stands, used clothing stalls, snack food providers) will be
located. On crowded streets in Arusha, there may well be such informal,
mobile businesses adjacent to salons. I regularly heard salon workers and
their clients complain about the presence of such businesses, which they
perceived as too noisy and too smelly (in the case of food vendors), and
generally as "bringing strife" (*wanaleta fujo*). These were not places for
clients and workers to interact, but places that, in the view of those in
salons, disrupted the salon's space. This separation of the street from the
salon is made tangible and visible by the white lace curtain that hangs
across the doorway of virtually every salon in town. Most salon owners
and workers said that the curtain was simply "decoration" (*kupamba*) or
"to beautify" (*kwa uzuri*) the space; a few noted that it kept the "dirt"
and "bad air" (*hewa mbaya*) of the street out of the salon. In each of these
ways, the lace curtain discloses as it conceals. It is necessary to separate the
salon from the street, to screen it from the perceived tumult of disordered
social life, even as the salon must participate in that tumult by revealing
the curtain to those who pass by. Like a woman wearing a *khanga* that
warns onlookers about the impropriety of invasive scrutiny through her
attractive appearance, the lace curtain shields the salon from the unwanted
intrusion of the street even as it provides a visible sign of the salon's respectability (*heshima*).

The interior of a salon: simplicity, elegance, respectability

The practices within the salon further develop this theme. When clients enter a salon, they remove their shoes and put on flip-flops provided for them. In this way, salon patrons say, a woman can remove her heavy shoes and feel clean. A clear break from the embodied routines of city life is implied in this simple act. The visual design of the interior of almost all salons is not particularly striking. A salon, which may be as small as any barbershop, perhaps eight feet by eight feet, need only have enough room for a chair, a large hair dryer, and usually a sink. Salons are well lit and have one large mirror. The overall effect of the space is uncluttered and simple. Unlike *kinyozi*, salons rarely have cut-out pictures of celebrities or song lyrics pasted on their walls. Perhaps one poster of a few hairstyles will be posted—but, again, this is much less common than in barbershops, where it is not uncommon to find three or four such posters. Although the appearance of the salon suggests simplicity, it is clearly the case that running a salon requires a good deal more capital than a barbershop. Hair dryers, which are necessary to the success of any salon, can cost a few hundred dollars. Barbershops can get by with a single pair of electric clippers, which are available for $30 or so. Hair salons also keep supplies of hair care products, which are both more expensive than men's hair care products and more routinely made use of in treating clients' hair. Labor costs are different as well. Most salon workers are older than barbers and may make a salary that is not subject to the number of clients the shop has. This is rarely the case for barbers, who depend on customers for their pay. *Kinyozi* are often built as shanty structures in unclaimed areas near the market, or even adjacent to housing from which they can draw electricity. No salon could possibly acquire clients with such an appearance. Haircuts at barbershops in 2000 cost as little as 25 cents; a basic relax and set, the simplest salon procedure available, usually costs $2. In all these ways, salons depend on wide connections of capital and commerce, qualities that barbershops celebrate, yet these are presented in the salons in much different ways. Salons, in my experience, never have television sets, and the radio provides unattended-to background noise. In contrast, much of the activity in the barbershop centers on these media. This, too, is part of the uncluttered, clean aesthetic of the salon, which works to keep the distraction of loud music and TV viewing out of the salon.

The Power of Intimacy: Respect and Corruption

In a host of similar ways, the salon is both linked to the wider world of commerce and style, yet aims primarily to establish intimacy among those who enter the salon and so assure the respectability of the institution as a known place. This is expressed through a range of practices. For example, it is not uncommon for mothers to bring their daughters into a salon and to tend to one child—perhaps combing out her hair—while the salon worker tends to the other. There is a distinctly sensual experience entailed in styling women's hair (see also Ferme 2001: 58). Even a relax and set requires that hair be combed, washed, and treated with relaxers before being dried and carefully combed into a particular style. Hair plaiting is also carried out in salons, although it is perhaps even more routinely performed in more informal settings, even among friends working in the market or in a sidewalk kiosk, passing the time between customers. This, too, depends on intimacy and a close care for the body. A woman having her hair plaited will spend a long time with her head in the lap of her hairdresser, who must carefully tease apart and weave together fine strands of hair close to the scalp. One salon worker told me that plaiting someone's hair was such hard work it made your body hurt, to which her colleagues agreed. Hair care providers, whether salon workers or simply friends, routinely comment on the qualities of the hair and scalp of the person they are treating, and they adjust their technique according to the hair's demands. All of these practices suggest that hair care is a shared experience among women, something the hairdresser and the client both participate in. Both are sure to have had the experience of plaiting someone else's hair and having their own plaited in ways that are attuned to specific bodily qualities.

Barbers, on the other hand, emphasize their technique, almost to the exclusion of the individual characteristics of their clients. They talk, as I indicated earlier, about how electric clippers have transformed the practice of haircuts. Men with dreadlocks almost always care for their hair themselves; rather than plait their hair, they twist strands of hair and tie them off at the end to create a simple braid. Moreover, every barbershop in town shuts down during the frequent power outages in and around Arusha, while most salons can still carry on with business. Salon workers, in spite of the innovations in their practice wrought by chemical relaxers, plastic extensions, dryers, and the like, do not think of their practice as a set of technical skills that they have mastered. Indeed, when a flyer for a beautician school run by a Danish company was circulated in town, a number of salon workers expressed outrage at the very idea of such a school. The competition for an ever-diminishing market share was seen as a threat, but most women thought of it simply as a scam: "Do you think *wazungu* can teach you how to care for African hair?" Tending for women's hair was something women felt they knew because they had been doing it for one another since they were children. Barbers might demonstrate technical mastery, and indeed, some had chosen to pursue course work in the profession, but the success of a salon depends on the way that intimacy is created and conveyed among women.

These forms of intimacy, sensual, social, and spatial, are indispensable to our understanding of how style (so closely associated with appearances) is created and secured—precisely because it is at risk—in Arusha. It is as though the spectacle of a beautiful coiffure that draws the eye requires the security and support of the respectable salon in order to keep this alluring display from becoming a kind of overexposure. Hair works to enclose the body even as it reveals it. Ferme (2001: 57) points out that among the Mende, "[t]he pliability of both hair and cotton served the purposes of concealment as well as elaboration," an assertion that does not fit easily into what I learned in Arusha. I never heard claims about hair hiding any aspect of the person, nor were there reports of illicit substances or spirits secreted into women's hair in salons, as is reported across West Africa.

There are, however, important parallels between the way that enclosure and display are articulated aesthetically, and the way that hair is cared for in salons. For example, one of the most common activities among salon workers is weaving, knitting, or crocheting small decorative items while they pass the idle time between customers. These items are often sold in the shop to clients. Far and away the most popular kind of items is called *kitambaa* (pl. *vitambaa*), which simply means "cloth." These cloths are small, square (occasionally round), loosely knit objects used throughout Arusha, and probably throughout Tanzania, as domestic decorations. These *vitambaa* can be used as small tablecloths, as a setting for a plate of food, or perhaps under a vase of plastic flowers. Most frequently these cloths are used *kutandika*, "to cover," household items—the cushions of a sofa, a cassette recorder, a television. Even a small plate of food may be covered by the *kitambaa* before being set on top of the cloth. These cloths are thought of as decorative and should be made in attractive, "shining" or bright colors that attract the eye. They both beautify and conceal (or beautify by concealing) what is otherwise unattractive: a weathered table, holes in a cushion, a bulky radio.

These cloths clearly combine aspects of enclosure and display; in fact, a house well stocked with *vitambaa* is plainly revealing that it aims to conceal. Not only are these items routinely created at salons, thus associating salons with the virtues of domestic security and this distinctive aesthetic tension, but the production of *kitambaa* is also explicitly linked to hair preparation. Both plaiting hair and knitting cloth are forms of *kusuka*, "weaving" (see also Ferme 2001: 49). All the salon workers I asked said that tending to hair and knitting *kitambaa* were similar kinds of work. "If you know how to care for hair," one woman told me as she knit a *kitambaa*, "your fingers are already used to this kind of work." One of the more popular patterns of *kitambaa* in 2000 was even called Curl Kit, after the imported home hair care products that were widely available in Tanzania in the 1980s and 1990s (Stambach 1999). These close associations between women's hair care and the production of household coverings suggest that the values of domestic security and propriety are brought into women's public practices. These values are fundamental to the respect that women aspire to in their productive lives. Hair may not conceal a woman, but well-groomed hair is a tangible display—the visible evidence—of a woman's body, which is undoubtedly meant to suggest the presence of something secured, valued, and productive.

These qualities of intimacy, security, and respectability are laden with conflict for women. The intimacy of salons, the shared material experience among women they offer, and the enclosed social ties they promote often make the women who frequent salons vulnerable to the accusation that their public appearance is designed to deceive and distort what remains hidden from view. In his boorishly satirical column in the *Arusha Times,* "The Dark Side," columnist Valentine Mark Nkrumah (June 3–9, 2000: 11) writes that salons are centers for "the juiciest gossip" that "can only be heard and told in the hair saloons, with curtains drawn and the head boiler in full function." There is no doubt that salons lend themselves to gossip; why else would an anthropologist hang out there? In this way, of course, they are little different from bars and restaurants, seamstress stalls, shoeshine stands, and even barbershops, all of which are public venues where intimate activities are undertaken. Beyond the gossip, Nkrumah cites the widely held claim that "office girls" used salons as venues for "secret rendezvous" with their bosses or other "rich tycoons." Plainly the materiality of the salon—its focus on beauty, bodily form, and a kind of public intimacy—makes the assumption that it lends itself to illicit sexual practices almost predictable. What is more troubling here is that the target of this gossip is the office girl, the kind of woman who is likely to have the income that permits her to frequent a salon, and a job where personal appearances are critical. This libel is telling in a number of respects. It is an indictment of the (male) salaried classes, whose privileges allow them to exploit young women hired, in the view of many, for little more than their sex appeal. Such critiques, which are commonplace in African editorials, cartoons, and street talk (Mbembe 1997), suggest that the contemporary cultivation of style in Tanzania, along with the proliferation of the means for pursuing it, are only available to a narrow segment of the population. This view leaves women as ancillary social forces to the economic advantages that liberalization has fostered; sexual dalliances are simply one of the perks of junior management.

In fact, I think the presumed links between salons, young women's illicit sexuality, and business practices are a good deal more insidious than this reading suggests. The fact that these encounters are presumed to take place in salons, or that lovers make use of the pretext of going to the salon, indicate that these sites for the promotion of style are held to actually introduce corruption into the productive process, taking time away from work, transgressing work relationships, and subverting production itself. The salon is an effective cover ("the curtain drawn") that, like the appearances they generate, is alluring and desirable, but such appearances are always deceptive, for they conceal as much as they reveal. Identifying salons as a site where the truth of office girls can be found (because that truth remains hidden) makes it seem as though women's business pursuits—whether running salons, or seeking employment that requires their services—inherently lack legitimacy. Such gossip about gossiping women is the male middlebrow equivalent of young thugs' claims that the city is not a place for women's sociality or productivity. Salons are emblematic of the pursuit of style, a pursuit that is in fact central (both as a means and end) to many women's productive practices. They are thus readily available targets for those who hope to undermine the viability of women working.

Critiques of Style

The material practices of salons and their prominence within local understandings of respectability, commercial enterprise, and aesthetics indicate that there is a great deal at stake for those pursuing style. The restraint, indirection, and enclosure that are characteristics of female modes of practice in an array of social activities in Tanzania are part of the built form of salons, and they structure salon workers' and their patrons' attempts to cultivate success and respect. But these very qualities, and their association with successful women, can make them vulnerable. In this case, enclosure is read as deception and secrecy. Conversely, the appearances that are produced by new forms of commodities—*mitumba*, jeans, carefully styled hair—are understood by both men and women as threatening to expose bodies (and persons) in ways that jeopardize the possibility of respect. One man, himself a barber, saw young women's use of curl kits as one example of the dangers of things being undisciplined because they were "out in the open," *wazi*. Girls who used curl kits were like girls who got in trouble at school: "In the past, boys had girlfriends, but they would always hide themselves (*wamejificha*). If you got a note from your *mpenzi* [a word that can mean either 'girlfriend' or 'boyfriend'], you would tear it up, if you met him, you would meet in secret. Now there is no respect, it's all out in the open! Tsst!" Hair, as we've seen with reference to shaved heads and dreadlocks, is a privileged site for the inculcation of discipline, which can motivate both women's ambitions to maintain well-groomed hair and the anxiety that hair that is overly attended to embodies not just a kind of trivial indulgence, but a form of transgression.

This kind of intense autocritique of public practice has a long-standing history in the Tanzanian nation; they are part of the "legacy of early independence African socialism in which citizens were politicized to scrutinize themselves and others for ideological conformity" (Stambach 1999: 234;

Used clothing (*mitumba*) sales

see Abrahams 1987; Rubin 1996). The scrutiny of style and its potential ambiguities also extends to men, and perhaps most importantly the relationship of men to women. Crucially, the critiques that men offer of other men whose interest in fashion is deemed inappropriate clearly conform to the general pattern, and further are explicitly articulated as gendered rebukes. This can be seen in some of the stock characterizations that young men commonly use to assess one another. In the 1980s, Kerner identified what she called "characterizations of personae" that circulated among youth in neighboring Moshi. These characterizations focused primarily on the aspirations of young men (Kerner 1988: 318–58). The personae are terms used to denigrate and parody, but in some grudging ways to appreciate the ambitions of young men (and young women figure only tangentially in these terms; Kerner 1988: 327). The characterizations described by Kerner are Check Rap, Check Bob, and TX Kubwa. Check Rap, on the fringes of the stylish set, is perpetually scrambling to make a living and immediately turns whatever profits he realizes into consumer goods—a new pair of shoes, a slick pair of pants. Check Bob is more entrepreneurial but is principally active in the informal sector. He is well versed in the latest slang, in foreign fashions, and in musical and dance tastes. TX Kubwa is a member of the elite. Money is not a concern, all of his goods are imported, and he exercises great political and economic influence, especially over women.

In Arusha today, only *Check Bob* remains a term in wide usage; more common personae are the Brother Man and *wapambe*, the followers of a wealthy patron. All of the (always derisive) uses of these terms refer to someone whose ambitions are essentially pretensions. There is some way that these personae are guilty of excess: they don't just aspire to success, which is hardly worthy of derision in Arusha, but they call attention to the fact that they are reaching. They think of themselves as "special," a term now used (in English) to suggest self-centered antisociality. What's more, this pretension is signaled by an excessive emphasis on appearances. This was certainly made clear to me by the scorn that barbershop thugs heaped on those who they identified as Brother Men. One morning, as I rode a crowded *daladala* into town, the conductor spotted a man standing at the bus stop wearing a black nylon shirt with a gray pinstripe, neatly creased black pants, and loafers polished to a high shine, and shouted, "Make some space for the Brother Man!" The term *Check Bob*, according to many who used it, has a visual implication. It means someone whose actions are aimed at making a spectacle (as in "Check out Bob!"). Similarly, *wapambe* literally means "those who decorate." They are the beautifying appendages to the elite, and so subject to more scorn than the elite themselves.

This emphasis on visual appeal also makes these personae akin to women in many respects. A Brother Man is not a real man. His opposite is the *kidumu*, "tough guy," who values his ties to his comrades, not the impression he makes (on women). *Wapambe* was a term used on the Swahili coast in the late nineteenth century to refer to slave girls, lavishly decorated to visually enhance the appeal of the *majumbe*, "big men," for whom they publicly performed (Glassman 1995: 129–30). In all of these ways, men see the exaggerated importance of appearances as a central problem of their social world. For those who adopt the "Tupac solution," this appearance is an unwanted intrusion that provides a basis from which to stage an assertive struggle. Conversely—but in keeping with the gendered character of these ambiguities—those who actively promote their own appearance, making appealing spectacles of themselves, are derided as womanly. Style is contentious, and gender is the cultural register of that contention.

Such contentions in Arusha are confirmation of the more general claim that "diffuse anxieties about the moral and material health of nations take root in female bodies" (Comaroff and Comaroff 1999b: 31). This seems an incontestable claim, as any number of social observers inhabiting any number of social worlds have noted. At the same time, the vulnerability that women experience with respect to style and appearance is grounded in a wider phenomenology of perception, embodiment, and sociality. This is not to dismiss the primacy of gender to these contemporary anxieties about style, or to suggest that intensive scrutiny of women is somehow really not about women but about something else. Indeed, a focus on the phenomenology of appearances allows us to specify the contours of how gender is constituted in social practice, and thereby to better understand why so much tension surrounding style is about gender. This also helps us to understand how problems of visibility—the requirement that value be displayed and/as concealed—also ensnare men in conflicts akin to those experienced by stylish women. More specifically, conflicts surrounding men's pursuit of style often raise questions that are centered on gendered personhood, as the contemporary personae of the Arusha streets indicate. These personae suggest that the proliferation of venues, media, and objects for the cultivation of new appearances is highly ambiguous and produces ambiguous genders: Brother Men—a reduplicated masculine, derided as feminine—and the male dependents of elites who recall extravagantly dressed slave girls.

Of course, men working in barbershops are working in the eye of this storm. In their own view, they do not emphasize appearances at all but instead provide a service that allows them to be transgressively independent (à la Tupac), defying propriety itself and generating tough bodies that are not at all visually appealing (but this toughness must nonetheless be visually confirmed). Perhaps not surprisingly, this potential contradiction made many of the salon workers that I knew call my barbershop friends "those Check Bobs," slavishly imitating African American imagery. What all of these characterizations further suggest is that the slippery field of the appearance trade is felt by many to have feminized social life more generally, while at the same time the position of women has been subject to intensive scrutiny, condemned at once for being too secretive and too assertive. The pursuit of style is above all suspect, even as it is absolutely essential to social advancement and (even more importantly) aspiration in Tanzania today, because appearances can always be deceiving. This fact has long been recognized across a variety of domains in Tanzania. Appearances are both powerful and dangerous.

At the same time, there is reason to suspect that the ambiguities inherent in the tension between enclosure and display have been exacerbated in recent years. It is certainly the case that both barbershops and salons have only come into existence in the form they have now in recent decades.

Indeed, economic liberalization schemes, first in the mid-1980s and then in the early 1990s, facilitated massive imports in hair care products, *mitumba*, as well as the media representations to promote their use (Stambach 1999; Tripp 1996; Gibbon 1995). These new commodity forms and the services to sustain them have proved to be among the more successful economic endeavors in contemporary Tanzania. In cultural terms, their success is even greater because in spite of public debates over salon-styled hair and thuggish barbers, well-groomed hair is indispensable to contemporary understandings of respectability. Nor is this just an elitist pretension, the style of Check Bobs and office girls. When he asked the street kids with whom he worked what they would like to have if they could have anything at all, the kids told the director of a small NGO I knew that they wanted proper haircuts—or at least some clippers so they could provide them for themselves. Style, perhaps especially the style of hair, is the currency of social recognition for many in Arusha. Yet these tensions indicate that many see this currency as a false coin. In a neoliberal era, the possibilities of global interconnection feel palpably present, as evidenced by the relative availability and affordability of stylistic innovations now legion in Arusha. Yet the inability of these forms to generate greater security and respect in everyday life has made them icons of deception and secrecy (Blunt 2004). The promise of access and aspiration invites suspicion when these promises remain unfulfilled. This global condition, embodied by new forms of style, is acutely felt and debated in gender's changing appearance.

6 Learning from Your Surroundings

Watching Television and Social Participation

The insecurities that characterize the debates around what we might call aspirational consumption and its attendant politics of appearances can be grasped as part of a wider problem of participation. The form, quality, and intensity of neoliberal modes of transnational interrelations have generated certain characteristic tensions in the social life of many in Arusha. These tensions are often felt as uncertainty about the value of the kinds of access to a globalized world that are available from the marginal situation of a place like Arusha. Are Tanzanians now able to keep up with times, or do they have a greater sense of their shared suffering, their collective pain? Are well-tailored used clothes and high-maintenance hairstyles evidence of one's respectability and sophistication, or mere trappings that conceal a hollow, even threatening antisociality? And are Tanzanians, as they engage in this heady new mix, active players on this emerging landscape, or are they merely confirmed in their wider irrelevance? This dynamic of inclusion and exclusion (perhaps we might even characterize it as inclusive exclusion) generates a pattern that formulates the shape of contemporary social life in Arusha.

The popular practices that flourish in Tanzania at this most recent fin de siècle plainly depend on the widespread dissemination of electronic media and technology, from radio and audio cassettes to VCRs and satellite television. Televisual experiences offer a prominent, if not privileged, means of assessing how Tanzanians grasp what the terms of participation on a global scale might entail. In part, a sense of their place in a wider world is realized through the kind of comparative process that is entailed in watching programming, especially from non-Tanzanian sources, as men and women in Arusha comment on the content of these broadcasts. Precisely because the televisual experience is a performative one in which audiences receive programming, the concretely specific ways that particular audiences watch television and the ideologies of reception (or, we might say, audience ideas about what watching television is all about) that inform these practices need to be explored. Each of these dimensions of participation, one having to do with Tanzanians' views of themselves on a global stage, the other having to do with Tanzanians' views of television reception, informs the other and reveals important features of television watching as a lived experience (Spitulnik 2000).

Khalidi's Story

Some of the implications for thinking about questions of participation and performance in the neoliberal world from one particular perspective in Arusha were highlighted in an arresting encounter. The encounter itself had little to do with TV audiences or with the soap operas that I will subsequently address, but it exemplifies the dynamics of participation frameworks that are relevant to TV viewing. One evening, I was called to the barroom table of a man I knew, the maternal uncle of a close friend. This man, whom I will call Khalidi, was nattily attired, his wire-rimmed aviator glasses and silver stickpin through his shirt collar making me feel more than a little grubby in my fieldwork gear. Khalidi offered me a beer while he sipped a Coke. As he drank his soda, he also chewed *miraa*, a taste he had acquired during time he had spent in Mombassa working as an importer. "This is my pleasure (*raha*)," he told me. "If the cops see me chewing this, I don't even care." Khalidi was currently working as a gemstone dealer, and in that occupation, he told me, he had had the pleasure of meeting a number of Europeans. "I always like to make friends with *wazungu* (white people), when I have the chance," he told me, and then he proceeded to describe in detail one important friendship he had made. A few years back, Khalidi had met a British woman from Manchester who was working for a local NGO. The two became fond of one another and enjoyed a lengthy relationship. Khalidi made note of particular places he cherished in his memory: how they had stayed at the beach in Zanzibar with members of his family; how he had even gone swimming with her in the pool of the Tanzanite Hotel in town. This English woman was also adored by his own mother and sisters, who prepared fabulous Swahili dishes for her; she encouraged them to publish their recipes in a book.

Khalidi had intended to travel with her to England to meet her family, but "business affairs" prevented him from making this trip. While she was away in the United Kingdom, Khalidi came to a difficult decision; he would have to leave this woman, and instead he would marry the woman with whom he had recently had a child. Indeed, I had first met Khalidi just a few days earlier in the rooms he shared with his in-laws, where he proudly introduced me to his second child, a little boy only a few weeks old. It wasn't right, Khalidi had decided, to leave the mother of his child without marrying her.

When his girlfriend returned from Britain, Khalidi revealed his plans to her. "The day I told her I could not stay with her, she cried right here on my shoulder. And she cried again when I took her to the airport to fly back to England." Khalidi finished his Coke and poignantly turned to me. "Now you see, I always enjoy meeting with *wazungu*, so I thank you."

Although this is not exactly a typical soap opera story, it does illuminate the dynamics of participation in a globalized world that I feel also underlie the practices of television audiences. Consider, for example, what it would mean to think of Khalidi's account as evidence of a kind of deterritorialization, which is one prominent way of characterizing the flow of persons and values and so denoting a mode of participation, in a neoliberal order of things (Gupta and Ferguson 1997). Do Khalidi's actions, we might ask, bespeak an easy bounding from one relationship to another? Is he seeking alternatives from disjoint possibilities in a hypercompressed but still fragmentary world? Is his refusal to pursue a relationship whose impact still lingers evidence of the absolute barriers that still constrain the possibilities of even the most affluent Africans? Or might the conjunction of these alternatives remake the meaning of these relations? Is this a story of family values or an example of how they are flouted? Was Khalidi's marriage threatened by this past relationship? Or is his family confirmed by the timing of these relations, which suggests that Khalidi's marriage is not about consumerist choices, is not about affirming traditional marriage, but rather is about a recommitment to a changing order of kinship relations?

However we interpret these possible motives and implications, it is clear that Khalidi's story exemplifies one variant of the kinds of conflicted fantasies that abound in Arusha, even, perhaps especially among, those with far fewer material means than Khalidi. The participation framework through which he struggles with these aspirations—here, telling me a story, buying me a drink, indulging in a semi-illicit pleasure—is central to these fantasies. For example, his understanding of his own experience in this concrete performative context depends on the presence of an interlocutor like myself, although, in fact, any *mzungu* (European) will do. What makes Khalidi's account especially compelling is not the facts of the matter as they occurred to him, but rather his ability to tell it, and to tell it to someone who in his view will appreciate the potential of the different social worlds engaged, and so comprehend what it means to him to consider them as alternatives. In fact, frameworks like this that cast others as central interlocutors through which such particular understandings of concrete experience can be realized makes these cultivations of aspirational sensibilities akin to the reflexive production of anthropological knowledge. In the same way, my project of assessing the nature of value production in the contemporary moment is (meant to be) more than just a comparative perspective exploring neoliberalism as it appears in one instance. Instead, it depends on the actions and motivations of Tanzanians so as to transform my own understanding of what actually constitutes neoliberal social reality. It also goes without saying that what I learned of Khalidi's story was framed by the constraints on my participating in it, but it was also facilitated by my presence, without which telling the story would have lacked a clear motivation, and the force of the values it exemplifies would have been obscure. These dimensions of participation as a performative and transformative process are central to television reception, and the frameworks it exemplifies and produces, in Arusha today

Anthropological Approaches to Media Reception: Cosmopolitanism Observed

Recent anthropological assessments of electronic media in this era of globalization have suggested that consumers of mass-mediated technologies, most characteristically television audiences, are engaged in fundamentally cosmopolitan practices. Such assertions might be understood as an ironic interjection intended to evoke a frisson by the juxtaposition of sophisticated, itinerant citizens of the world with domestic, inert recipients of the televisual spectacle. This presumed divide between active culture producers and passive consumers, a theme clearly articulated in the burgeoning literatures on both consumption and popular culture more broadly, is hardly tenable. So, too, the notion of cosmopolitanism, or the recognition of plural cosmopolitanisms, as many have noted (Abu-Lughod 1997; Foster 2002; Pollock et al. 2000), is meant to destabilize presuppositions about the parochial character of social and cultural practice. As Abu-Lughod (1997: 122) notes in her ethnography of Upper Egyptian soap opera viewers,

"[T]elevision is an extraordinary technology for breaching boundaries and intensifying and multiplying encounters among lifeworlds, sensibilities, and ideas." Accordingly, an analytical emphasis on cosmopolitanisms can draw attention to how people the world over act, and also understand themselves to be acting, in ways that both depend on and serve to establish transregional connections among wide-ranging locations.

Important as these insights are, there are any number of risks entailed in assertions of cosmopolitanism, not the least of which is the fact that this contemporary "sense of mutuality" bears the burden of a complex history laden with untenable assumptions, those "universalist claims to world citizenship, based on the spectacular success of the Enlightenment as a pedagogical and political project" (Pollock et al. 2000: 580, 581). Consider, for example, de Certeau's account of what could taken as a paradigmatic feature of cosmopolitanism as this sensibility has come to be understood in many contemporary assessments of postcolonial realities. In "Walking in the City," de Certeau illustrates this sensibility with a now impossible experience: that of gazing out from the observation deck of the World Trade Center:

> To be lifted to the summit of the World Trade Center is to be lifted out of the city's grasp. One's body is no longer clasped by the streets that turn and return it according to an anonymous law; nor is it possessed, whether as player or played, by the rumble of so many differences and by the nervousness of New York traffic. When one goes up there, he leaves behind the mass that carries off and mixes up in itself any identity of authors or spectators. An Icarus flying above these waters, he can ignore the devices of Daedalus in mobile and endless labyrinths far below. His elevation transforms him into a voyeur. It puts him at a distance. It transforms the bewitching world by which one was "possessed" into a text that lies before one's eyes. It allows one to read it, to be a solar Eye, looking down like a god. The exaltation of a scopic and gnostic drive: the fiction of knowledge is related to this lust to be a viewpoint and nothing more. (1984: 92)

The cosmopolitan experience of the city has been shaped, at least since the Renaissance, de Certeau suggests, by the drive to gain a totalizing perspective, a "viewpoint," as he puts it, that is simultaneously everywhere at once and nowhere in particular. Unmoored from the strictures of bounded locality, cosmopolitans find themselves at home in the world, capable of inhabiting all specific places (at any given time) in a topos of equal and interchangeable locations. This consciousness, both alienating and exhilarating, distancing and alluring, when taken as an analytical perspective on cosmopolitanism and not merely an example of it, may obscure the ways in which postcolonial sociocultural practice is concretely constituted in space and time. Indeed, de Certeau himself suggests that this panoramic pictorial approach to the city fundamentally misunderstands the nature of spatial practices, like walking in the city and other "pedestrian speech acts" (1985: 106) through which urbanites (and the cosmopolitans among them) enunciate and dwell in place.

The television genre of soap opera might be approached as a form that seems similar, in some respects, to the Icarus-like visual spectacle de Certeau describes. Soap opera seems to offer its audiences "images that do not arise from the life world of any socially defined community" (Das 1995: 170)[1] and a vantage point that is both all-knowing and intimate at the same time. The television serial form, with its global distribution and its production in a host of national settings, including Tanzania, seems the very model of an unfixed object, appropriate to an audience attuned to a voyeuristic, possessive fantasy. Such formal properties make it possible for Abu-Lughod to assert that viewers of Egyptian soap opera are "part of the same cultural worlds we inhabit—worlds of mass media, consumption, and dispersed communities of the imagination" (1997: 128). This assertion is problematic. Surely the forms of global connectivity exemplified by soap opera make it possible to envision the world as a unified, common place. Yet the critical question for anthropological investigation is: do we all inhabit this world in the same way? My contention here is that when we shift our attention from ubiquitous forms of globalized imagery, like soaps, to the ways in which those forms are engaged, we can begin to address the articulation of diverse and particular regional worlds, which is crucial to cosmopolitan sensibilities.

Indeed, Abu-Lughod also insists that cosmopolitanism is valuable as a rubric in the analysis of television audiences so long as it is understood to be embedded in "particular configurations of power, education, and wealth in particular places" (Abu-Lughod 1997: 132). Making similar claims, Foster (2002: 135) has made imaginative use of the notion of "imagined cosmopolitanism," updating Anderson to suggest that television can be understood as a medium through which "Papua New Guineans are differently attempting to fashion themselves as subjects . . . within a cosmopolitan frame of reference." His analysis is especially noteworthy because he demonstrates the ways in which the cosmopolitan character of Papua New Guineans' understanding of themselves entails an understanding of their marginalization and subjugation to more powerful forces within that cosmopolitan frame. Foster's analysis draws our attention to the ways in which self-fashioning as a "transnational subject" can "exact a certain price" (2002: 138). In these respects, the cosmopolitan frame of reference as analysts of global television audiences describe it is organized in ways aligned with the thug-like fantasies that I have already described. In both instances, for an increasing segment of the world's population, participation in a transnational order of things carries with it a sense of their simultaneous exclusion from that transnational purview. Again, we see a characteristic contradiction of the current neoliberal moment articulated in its popular cultural practices.

Cosmopolitanism as a wide lens through which to assess media consumption offers the possibility of situating specific audiences within a transregional world. When understood as a plural phenomenon, it further provides a means of complicating our assumptions about the kinds of persons who are interconnected across space and time, as well as the character of those connections. That said, we still need to clarify how we can make use of cosmopolitanism's possibilities and what kinds of insights into the specificity of audiences this term can provide. If, for example, it illuminates principally "configurations of power, education, and wealth," how is it different from a focus on political economy or the sociology of cultural production? What might a cosmopolitan configuration look like, and how might it be distinguished from a merely global order? How, in other words, does cosmopolitanism serve both as a mode of organizing social, cultural, and material relations and as a consciousness of that organization itself? We can address these matters by looking at concrete cases of television viewing in Arusha. One critical problem that is often begged by the assertion of cosmopolitanism is, what sense or senses of place does television create and presuppose? Does the notion of cosmopolitanism confound a sense of place? Is cosmopolitan identity or aspiration intrinsically deterritorialized, disjointed from the particularities of a regional spatial nexus? Or does a cosmopolitan frame of reference bespeak the regional worlds through which it is generated?

The notion of cosmopolitanism can be used to investigate claims about belonging, and a sense of belonging entails the production of a frame of action in which participants feel their claims have validity. Thus, an apt method for addressing the complex articulation of disparate worlds is to treat various elements of television watching as features of a participation framework in the way that much linguistic analyses and studies of performance treat complex discursive actions.[2] From this perspective, cosmopolitanisms can be assessed as a certain kind of competence, the relative capacity both to conjoin multiple frameworks of action and to facilitate shifting among these alternative frameworks so that they are encompassed by a common horizon. As Larkin (1997: 406) puts it, audiences for popular media "participate in the imagined realities of others cultures as part of their daily lives." This kind of capacity for "transposition" (Hanks 1995: 211ff.) suggests that the place of cosmopolitanism is not conceived of either as a thoroughly decentered landscape made up of incompatible and divergent zones or as a unified field of entirely commensurable regions. Such decentered approaches to space, which have become legion in contemporary analyses of popular culture, exemplify a voyeuristic orientation to spatiality while participation frameworks ground us in the spatial practices (which also entail temporal implications) of situated social actors.

Serial Forms and Features

Television broadcasting of any variety is extremely recent in Tanzania. Until 1994, there was no television broadcasting in mainland Tanzania. Broadcasting was dominated through the 1990s by Independent Television (known everywhere as ITV). When I first watched television in Arusha in 1999, ITV was advertising itself as "the only station in the whole nation," suggesting a clear link between broadcasting audiences and a Tanzanian sense of nationhood. But it also suggests, if perhaps ironically, the fragility of that Tanzania nation because it can (or could) only sustain a single broadcast television network. ITV itself is a subsidiary of IPP Media. This corporation, founded and still chaired by Reginald Mengi from Kilimanjaro, is a media giant; today, it also owns three radio companies, ten newspapers, and publishing outlets in both Kiswahili and English, as well as a second television company, East Africa TV. IPP Media is also a powerful purveyor of consumer goods more generally. The IPP Group, of which IPP Media is but one component, "encompasses a Financial Consulting firm— IPP Consulting—a bottling company in joint venture with Coca-Cola— Bonite Bottlers Ltd.—[and] Tanzania's leading manufacturer of soaps and toothpaste—Bodycare Ltd" (Warren-Rodriguez, http://www.nowpublic .com/reginald_mengi_east_african_industrialist_and_media_tycoon). Mengi has clearly been extraordinarily successful at creating a synergy in Tanzania's neoliberal moment. However, the nature of his domination of media and consumer goods markets has also meant that Mengi has been the subject of many rumors, most of which turn on anxieties over the ways that he has begun to use his position to sway Tanzania's political processes. Multiparty democracy, broadcast television, and something of a consumer revolution were all initiated in the mid-1990s in Tanzania, the core components of *mageuzi*—"changes." It is hardly surprising to find that responses to transformations in the relationship between the state and its citizenry are often articulated in concerns about commodity forms in general and electronic media in particular (Stambach 1999; Shipley 2004).

In the summer of 1999, the most popular television show of the moment in Arusha was *Sunset Beach*, the American serial produced by NBC. It was shown each night on ITV. Although a few shows broadcast on ITV were produced in Tanzania, including news reports, some sports programming, and a weekly Muslim prayer report, most shows—and far and away the most popular ones—were foreign imports. Not only American and European programs but also South African soaps, first *Egoli* and subsequently *Isidingo*, the telenovela *La Mujer de Mi Vida*, produced by Univisión, and today the Filipino soap *The Promise*, enjoy a substantial following. Many programs, though, were cast-off American soap operas, comedies, and action shows. ITV airs many shows that enjoyed a relatively short run on American television (*227*, *Parker Lewis Can't Lose*, *Renegade*) as well as serials that are in syndication (today, *The Bold and the Beautiful*, preceded by *Acapulco Bay*, which replaced the still-beloved *Sunset Beach*).

These serials are broadcast not as daytime television (except on satellite transmissions, where some serial or another is available at almost any hour of the day) but as nighttime programming. *Sunset Beach* was broadcast daily on ITV at 10 PM during 1999, but it was also shown during the day on satellite. I was able to watch television in a number of venues; a good many barbershops have televisions, including satellite transmissions, as do some bar-restaurants. I watched television daily, sometimes for brief periods, sometimes for a few hours, during my time in Arusha in most of these locations, and I was also able to watch a good deal of TV in private residences. All of the imported programming is broadcast in English. None of these foreign shows are subtitled or dubbed into Kiswahili, although *La Mujer de Mi Vida* and *The Promise* are dubbed from Spanish into English before they are broadcast in Tanzania. This linguistic dimension of these popular serials certainly complicates the modes of reception available to audiences. Most of the Tanzanians I knew in Arusha who were interested in television and followed a particular show did not have any particular fluency in English. In many cases, schoolchildren with a high degree of comprehension would translate the dialogue or simply explain plotlines to a wider audience. In any event, a lack of fluency in English hardly prevents anyone in Arusha from enjoying a soap opera like *Sunset Beach*. As even casual observers of American serials know, the dramatic tension and narrative arc of the serial form itself are conveyed through a number of formal conventions—gestures, facial expressions, and especially the use of musical scoring—that do not depend in any simple way on the dialogue (see also Larkin 1997). Indeed, it is problematic even to assert that soap operas have a discernible narrative form since their quintessential feature is a seriality that results in a lack of closure.

Yet far from making these broadcasts incomprehensible, these formal repetitive and recursive features facilitate understanding. Thus, non-English speakers in Arusha had no trouble identifying the character of individual personae or understanding the interpersonal and interfamilial tensions essential to a serial's unfolding; these elements of the soap opera are revealed over multiple viewings in the recursive, highly formal qualities of this media genre. Moreover, soap operas are also valued in Arusha (as elsewhere; Geraghty 1991: 130) for the sheer spectacle they present. I regularly heard men and women comment on the lavish clothing of the characters, the elaborate furnishings of the domestic spaces they inhabited, and the beautiful scenery of the outdoor shots. These concrete qualities of the highly formalized genre of the soap opera are critical, performative features of the program that can structure modes of audience reception in important respects in Arusha.

Reflexive Consumption: Approaching Imported Media

A substantial and important literature addresses the ways that both global and African audiences engage with imported foreign-language electronic media. Miller's (1992) ethnography of Trinidad provides a model for many such studies. His work on audiences for *The Young and the Restless* in Trinidad follows directly from his approach to consumption and material culture more broadly insofar as he argues that the reception of this serial contributes to what he calls the a posteriori construction of local culture. Soap opera, says Miller, is best understood as part of local Trinidadian culture, not simply because Trinidadians appropriate its meanings and values, but because of "its role in the refinement of the concept of Trinidad as the culture of the bacchanal" (Miller 1992: 179). In short, watching *The Young and the Restless* in Trinidad helps to produce the cultural difference that Trinidadians understand as local. Here, locality is not simply given (a priori, as Miller would have it), but rather emerges as the creation of a specific community's engagements with global processes—here, of mass mediated broadcasting.

Miller's approach is relevant to my own insofar as it emphasizes the fact that local forms of cultural difference are inflected and articulated through media, but even more specifically the ways that a sense of belonging can be cultivated by audience participation even in foreign products. Trinidadians' grasp of bacchanal and their understanding of themselves as sharing, if not all equally or uniformly, in the "culture of bacchanal" are realized by viewers of *The Young and the Restless*. What Miller's account does not explore, though, are the ways that this specifically Trinidadian sense of belonging are also embedded in the material flow of global media and in a cosmopolitan sense of interrelatedness. The cosmopolitan frame of reference might provide us with a reflexive sense of Trinidadians self-fashioning as they stand in relationship to—in conjunction and disjunction with—the images and personae of a specifically American serial.

A number of studies of African audiences for imported media have been more critically engaged with such questions. Both Larkin (1997) and Fuglesang (1994) examine the importance of Indian films and videos in two African societies. Each deals with a predominantly Muslim community; Larkin works with Hausa society in Kano, in northern Nigeria, and Fuglesang with Kiswahili speakers in Lamu, Kenya. What is clear in both Larkin and Fuglesang's work is that the particulars of these audience's communities make a difference. The meaning of Bollywood for both is generated by the perspectives from which these Muslim audiences view these films. As Larkin (1997: 411) notes, many Hausa claimed that Indian films are popular in Kano because their culture is "the same as" Hausa culture. Similarly, Fuglesang (1994: 165) holds that the "romantic version of love (and sex)" found in Hindi films "appears to be most acceptable and akin to the sentiments and sensibilities of young women in Lamu."

However, neither argues that the African cultural context of the audiences accounts for the popularity, let alone the intelligibility, of Indian films. Indeed, both assess the interpretive processes of their respective audiences in similar terms. For Fuglesang, Indian film in Lamu works to fabricate a fantasy, and the plenipotentiary qualities of fantasy are at play for those in the audience. "Fantasy," she writes (1994: 179), "can be an escape into a dream world, or it may be a way to forget pains and sorrows, but it may also be resistance, a way of creating 'a space for oneself.'" It is this space for oneself that the global dissemination of media cultivates. Indian films do not replicate or oppose Kiswahili values and relationships but instead provide a counterpoint to the experience of the viewer in Lamu (Fuglesang 1994: 178). In discussing one young viewer, Fuglesang (1994: 177) noted that "the film story helped her reflect on her own situation and allowed her to fantasize about her boyfriend, enabling her to endure the dreariness and pain of what had happened in reality."

Larkin takes a fundamentally similar approach:

> The reasons why Hausa viewers recognise commonalities between their cul-
> ture and Indian culture are many and varied. In an Islamic African society the
> films are popular because they engage with the disjunctures of social change
> elaborated in terms that are familiar to Hausa society yet also distinct from
> it. This coexistence between likeness and dissimilarity is important because it
> is in the gap that the narratives of Indian film allow the exploration of social
> relations. (1997: 418)

Although Larkin focuses less on the individual viewer's experience than
Fuglesang, he also argues that Indian films stand in a kind of tension or
counterpoint with Hausa social life that the audience can productively
make use of in order to negotiate their relationship with modernity.

Both Fuglesang and Larkin, along with a host of others interested in the
active role of audiences (Barber 1997), argue that imported media—films,
videos, and television programming—permit audiences to productively
explore cultural difference. Meaning lies not in the cinematic or televisual text or in the audience's prior dispositions, but in the opportunity
for reflection on the alternative possibilities, the space between reality
as it is and as it might be, that the film/video viewer experiences. The
notion that televisual media create this space (that is, a productive gap
that fosters resonance and dissonance), while valuable, also needs to be
examined critically.

The idea that television viewing is principally a reflexive practice runs
the risk, I suggest, of transforming the cultural contexts in and through
which television broadcasting and watching are produced—and not simply the program narratives themselves—into texts that can be subject to
comparison. This model runs parallel to Geertz's (1973) arguments about
Balinese cockfighting as a dramatization of status hierarchy that permits
participants to interpret and experience and thus to reflect on the theme
of status in the Balinese social order. Claims that focus on the reflective
character of audiences tend to the meaning of performative processes in
the creation of a spectacle: the media image becomes a projection that is
abstracted from its cultural context and presented to the audience for their
evaluation. In this way, to follow Larkin's case, it is not only Indian films
and Hausa love stories that are distinct and comparable representations, but
also Indian culture and Hausa culture themselves that become alternative
responses to prevailing conditions of modernity. Audiences thus interact
with mediated performances, generating new imaginative forms.

This formulation of audience participation depends on a set of ab-
stractions that see culture as embodied by a set of images available to be
selected, recombined, and subverted by viewers who occupy (or generate) this space between the array of possibilities presented. It may well be

the case that the mass mediation of cultural spectacle, which has become pervasive with the proliferation of televisual experience, cultivates such an understanding of cultures as reified collections of possibilities, emotions, and desires. In this way, audiences are inclined, even predisposed, to describe their experience in terms that emphasize their interpretive virtuosity or the contradictions they experience when confronted with alternative material forms. This is characteristic of consumerist modes of subjectivity more broadly. It is problematic, though, to see these forms of self-creation as having significant analytical value; they really exemplify the very kinds of processes they are meant to account for. Audiences are not simply weighing the merits or implications of their own social world against an alternative when they participate in the fantasies of televisual (or other) spectacles. Their participation is organized and constrained by the cultural conditions of possibility through which they act. Audiences are not merely observers or even interpreters of cultural images; observation and interpretation are themselves culturally informed practices.

Television watching is a productive action, and in that sense, it is constituted by wider social process of producing value. Here I examine the kinds of values that serve to orient television viewing and that are generated through such practice. What is the point of watching television? What does it achieve? How are the values that shape this mundane practice realized in the participation frameworks that organize audience's television viewing in Arusha—participation frameworks that are themselves refractions of a social horizon (Hanks 1995: 202)? To address these questions requires discussion of the particularities, and perhaps even peculiarities, of audience activities in Arusha.

Audience Performance

Television watching in Arusha, especially of English-language or other non-Kiswahili-language programming, is a complex communicative practice. Any electronically mediated utterance is conveyed and received through a dynamic network that becomes increasingly elaborate over time as media forms produced in a concrete sociocultural context, perhaps even targeting a specific demographic group, become distributed and replayed to diverse audiences (Spitulnik 2000). The circuits of media—the combination of programming and broadcast genres available to any particular audience over time—come to establish the context through which media consumption is interpreted and evaluated. That is, particular histories of media distribution provide a powerful way of framing this form of communication. In the Tanzanian case, this has concrete implications. The fact that all television broadcasting has occurred within the last decade and that it consists largely of imported shows shapes audiences' sense of the novelty of television and of the way that television exemplifies rapid, contemporary social and political change, a fact noted by many even while watching television or videos. For example, it figures in Tanzanians' struggles to determine the place of Tanzania in the wider world that these transnational media represent.

Further, the programming decisions of broadcasters seem to have implications for the way that genres are established. Serials in Tanzania are shown in the evening hours during the week, during the day on weekends, and at almost any time of the day via satellite broadcasting. This means that these programs may not carry the same genre expectations that they do in the contexts in which they were produced. The routine conventions that an American audience may associate with soap operas as a genre, and that they may especially attribute to soap opera audiences, are established by the fact that they are broadcast during daytime hours and that they promote commodities attuned to a particular, highly feminized vision of domesticity.[3] The fact that these programming conventions are belied by the conditions of their distribution in places like Tanzania—to say nothing of the fact that Tanzanian assumptions about consumption, domesticity, and gender are distinctly different from American ones—means that it is quite possible for serial programs to carry much different genre expectations, including the possibility that soap operas convey a cosmopolitan sensibility.

The complexity of participation frameworks is also manifest at the immediate level of television watching. Viewers often depend on one or perhaps several translators, who may either translate or simply summarize the dialogue of an English-language program. Moreover, it is common for audiences to watch television with the sound turned off. This is especially true in places of business, like bars and barbershops, where audience attention to the programming is intermittent. In many of the businesses I frequented, the television sound was kept off while a radio played. The television sound might be turned up only for particular programs or at the request of clients. These are commonplace but by no means trivial uses of television. A small business may incur substantial expense to set up a television, which will often include a cable connection, a satellite feed, and in some instances a VCR. A television will, at least initially, bring in a crowd of people, at least some of whom become paying customers. Moreover, viewers regularly interact with television broadcasts even when no sound is played. For example, as we sat watching a silent broadcast of a

British worship service that consisted of a rock concert set in a vast church, two of the young men watching the show commented on the size of the crowd and the spaciousness of the church, noting, "The European (*mzungu*) must love God a lot! I thought that was a stadium, but it's a church!" His friend added that most musicians in Europe got their start in the church, which was good for him because he aspired to a similar career through his church activities. Even this simple exchange exemplifies the ways that audiences in Tanzania use participation frames to locate themselves in relation to the places and values (here, Europe and religiosity) embedded in television broadcasting.

Framing the Soap Opera

What are the kinds of conventions that frame the participation of soap opera audiences in Arusha? The narrative structure of soap operas was not a particular focus of interest for the serial watchers I knew in Arusha. Nor had a kind of connoisseurship in fandom emerged in Tanzania, with devoted followings attending to the broadcasts or recirculating plotlines and redeploying characters in other media, as is the case with so much other engagement with popular culture (cf. Jenkins 1992). What is more compelling about the way that Tanzanians engage with soap opera is the way that their interest in this genre resonates with wider patterns of consumption and self-fashioning. For example, although we occasionally discussed story lines, and even more frequently character personalities, as we watched the show or talked about it during the day, the people I spoke with in Arusha about *Sunset Beach, Egoli,* or *The Promise* even more regularly exclaimed their conviction and surprise that these shows were, as they put it, "live" (the term is always used in English; I have never heard a Kiswahili equivalent). This was not meant to imply that the show was a direct, immediate broadcast from somewhere. Rather, the live-ness of *Sunset Beach,* as well as a variety of other serial broadcasts, such as *Egoli* and *Isidingo* from South Africa, related to the actuality of the personae and their relationships. *Sunset Beach,* from this widely held perspective, was a kind of reality TV avant la lettre. This understanding of soap opera as a lived form, in some sense not a performance at all, is telling. It certainly reveals something about urban Tanzanian's speculations about *wazungu* (that is, European/American) lifestyles. It is especially important to consider what this understanding tells us about how Tanzanians identify themselves as the audience for such a transmission. This prevalent concern with the live-ness of such shows reveals an interest in the coeval positions of Americans and Tanzanians in a common spatial and temporal horizon where experience can be situated (Fabian 1983). These coeval positions generate both continuities and discontinuities in the experience of the audience and of the televised. As Wilk (2003) has suggested, the coeval, and to a lesser degree copresent, dimensions of broadcasting, which he calls "TV time," can constitute a kind of temporal and spatial compression that permits audiences to feel that they are sharing in a performance or an enactment—or at least that they have a claim on it.

This entitlement to a coeval horizon helps watchers establish the relevance of the broadcast to their own lives. Still, it is important to point out that this reception of, for example, *Sunset Beach* as a series of live broadcasts also highlights important perceived discontinuities between audiences and broadcasters. This break can be seen in the reasons many people provide to support their conviction that the show broadcasts actual lives: "That Ben and Meg, they must really be a couple. How else could they sleep in the same bed? Could she really have another husband and do that?" These explanations suggest that what makes the temporal sharedness—the fact that *Sunset Beach* is "live"—necessary is the impossibility of the characters being as they are and doing what they do if the broadcast were merely a performance rather than unmediated reportage. If the soap is merely a performance, if the coevalness is denied, then it becomes impossible to interpret the show—impossible not just as a drama or a piece of imaginative activity, but as the product of real social activity conducted in that way.

The necessity of live-ness as a performative and interpretive feature of this genre has further implications. It suggests a certain irrefutability to the broadcast. After characterizing the telenovela as "a great 'live' show," one man told me, as we watched *The Promise* in a lunchroom, that people loved *The Promise* because "it shows life on the inside, completely!" (*inaonyesha maisha ya ndani, kabisa*). That is, it revealed what are otherwise hidden realities, and in this way (and in contrast to most other broadcasts—and much of the rest of popular practice) is not just about appearances but about showing something more intimate and more profound. Recall again the way that much popular practice in Arusha plays on the anxieties generated by the revelations and deceptions of appearances. For something to be live implies that the performance is not just on the surface, not merely an appearance, but something inside and therefore more valid, even true. This understanding of live-ness as a quality (again, the term was always used in English) was confirmed for me in what might seem a diametrically opposed context: in speaking with Pentecostal Christians attending a crusade in Arusha in 2006. In this context, in discussing their acceptance of Jesus (again, something that happened, according to their own testimonies, "inside their souls"), many said they knew the "powers of God" (*nguvu za Mungu*) were working in their lives because they could see these powers "*live, kabisa!*" (completely live!) in their lives, perhaps through healing, their release from demonic possession, or other wonders (cf. Engelke 2007). The live quality of these broadcasts is part of the participatory framework through which they are assessed. Live-ness makes it possible to make sense of these genre performances as it indexes the immediacy of the relationship between performers and their audience and so confirms the validity of the performance experience.

I should note here that the seriousness with which this participatory framework of live-ness is taken is revealed by what happened to *Sunset Beach:* it was abruptly canceled in July 1999. This was a censorious act, said many, undertaken by those opposed to the way that *Sunset Beach* and other soaps (but especially this one) worked *kupotosha jamii*—that is, to undermine the family. This account of the serial's cancellation, offered by both adversaries and devotees of *Sunset Beach,* for many viewers confirmed the truth that such broadcasts must be live, that it must reveal the actual reality of other ways of life, because it was clearly perceived to pose a palpable threat to Tanzanians.

Educational Television

Of course, the very possibility of conducting one's life in "that way," as televised on *Sunset Beach* or *The Promise,* in Arusha is what makes programs like this compelling viewing. The viewers I talked with in Arusha about soap opera explicitly commented on the pronounced contrast between what they viewed on TV and what life for them was like in Tanzania. They noted this contrast not by their direct description of the content of this or any show, but in the way they accounted for their viewing preferences. With a remarkable degree of unanimity, soap audience members I spoke with told me that they watched serials because "these programs teach us/educate us" (*vipindi hivi vinafundisha/vinaelemisha,* both variations reported). This interest in the educational value of soap operas illuminates yet again both the links and the breaks between what Tanzanians think they are watching and how they feel themselves to be living. As an educational medium, soap operas depend on a perceived gap in knowledge and understanding that these programs can help fill. This gap facilitates processes of teaching and learning that motivate TV audiences. Further, this insistence on teaching also serves to establish the soap opera as a form that conforms to emerging program categories or genres of popular culture (Fabian 1998). As a genre, such educational television works to establish hierarchical—which is to say, power-laden—criteria that permit Tanzanians to make aesthetic and social judgments about broadcasting and audiences.

Not just soaps but other broadcasts, videos, and films and are routinely evaluated and enjoyed with respect to their educational benefits. Shows like *Sunset Beach* are more educational in comparison, for example, to locally produced—and much less admired—Tanzanian serials, which are "just for laughs" (*wanacheka, tu*). In addition, I noted that other American programs were denounced or dismissed because they were not of value, and this dismissal was related to the criteria by which educational genres were judged. In 2003, for example, I watched an episode of *Jerry Springer* on a satellite broadcast with a small group of men and women gathered in a barbershop. Although there was some fascination with the show, it was explicitly not valued in the way any serial program was. Indeed, many other viewers of this show with whom I spoke suggested to me that the show was not a good one because it was not "real" (*kweli*) but must have been "fake" (*feki*). Unlike soap operas, it was assumed by most people I spoke with about such talk shows that the segments could not possibly be live (in the sense already discussed) because no one could really act in the way guests on these shows routinely acted. Similarly, audiences for professional wrestling programs were convinced the shows were fake ("Are they really being hit? Where is the blood?"). Here, it was commonly reported that the motivation for these wrestlers was suspect because rather than wrestling for real, they were only performing for money. The criteria by which such shows are evaluated confirm for them the importance of live-ness as a quality that permits these shows to serve a legitimate purpose. This quality further speaks to many Tanzanians' sense of themselves as audiences that can share in or belong to the world where these performances take place. Thus, many people used *Jerry Springer* not as an example of television's educational purposes, but of the still irreconcilable divides between the *tabia* (the character and conduct) of *wazungu* and Tanzanians.

To say that soap operas are part of a genre of educational television does not mean that all audience members evaluate serials in the same way, which is certainly not the case in Arusha. Rather, it permits us to recognize that different audiences and different audience members can make opposing judgments relative to similar or identical criteria. Thus, one mother I knew rejected *Sunset Beach* on the grounds that the show doesn't teach anything while her daughters found it educational. Further, genres such as these are not simply evaluations of the broadcast texts or objects; they offer categories for judging the televisual performance as a whole. From this perspective, judgments about educational shows are also judgments about the various modes of participation that define soap opera audiences. To demonstrate this point, I need to situate the genre criteria of education in wider fields of social action in Arusha. When I asked people what a show like *The Promise* taught them as an educational experience, I was invariably told that you learn about your "surroundings" or "environment"—*mazingira*—through shows like these. For most, the environment that one could become educated about had to do with human relationships, family, business, and sexual ties. The complex entanglements and manipulations that are the bread and butter of serial television were taken by many viewers as object lessons in what life is like. For others, the educational benefits of soap operas were more distancing; for them, the relevant surroundings of the show were cautionary tales about the dangers of wealth and power and disrespect for family members.

But, I often asked, could you compare the surroundings televised on *Sunset Beach* with the surroundings of Arusha? A great many people said no, the relationships and values depicted in this soap could not be found in Tanzania. It was impossible, for example, for lovers to act in such public ways, or for children to manipulate their parents' lives or relate to them in such a direct manner—the same qualities of inappropriate *tabia* that disqualified *Jerry Springer* as a true program. Even more interesting than this perceived gap between Tanzania and this televised fantasy were the claims that some viewers made that the environment in Arusha was changing so that some now people acted in ways that could be watched on soap operas. This point was made clear to me as I chatted with Saidi after we watched not a soap but a Jackie Chan video, *Who Am I?*, an action-packed thriller about a military agent seeking revenge against a team of global assassins. Saidi immediately told me the film was great because "It's educational; it has a lot of lessons" (*"Inafundisha; Inamaelezo mengi!"*). Again, I was curious about what he, a young sign painter from Tanga, could learn from a film like this one. "About your surroundings," he said. After I pressed him further, he responded, "It shows you what life is like. You can find yourself in a situation that you think is impossible, but just like that soldier is successful, you'll find that there is a way that you can be successful too." He went on to talk about what life in the city was like, how people could seem to support you but then turn out to betray you or have their own agenda. A film like this not only shows viewers that this is what the world is like, but also shows that it is possible to succeed even in a world as contentious as this. Saidi added that there were different kinds of films and videos. Some were just for pleasure—*starehe*—while others, like this, were educational and could help viewers understand their surroundings. Some folks, Saidi continued, go to bars after work to deal with their "thoughts" (*mawazo*), but others preferred to watch videos like this one to learn something—"*hazina ubaya!*" ("What's the harm in that?").

I had almost identical conversations with soap opera viewers. Soap operas teach viewers about their surroundings, for just as soap operas reveal things in their inside look at the intimacies of the lives of others, so too do soap opera viewers frequently face family conflict, and—especially—duplicity in social relationships in the world today, and—especially—in a city like Arusha. The surroundings depicted, according to those viewers claiming to learn about their surroundings, are in the first place social relations. The material circumstances of these settings were only relevant insofar as they were part of the way they revealed the complexity, ambiguity, and deceit in human affairs (as, for example, when it's assumed that a spouse has married for love and not for wealth, a circumstance that is almost always suspected as a motive in almost any marriage, regardless of how meager the wealth involved in Arusha). Part of what is interesting about the claim that the surroundings enacted in a soap opera are akin to the surroundings one encounters in one's everyday life in Arusha is the way that this claim allows soaps to validate a particular understanding of social life as complex, duplicitous, and ambiguous, a validation that is expressed and confirmed in the interpretive claim that such broadcasts are live. The more soap operas reveal the hidden antagonistic intricacies of social reality, the more persuaded viewers are that their social reality is intricately antagonistic. Here, I would concur with Miller's assessment of the way that *The Young and the Restless* contributes to Trinidadian views of their own social character: beyond just identifying with the dangerous entanglements televised in soap operas, Tanzanian watchers are remaking their sense of their own entanglements as viewers. In this way, they are learning about their surroundings in a Bourdieuvian fashion, by cultivating a disposition toward a world they create through their actions, including their active soap consumption.

The assertion that what makes the surroundings in Arusha and those depicted on the screen compatible, or potentially so, is the way soap opera surroundings can educate viewers about themselves reveals something further of the viewers' active engagement in the televisual performance. As Saidi suggested, the educational process is itself part and parcel of the surroundings where it is carried out. Just as the surroundings are contentious and ambiguous, so too is learning lessons an arduous task. It is not a form of *starehe*—"relaxation"—like watching games or drinking in a bar (to use Saidi's examples), but rather a way to address the thoughts that one experiences in the course of everyday life. The theme of education, then, as part of the value production process of television viewing (that is, what it is that makes watching soap operas meaningful and valuable) resonates explicitly with wider processes. The conflict-laden experience of "having thoughts" (*kuwa na mawazo*) confirms the fraught character of social reality, is expressed in the felt experience of pain, and can be worked through in the social practices of survival, acknowledging this pain and seeing it as a qualification to act in a world defined by conflict. In the same way, viewers who are educated by viewing the surroundings broadcast "live" on soap operas are attuning their felt sense of having thoughts, which they can acquire and transform through education, to the reality of deception and antagonism that they confront in Arusha and find confirmed for them in *Sunset Beach*.

This remaking of subjectivity as part of the participation in televisual performance is also something noted by many viewers in Arusha. Thus, those who claimed that one could learn from the surroundings depicted on soap operas also held that those best able to do this "were educated" or "had studied" (*waliosoma*). An educated audience thus finds points of connection in the surroundings represented on a show like *The Promise* or a film like *Who Am I?* (or, lest we forget, *Commando*). Again, these viewers' claims do much more than suggest the extent to which an audience does or does not identify with what it watches. Instead, these assertions show the criteria of the genre that includes soap opera (that is, educational TV) are also being used to gauge the character of the audience that watches it. Here, too, the televisual performance offers a framework for action in which one must be qualified to act. These viewers seem to say, if you are educated, then television can teach you.

The way that diverse audiences are produced through the creation of distinct genres of programming is further articulated through gendered practice in Arusha. There is no sense in which soap opera forms a woman's genre, as many commonplace understandings of these programs in might assume. This is not to say, though, that men's and women's expectations or tastes are identical, or not systematically developed. In fact, both women and men are avid viewers of soap operas, although beyond the concern with education that men and women share, the aesthetic experience of the soap opera form is weighted differently by men and women. Women typically became most engaged with serials when they perceived the subject matter as especially sentimental. More specifically, plot elements that were especially "saddening" (*inasikitisha*) or "heart-wrenching" (*inagusa roho*) were captivating for many women. Conflicts, especially between parents and children, were the ones most typically commented on. These criteria were certainly not limited to soap operas. Women are the predominant audience for precisely the kinds of Indian films both Larkin and Fuglesang describe, and the sadness of these stories is inevitably cited as part of their appeal. I also watched a video of the film *Witness* with two older women in their home; both of them found it moving and sad because of the dangers faced by the young Amish boy and the uncertainty of Harrison Ford's character's ability to protect him. On the other hand, men were drawn to soap operas, but for different reasons than women. Many men told me they preferred programs with "tension" (used in English) where the conflicts between characters were realized less in the sentiments evoked or depicted in the narrative than in overt dramatic confrontations. Thus, men could readily embrace soap operas for the scheming manipulations of the characters in the same terms that they professed to enjoy films with Arnold Schwarzenegger and Jackie Chan.

Let me offer some further illustrations of how such participation frameworks are realized in practice. My first example concerns audiences for popular music in Arusha. A number of English- and Kiswahili-language tabloids are readily available in town. Some of these are published in Tanzania, and many of the most popular come from Kenya. Readers of these papers typically follow the exploits of international celebrities, from musical artists to sports stars, items that are a staple all such tabloids worldwide. In Arusha, one of the most popular papers is the Sunday edition of the *Daily News* from Kenya, which is prized for its section on popular music, usually found on the center page. Each week, one international artist is covered in detail, with excerpts from a Reuters interview, several recent pictures, and most importantly, the transcribed lyrics from the performer's most recent hits. Many young men and women, many of them well into their twenties, kept elaborate scrapbooks made up of materials culled from these tabloid centerfolds. Occasionally these scrapbooks—simply called *daftari*, or notebooks—were highly intertextual, consisting of notes received from friends, headlines pulled from multiple papers, and photos of the celebrities that were often subsequently removed from their place in a notebook to decorate a family sitting room or a workplace. The most consistent feature in the dozen or so notebooks that people shared with me were page after page of carefully handwritten copies of the lyrics published in the Sunday papers. This practice of serial transcription seems to be carried out by a truly diverse group of people, as young as twelve and as old as thirty, young men and women, and fans of different kinds of music and style.

This kind of writing practice, which has a long history among school goers in East Africa, and the intentions of the youth who keep these notebooks resonate with the complex meanings under consideration. Most people I asked told me that they wrote out the lyrics in the papers because such exercises are "educational" (*yanafundisha*). This notion of the educational value of participating in popular culture is interesting in a number of ways. To begin with, it suggests the connection of these kinds of activities with schooling, and indeed, most youth who keep notebooks said that they began the practice while they were in school. Many of them, not surprisingly, linked this kind of transcription to lessons in reading and writing in English, and so kept it up in order to improve their linguistic capacity. At a wider level, such claims about the educational significance of these transcriptions are in keeping with the meanings that audiences of soap operas give to their actions. This example of transcription and its explicit connection to education poses a challenge to what is typically thought of as audience reception. For although such audiences are characteristically theorized as consumers of pop culture producers, actions like these serial transcriptions suggest that the categories of production and consumption are not so neatly distinguishable in actual practice. After all, rather than simply cutting and pasting the newsprint lyrics onto different surfaces, these fastidious transcriptions serve to demonstrate, as the category of *education* implies, a kind of competence that requires popular cultural participants to develop their own ability to master these texts. In describing this writing as educational, in other words, these youth are emphasizing their ability not just to copy or assimilate these texts, but to make use of them (see also Ranger 1975).

Qualifying Audiences

Participatory engagements in popular culture may also lead us to an understanding of how global forms of media like serial television structure and are structured by local tensions. In watching television in public venues in Arusha—bars and restaurants, barbershops and salons, private residences—broadcasts of soap operas and other dramatic series frequently generate contrasting commentaries on topics ranging from wealth to fashion, but most commonly marriage and family relations. Occasionally these commentaries are expressed in the form of open debates that erupt—and could persist in discussions around town for several days—over, for example, the role of parents in deciding the marital fortunes of their children, or the nature of family ties among children and grandchildren after divorce. Often these debates proceed along unanticipated lines. In one instance, two senior men, each heads of their households, offered different perspectives on a dramatized divorce case, in which an abused wife sought to keep her husband from getting custody of their child. Their debate took place among a group of five other men of different generations in a small barbershop. One of the men insisted that this mother and wife needed protection, that she had "rights" (*haki*) that must be recognized, and above all, that as the mother of her children she would best provide the support of a "family" (the term used in English, along with *jamii*). The other man insisted that cases like this one showed, conversely, how kinship was threatened. A wife like this needed to be "taught" to "endure" (*kuvumilia*) such a husband by the members of both her natal and marital families. Moreover, the question of custody had to be decided in the father's favor, because he was the unquestioned father of the child, and to deny him access to his child would undermine his clan (*ukoo*). It was clear from the participants' contributions to this discussion, and from subsequent discussions I had among other men and women about this discussion, that the two perspectives they took on gender, marriage, and kinship more broadly were representative of prevailing conflicts over just such questions in perhaps especially urban Tanzania today.

Soap opera viewers plainly see that marriage and kinship are at issue and are available to be debated through their televisual performance. The terms in which kinship is understood—family as opposed to clan—plainly prefigure various positions in this debate. The televisual models of kinship presented on soap operas can in no way be said to determine the significance of these categories, which are embedded in much wider transformations in Tanzanian sociality.

Indeed, the family/clan divide encodes a broad array of relationships, forms of status, and wealth; each is a rubric for a distinct configuration of social values and persons. Those who are more likely to speak of the importance of family tend to have a higher class standing and higher levels of formal education. Their ties to urban areas are likely to be more entrenched than those who understand their kinship ties as dependent on clan organization. Further, this distinction bespeaks different understandings of the expectation that kin have for one another—of the obligations, for example, of an urban businessman to his rural lineage mates, or a father to his sons and daughters. For example, in a related debate (one not televised on any American soap opera), advocates for women's rights to inherit property from their fathers spoke in terms of shared membership in a family, and even demonstrated this membership by reference to the shared DNA between parents and all of their offspring to make their claims. In contrast, those who opposed granting daughters the right of inheritance spoke of the inviolability of clan wealth and of the obligations of a husband's clan to provide for his wives. A daughter, said those defending such a position, leaves her house behind, while advocates for the family saw these bonds as enduring beyond households. The point is not simply that there are distinct gendered implications for understanding of kinship and sociality embedded in this contrast between family and clan, which there clearly are. These two terms represent key elements in a broad ideological contrast—one that has no doubt been abetted by the rise of neoliberal policies, with their emphases on individuals, rights, and family values, as numerous studies of these cultural forms have demonstrated (Comaroff and Comaroff 2000; Weiss 2004).

Further, this contrast has critical implications for the actual material conditions of people in Tanzania, including the conditions that shape their ways of participating in televisual performance. The contrast between family and clan organizes audiences' engagements with the media even as it is remade in the process. It is clear, for example, that advocates of both the family and the clan were equally avid fans of soaps like *Sunset Beach* and were equally capable of suggesting that they undermine the family, however this discourse is grasped. At the same time, the act of watching these local tensions played out in the soap opera medium can help to structure those tensions by validating the specific criteria through which both television watching and marital relations are evaluated in those local contexts. This helps explain why the other members of the audience for this debate about *Sunset Beach* and its depiction of divorce characterized the difference between the two men in terms of education: the man who supported the wife's parental position was judged to be "someone who has studied." This is a concrete illustration of the ways that, as many Tanzanians put it, television can "teach those who are educated." It further demonstrates, as Spitulnik has noted, the fact that media "forms both presuppose and create the contexts for their interpretation" (1993: 297). From this perspective, we might say that such audiences not only aspire to participate in the worlds they watch, but by watching their preferred broadcasts, they also assert their qualification as participants within the wider performances of television and other forms of popular culture. The participation framework suggests, therefore, that the idea of audiences creating a space for reflexive self-understanding relative to distinct depictions of modernity is problematic. Although for many Tanzanians there is a perceived gap between life as it is lived in Arusha and life as it is live on a soap opera, there is also a sense that the act of watching television emerges within contexts that are shaped by much more than the medium and its representational content. The pragmatic forms of action through which audiences engage with television and the evaluative criteria they use when watching—for example, the distinctive interest in education and coevalness—suggest that the meanings that audiences bring to bear on these performances are structured by local requirements of participation. More than just choosing a path for themselves or seeing personal sentiments played out in an enacted performance, television viewers are making, defining, and qualifying themselves as participants.

This mode of participation tells us something crucial about cosmopolitan sensibilities in postcolonial contexts and about the spatial dimensions of these sensibilities. Television (video as well as broadcast) audiences in Arusha, with their explicit attention to crucial differences between surroundings as sources of education, inhabit a world that is neither a series of disjunct, fractious positions nor a homogenous order of desire into which they are inevitably drawn. Rather, their viewing practices and critical evaluations of television and themselves are situated in places that take on their concrete character when they are transposed as specific positions encompassed by a common horizon. These particularities of place matter because they make it possible for television viewing to be effective. That is, they permit viewers to shift between various local perspectives and so become educated about, and thus qualified actors in, the surroundings they inhabit.

Participation and Difference

How might this approach to media reception have consequences for contemporary anthropological theorizing about mass media? How, for example, might it relate to prevailing ideas about the cosmopolitanism sensibilities of audiences? How might it perhaps inform the very notion of what constitutes the cosmopolitan? For this discussion, let's return to my encounter in the bar with Khalidi. In many ways, Khalidi exemplifies a kind of cosmopolitanism. Not only his life's experience but his accounting of it are grounded in a transnational context. When situated in this context and understood as a way of participating in the transposing of diverse perspectives across different viewpoints within that framework, we can see that Khalidi's story offers a means of transforming the value of his own lived experience. Does his narrative demonstrate a betrayal of his kinship connections in Arusha, or does he affirm the strength of his commitments to them—a commitment that is realized, in this case, as a kind of sacrifice? Larkin (1997: 420) has noted that "[s]acrifice is significant to postcolonial societies negotiating the rapidity and direction of social change," and as a result has become a prominent theme in Indian films and Hausa vernacular literature. No doubt it is structured differently, if it is thematized at all, in American soap operas. It is further worth asking about the character of this sacrifice, especially of the sort exemplified by Khalidi's actions. Is sacrifice a means of reconciling "the tension between modernity and tradition in postcolonial societies" (Larkin 1997: 419)? Might it be grasped less as a resolution than as part of the price exacted from those who pursue cosmopolitan aspirations (Foster 2002: 135)? Or yet again, can Khalidi's sacrifice be taken as an assertion of the value of other modes of affinity, not as a loss but as a positive transformation?

What permits all of these possibilities to coexist and inform one another is the way that Khalidi and I participated in his reporting his story to me. It is his capacity to project an "other" from the transnational purview as part of the framework in which these events occur that transforms the meaning of his affair, his marriage, and his family in profound ways so that they are not simply the fulfillments of social obligations or aspects of a torrid past, but the specific expression of an unfolding relationship between these possibilities. He confirms that he is qualified to tell this story by telling it to an American, who embodies not just the perspective of the other against which the choices (or sacrifice) he has made can be seen as a kind of loss, but who also embodies, by his physical presence in a bar in town, drinking and exchanging thoughts, the interconnection between the distinct possibilities within the unifying framework that his story creates. By telling the story to me, he demonstrates that he is fully a part of the worlds he describes, and so he can effectively act in them. Ultimately it is not the incompatibility of alternatives but their comparability that allows Khalidi to appreciate and comment on the nuances of his encounters. This capacity to participate in a world of synthesized differences (and so not the same world that Americans inhabit), to draw comparisons, to see difference as a source of value and transformation, to be educated (in the words of Arusha's soap opera viewers) about one's surroundings—these are what those who participate in a cosmopolitan frame of reference hope to achieve. What is equally clear is that participation in such a world must be grounded in particular surroundings. The cosmopolitan inhabitation of space is a not a shifting between indistinct and interchangeable zones. Rather, it is a situated perspective in a specific world.

Television viewing can similarly be grasped as a kind of performance, and as such, it requires us to pay attention to the way that viewers participate in their experience as an audience. From this perspective, a framework for participation can be discerned in the viewing practices of television audiences in Arusha, one in which viewers make use of a specific, meaningful criteria to evaluate the content of the media they watch and to evaluate themselves as an audience qualified to effectively comprehend. They thus fully participate in their televisual experiences. In this way, reception can be understood as a dynamic, reciprocal process in which audiences do not merely interpret or reflect on the possible meanings of the spectacles they consume, but also remake the reality of the fields of social activity they inhabit. In their own terms, television viewers in Arusha are educated about their surroundings. They thus make important comparisons between worlds and come to know the "live" reality of their lived worlds anew.

7 Chronic Mobb Asks a Blessing

Apocalyptic Hip Hop and the Global Crisis

In the summer of 2000, I returned to Arusha in Northern Tanzania armed with a copy of *The Source*, the self-described "magazine of hip hop music, culture and politics," which I expected would be a hit with many of the young men I knew in town. Indeed, this large glossy issue quickly circulated through the streets of the city center, and many of the young men—and a few young women—who combed through it valued it especially as a source of stylistic inspiration. The magazine was lauded as *katalogi* ("catalog"), a term in contemporary street Kiswahili that refers primarily to a way of dressing in contemporary, youth-oriented clothing and accessories; it also refers to the multiple media through which such fashions are displayed. One afternoon, a month after my arrival, I sat down to peruse *The Source* with a few guys who were hanging out in front of a kiosk. As one of them flipped through its pages, he made comments typical of other such browsers: "I don't like those pants," "Those shoes are fierce," "That Eminem is crazy!" But he slowed down to read an interview with the artist Q-Tip, MC for the crew A Tribe Called Quest, and tapped the accompanying picture with his knuckle. "*Huyu, anapiga swala tano*"—"This guy," he noted, "hits five prayers," that is, he prays five times a day. This remark points to the way in which participation in the stylistic possibilities of hip hop—its music, culture, and politics—also provides a great many youth in Arusha a means of defining and affirming their religious affiliations.

Such stylistic possibilities are especially significant, perhaps even pressing, concerns in contemporary Arusha. At the turn of the twenty-first century, Tanzania, and in particular the Aru-Meru region in which Arusha is situated, has been engaged in highly public, often turbulent deliberations over the nature and meaning of religious association and spiritual practice. In the early 1990s, fractious and openly violent conflicts within the dominant Lutheran diocese across Mount Meru and Mount Kilimanjaro attracted the attention of national church and state authorities (Baroin 1996). By the end of the decade, these contentions had been further fueled by Pentecostal fervor, which today attracts an interest across the region that goes far beyond internecine Lutheran conflicts. Moreover, religious affiliation has had an abiding significance in the historical transformation of Arusha's social and spatial organization. Colonial policies promoted the presence of Muslim Swahili traders as proper urbanites in the residential areas of Arusha town, while inhabitants of the mountain communities from Kilimanjaro and Meru were assumed to be rural peoples and thus outsiders and migrants in town (Peligal 1999). Today, however, many descendants of these long-standing urban and Muslim residents, as well as Muslims who come from areas all across northern and central Tanzania in order to work and live in Arusha, frequently see themselves as besieged by what they understand to be powerful, privileged external forces—in particular, Chagga and Asian entrepreneurs. Indeed, turmoil surrounding national electoral processes in both 1995 and 2000 have prompted many of Arusha's Muslims to insist that their very citizenship is at risk. "This is becoming a Christian nation" is how many young Muslim men in Arusha assessed the contemporary political climate. For good measure, and also for ecumenical scope, there is also a broad, perhaps even consuming, concern within contemporary Arusha for the resurgence of malevolent spiritual forces of various forms. Meruhani spirits from the Indian Ocean threaten the fertility of newly betrothed women in town, and even the *Arusha Times* reports, "Ten female pupils [ages nine to thirteen, both Christians and Muslims] of the Naura primary school in Arusha municipality, recently collapsed in fits of hysteria after allegedly being strangled by what they believed to be 'demons'" (Nkwame 2002; see also Smith 2001 for similar events in southeastern Kenya).[1]

These tensions are not offered as a prelude to a wider discussion of the nature of sectarian conflict in Arusha. Still less could I hope to characterize a range of specific positions—Lutheran, Pentecostal, or Muslim—as they emerge in these interactions.[2] These tensions do illustrate a repeated observation about contemporary Tanzania (Baroin 1996; Kelsall n.d.; Stambach 2000a, 2000b): in a period of densely articulated and rapid social, political, economic, and cultural transformations, discourses that emphasize problems of religious affiliation and identity have come to the fore in the Tanzanian public sphere. Beyond this observation, these religious discourses, and their current predominance, are best understood not as responses to the shifting Tanzanian landscape, but as themselves implicated in the changes they articulate. My central concern, therefore, is to understand how religiosity itself is (re)created within dynamic socio-cultural fields such as those prevailing in Arusha today.

Consider, for example, the range of social processes that greatly accelerated in Tanzania during the 1990s—processes like the proliferation of print and electronic media across the nation; the collapse of what were already tenuous public services as a condition of structural adjustment; the official rejection of African socialism (*ujamaa*); the consequent meager, but nonetheless powerful, influx of capital into formal sectors of the economy; the institution of multiparty democracy and the attendant crises of both presidential electoral cycles; and the continuing spread of the AIDS epidemic throughout the nation. This litany locates a specific history of contemporary Tanzanian society and politics, and gives evidence of the effects and implications of globalization. Indeed, the intersection of popular cultural practices with contentious religious affiliation is a prominent site on this local-global terrain, perhaps especially so for youth who feature as both targets and agents of these powerful social projects. By situating current spiritual concerns within these simultaneously local and global processes as intrinsic, constitutive dimensions of diverse and extensive transformations in Tanzania and elsewhere, it becomes possible to problematize the prominence of these religious discourses and to draw attention to the ways that spirituality has been reconceived by these recent historical shifts.

Pop Culture, Postsocialism, or Youth in Tanzania

A host of critical studies on the African production of modernity (Geschiere 1997; Meyer 1998a, 1998b; Larkin 1997; Barber 1997; Burke 1996; Weiss 1996; Comaroff 1993; Masquelier 2001; Piot 1999) have made it impossible to assert that the kind of religious claims made in Tanzania today are vestiges of recalcitrant tradition that provide a moral compass in a sea of global change. Further, when we talk about popular culture in its globalized forms, it is important to recognize that these modes of cultural production include not only FUBU sweatshirts and Fila sneakers, Destiny's Child and the Disney empire, but also circulating cassettes of eminent Maalams and stadium-filled revival services. It is especially interesting to note that within this multitude of disparate forms, current popular practices in urban Tanzania reveal important convergences between what are routinely seen as oppositional discourses such as morality and desire, piety and pleasure—the devotional practices and *katalogi* clothing both represented through *The Source*. Because my argument concerns the reformulation of religiosity in urban Tanzania, I am especially interested in the confluence of these seemingly contradictory discourses and practices that hip hop performance often embodies. A close examination of this confluence reveals how themes of piety and moral caution structure the possibilities of the hip hop world, and reciprocally, how global hip hop reformulates religious commitments.

Recognizing and articulating this conjunction between religiosity and rap within urban Tanzanian popular culture is hardly a narrowly circumscribed endeavor. Hip hop incorporates a wide array of activities, including modes of dress and dance, visual arts (including graffiti and tattooing), and sonic forms like DJ mixing and scratching, all of which are present in some degree in Arusha. As diffuse as hip hop is, the field of religion (if such a discrete entity even exists) is, of course, even more expansive, amorphous, and intensely debated. Hip hop and religion are not usefully thought of as distinct forms that are brought together in a specific time and place, but their themes can inform one another in concrete social practice. There is, perhaps, a risk that this convergence of (often explicitly articulated) concerns on the scene in Arusha simply dissolves as a phenomenon, or dissipates it into the broad context of culture the moment it is subject to any scrutiny. There is no definitive take on hip hop or religion that will demonstrate their mutual construction in Tanzania. Still, there are certain core themes and dynamics in the practices I found in Arusha that serve to define and create the character of living the life in its religious and hip hop senses.

This hip hop/religion convergence also points to some important issues for the more general study of youth within prevailing globalized conditions. A number of scholars have recognized that the circumstances faced by young people around the world today have been profoundly shaped by widespread neoliberal political economic reforms. "The cumulative impact" of these reforms, writes Cole (2004: 573), "has been to create contradictions for youth by simultaneously targeting them as consumers and making them particularly vulnerable to socioeconomic exclusion" (see also Comaroff and Comaroff 2000; Weiss 2004). "Why youth now?" is a question best asked by situating it within this general tension between exclusion and inclusion, a tension exacerbated and specified in the recent history of Tanzanian economy and society. The young men (more than women)[3] who work and hang out in informal sector—the barbershops, salons, bars, and bus stands, that I have worked with—constitute a large audience for the consumption of hip hop media and commodities and are also among the most deeply interested in the current maelstrom of urban Tanzanian religious discourses. Indeed, it was groups of young barbers who took me to the rap shows in Arusha where verses about religious righteousness and moral caution were eagerly performed. The coupling of this moralism with consumerism indicates that the neoliberal production of value as self-fashioning is accompanied by a profound ambivalence. A contradictory consciousness that shapes the experience of youth is manifest at a number of levels. In part, those who most fully endorse the prospects of global cultural production exemplified by hip hop are also most acutely aware of how severely limited their access to that world is. This leads to a sense of frustration and occasionally despair that is palpable in most social milieu in Arusha. Moreover, a simultaneous embrace and mistrust of such social projects as education, the media, political reform, the market, and commodity forms is apparent in this ambivalence. That is, the most prevalent and celebrated forms of social engagement—those that promote such consumerist self-fashioning—are also subject to widespread critique as unsatisfying, illusory, and (as we shall see) unreal sources of value. In other words, youth often sense that they are confronting a crisis, and further that the very resources that might permit them to overcome that crisis may themselves be inaccessible, or worse, illegitimate.

Theorizing the Global Hip Hop Nation

It is only in recent years that the scholars of hip hop have begun seriously to examine the global dissemination and production of its musical and cultural forms. This is not simply because hip hop went global well after it had already gained a tremendous following in the United States. In fact, even in Tanzania, there has been a flourishing hip hop scene since the early 1990s. Rather, it reflects a core concern of hip hop artists and aficionados themselves, one which has been taken up as a theoretical principle by many of its analysts. This is what might be called a relentless commitment to locality, a notion that what is probably the critical feature of hip hop performance, crucial to its aesthetic, and perhaps even moral value, is its authenticity. In particular, a great many devotees of rap most appreciate what they call the "realness" of its performance. And as Krims (2000) indicates, these qualities of authenticity and realness are characteristically expressed in judgments that are firmly tied to time, and perhaps especially to place. He observes, "It is not at all an obscurity, among listeners, to refer to someone as having an 'old school flow,' or even an 'early 90s West Coast flow,' or a 'new-style Queens flow.' Such terms are fodder for record company ads, artist interviews, song lyrics, and discussions among fans" (Krims 2000: 44; see also Forman 2002 passim). Even a figure such as Eminem, often vilified as a crass, commercial misappropriation of African American practices, can be lauded for his authenticity: "Three kinds of authenticity are initially evident [in hip hop]. First, there's a concern with being true to oneself. Rap illustrates self-creation and individuality as a value. Next, there's the question of location or place. Rap prioritizes artists' local allegiances and territorial identities. Finally, the question becomes whether a performer has the requisite relation and proximity to an original source of rap. Eminem is firmly grounded in these three kinds of authenticity" (Armstrong 2004). Although such essentially aesthetic categories are indispensable to an understanding of hip hop's cultural productions (in everything from the self-identification of performers and audiences, to the international marketing of a potent commodity), a concern with bona fide origins is central to many analytical assessments of worldwide hip hop. Thus, Potter (1995: 146) writes, "As [hip hop] gains audiences around the world, there is always the danger that it will be appropriated in such a way that its histories will be obscured, and its messages replaced with others." It is as though global rap music were a (notably pale) imitation of the Ur-sounds created in the South Bronx of the 1970s.

Recent scholarly works have challenged the assumption of African American origins as a critical feature of hip hop's authentic character, which is at risk of being diluted and misrepresented through hip hop's mass mediation. The works of Krims and the comprehensive collection *That's the Joint* (Forman and Neal 2004) as well as the essays collected in Mitchell's volume *Global Noise*, for example, argue that a concern with the putatively essential and original qualities of hip hop disables our understanding of its truly global realizations. In general, these critiques of authenticity follow from what are now pervasive anthropological perspectives on globalization more generally. Global hip hop is shown to participate in the worldwide production of locality through a process of indigenization, which involves the assertive appropriation of rap music and hip hop forms by performers who incorporate local linguistic and musical idioms, as well as wider popular (especially) political concerns in the creation of a hybrid art form (see Mitchell passim). As Urla (2001: 181) writes in a discussion of one Basque group, "Negu Gorriak's performances of a hybrid Basque rap may [best be] understood not as an Americanization or imitation but as a strategic deployment of signifiers that affords youth a window into their own situation and what it shares with that of racialized minorities." Concerns with authenticity in the transnational context of hip hop performance may be less relevant to its productive possibilities than the dynamics of rap as a kind of global idiom through which profoundly local conflicts can be reimagined and acted on.

These critiques of appropriation as inauthenticity are crucial. Indeed, related critiques have a long and important, if frequently overlooked, history in the social scientific understanding of African social practice in particular (Mitchell 1956; Ranger 1975). Yet we should not dismiss altogether the relevance of authenticity as a principle of cultural production. A number of critics have recognized the ways that images like pastiche, when used as interpretive categories, have the effect of dehistoricizing the material they are intended to address (Gilroy 1994; Mitchell 2001: 10). Arguments that emphasize the capacity of performers to select among an array of idioms, vernaculars, styles, and sounds tend to extract these processes of recombination from the contexts, both meaningful and material, in which they are possible. This runs the risk of celebrating what are highly specific notions of freedom and value embedded in consumerist models of choice. Further, it is not entirely clear that hybridity and ludic indeterminacy are the terms through which practice is made meaningful in the lives of those engaged in these activities. As Friedman asks in his characteristically polemical discussion:

> If the city landscapes in Stockholm now combine ethnically and linguistically mixed populations and store signs in American English, if We observe (at the airport) the Nigerian, Congolese or Papua New Guinean sporting a can of coke and a hamburger . . . is this to be interpreted as creolization in the sense of cultural mixture? Is it to be interpreted as hybridity in the sense of the liminal sphere between the modern Western and the pre-modern, non-Western . . . What is really going on in such referred-to realities? Does anyone have to ask or is the observation enough. What about other peoples' experiences, intentionalities and lives? Are not such hybrids defined as such because they seem to be betwixt and between our own "modern Western" categories (that is, hybrids) for us? (2000: 640–41)

This critique of the hybrid as an unexamined premise of our own social and analytical categories is crucial, not simply as a corrective to overtheorized and underinvestigated models of globalization, but also because it makes it possible to address the ways that these apparently plural realities are experienced and increasingly valued in much of the world. The notion of authenticity as an analytical category that establishes a kind of genealogical distinction between the original and the imitation or the pure from the contaminated is certainly not valuable. However, it seems equally crucial to recognize that some understanding of authenticity as a category of interpretive judgment is central—perhaps especially in popular cultural circles—to contemporary notions of taste, experience, and, more broadly, to conceptions of social being. Affirmations of authenticity, expressed in hip hop circles in Arusha and elsewhere as a concern for realness, have flourished rather than dissipated with the ready availability of a global and manifold set of styles and images. These values, along with this concern for allegiance to an unmediated, true reality, increasingly dominate the lived experience of those caught up in transnational processes like global hip hop, reformist Islam, and evangelical Christianity. This commitment to realness and anxieties about its beleaguered condition in the world today therefore offers a means for exploring the conjuncture of these diverse moral discourses across a range of popular cultural practices in urban Tanzania today.

The One True Religion and Reality Rap

Many contemporary religious inclinations in Arusha, as in much of (especially urban) Africa, emphasize the importance of specific, fixed attributes of identity—authenticity, in effect—as foundational dimensions of social and personal being. Briefly, participants in popular Muslim and Christian practices insist that their way of life is truer and more accurately reflects reality than other sectarian and secular positions. In the summer of 2000, I regularly engaged in conversations with groups of young men deeply committed to securing my personal salvation by persuading me that Islam was, as they put it, "the only true religion." These discussions generally focused on a kind of hyperrationalist critique of Christian dogma (as these Muslims understood it), for example, rejections of the Trinity as counter to the doctrine of monotheism, dismissals of Christ's divinity as violations of the fundamental distinction between human materiality and God's transcendence, and assertions that Christians elevate their clergy to the status of divinity. These rationalist assertions were paired with an insistence on the absolute veracity of the Koran, not just as a sacred text but as an encyclopedic source of all human knowledge. These young men described the Koran as more than a guide for living; it was also a source of empirically verifiable knowledge. "*Kila kitu kimeshaandikwa ndani*" ("Everything has already been written in it") is how many put it. Indeed, they framed the Koran as a guide for proper scientific investigation, its foreknown truths awaiting demonstration by research. Many of the Muslims I know exhibited this experimental attitude with Internet reports about scientific practice in the West inspired by readings of the Koran.

Claims like these indicate that Islam is increasingly understood by many contemporary young Muslims, as Swedenburg suggests in his discussion of French Muslim rap, as "an attitude that [is] very rational and scientific, but most importantly, mystical" (2001: 70). Indeed, the mystical character of Islam is in effect revealed and confirmed by the rational and empirical truths that a true understanding of Islam discloses. Thus, the irrefutable truths revealed in the Koran and already proven through human, historical observation also provide evidence, for many of the young Muslims I know, of the certainty of Koranic revelations yet to come. And so at the turn of the last century, it was not surprising to find these same young men asserting the scientific proof of Koranic authority also offering predictions about the "end of days" (*Nusu Kyama* in Kiswahili), citing obvious contemporary evidence that portends the appearance of a false God and world destroyer who will reign over humanity before the righteous are granted celestial immortality. Apocalyptic assertions like these have a long history throughout the Muslim and Christian world, and they are by no means novel in this context. What is compelling, though, are the ways that such mystical and transhistorical assertions are explicitly tied to the empirical and rational validity of the Koran. Such apocalyptic visions, in other words, are embedded in pronouncements about its broader integrity and authority. This textual absolutism, in urban Tanzania and elsewhere (Masquelier 1999), becomes a critical grounds on which adherence to Islam as a true and invariant practice—that is, as the foremost authentic religious identity—is proclaimed.[4]

Supreme truth and authenticity are often posited as critical features of what Tillich calls the "ultimate concerns" of religion. But notions of truth and authenticity are equally crucial analytics in the world of hip hop. As Forman notes, "the boundaries between real or authentic cultural identities and those deemed inauthentic are carefully policed from within the hip hop culture, and the delineations that define 'the real' are taken with deadly seriousness by those who ascribe to hip hop's cultural influences" (2002: xviii). Fans of widely divergent hip hop styles and rap music genres recognize this pronounced identification of authenticity with "the real" (Krims 2000: 54ff.). Yet all such stylistic variations and virtues are said to constitute ways of "keeping it real" and so assert the preeminence of authenticity in the guise of realness as a shared symbolic value.

In urban Tanzania, these concerns and commitments are equally important to hip hop. One young man, Rahim, told me why he thought rap was so popular in Arusha, and why he himself had composed rap verses. "It's a voice (*sauti*)," he told me. "Youth," Rahim went on, "have no voice. You cannot get a minister or a businessman in an office to hear your complaints, so you need a loud voice. You need to 'represent' the youth." In keeping with this construction of truth and its symbolic assertion, Rahim added, "We need to speak about *reality* as it is for youth, and rap is the music that has this voice." Rahim's assertions depend on an understanding of an unassailable truth, a "reality," as he puts it in English, or *hali haliisi* in Kiswahili, using terms and claims lifted directly from a widespread hip hop vernacular. More specifically, and somewhat paradoxically I would argue, Rahim insists that this raw, unmediated reality actually requires some means of demonstrating its truth in order to realize its implications. That is, it requires a voice to give expression to this truth. Further, this voice is characterized not as a style, interpretation, or even a way of knowing and speaking, but simply as an embodiment of the fundamental reality it expresses. Voice here is evidence of the authenticity with which it speaks. It is unassailable because it is a true expression of lived reality as it actually is.

To give voice in this way is—to use Rahim's language, a vernacular (in English) plucked from the global hip hop order that he extols—to represent. This term in such usages is understood not as a means of speaking on behalf of some underrepresented voiceless constituency, but as a way of expressing a commitment to the truth of the reality that constituency lives. As Krims describes American hip hop sounds: "[I]f one of the principle validating strategies of rap music involves 'representing' and 'keeping it real'—in other words, deploying authenticity symbolically—then that ethos is formed (and reflected) differently in each [rap] genre" (2000: 48). It is further clear that those modes of hip hop performance that emphasize the immediate and unmediated character of reality are equally concerned with the importance of giving voice to that (otherwise unvoiced, and underrepresented) reality through rap music. This is exemplified in such claims as Chuck D's celebrated celebration of rap as "the black CNN we never had" or MC Eiht's statement, "I just talk about the 'hood. That's just spittin' the real" (Forman 2002: 251, 93). Here is a characteristic tension in hip hop cultural production, one that is also plainly evident in urban Tanzanian accounts. Representing, or giving voice, is on the one hand a direct embodied expression ("a loud voice," "spittin' the real") that partakes of a given and incontrovertibly true reality; and yet on the other hand, it is also a means of confirming and establishing—literally creating—the specific qualities and character of the real itself (Dinwoodie 1997). Indeed, the realness of the voices that represent are constantly subject to scrutiny and critique by those they would claim to represent. This tension is different from the much ballyhooed crisis of representation because it is the real itself that is both explicitly embraced as an authentic truth, and thus the subject of perpetual challenge, and (as Forman 2002 puts it) also policed by those who participate in hip hop's performances. For these participants, it is as though reality itself were at risk.

Knowing Reality

It is this sense of reality being at risk—an apocalyptic contention intrinsic to the perpetual efforts of hip hop participants to ensure that reality is acknowledged and that voices are representing, thus keeping it real—that both transcends and connects global and local orders of meaning and practice. Such a shared and differentiated perspective clearly posits some notion of authenticity as a central symbolic quality, even as the paramount value. Yet this notion of authenticity is not concerned with adhering to the foundational tenets of some originary source of meaning, or an essential way of being that is either incompatible with other modalities, or in danger of being diluted or corrupted by those who would appropriate it. Shiite Muslims in Arusha, for example, can embrace the Koran as the unvarnished truth without feeling the need either to immerse themselves in Arabic or to renounce the significance of other social cultural products like hip hop clothing, rap music, or the popular press as inauthentic scourges of meaning. Instead, these young Muslims grasp the Koran as an immediate expression of their own concrete existence, a body of knowledge confirmed in their own sensible world of experience, that gives this text both its sacred character and its ultimate reality. The Koran, to use a familiar vocabulary, represents their reality.

This thematic of authenticity is as evident in hip hop's commitment to keeping it real as it is in the fascination on the part of many, including those in the hip hop world, with apocalyptic pronouncements. An understanding of the real as a phenomenon that is in danger of displacement or even disappearance plays a prominent part in reconfiguring social worlds in Arusha as well as in reconstituting religiosity. What this perceived assault on reality indicates is a broadly shared ontology. In turn, this implies that there is actual ontological work to be done by popular practice, both as an audience and a congregation. Participation goes beyond upholding abstract, even sacred, principles, in maintaining moral strictures, or in accurately reflecting the circumstances of your peers; it requires engaging in these practices as a means of sustaining reality. This ontological crisis demands, in particular, that you make your voice an expression of your being-in-the-world, so that your identity or self-representation partakes of the reality it upholds.

This specific dynamic is a feature of both hip hop performance and religious devotion for many youth in Arusha today. To describe this dynamic I want first to sketch out certain features of participation in popular culture in Arusha more generally, then show how these modes of participation serve as important means of demonstrating and concretizing the sociocultural process of establishing authenticity and the real. I will also attempt to show how the themes of realness and its fugitive character are given a voice realized in certain performances of popular culture, embodying specific qualities of this real world. To illustrate this process, I will show how voice is explicitly realized in the verses of Tanzania rap music, both mass mediated and less widely distributed, that I heard in Arusha in the summer of 2000.

The educational value of popular culture, as in soap opera viewing, is often cited as one of its most compelling qualities. This concern concretely shapes the practices of many devotees of pop culture in the transcription of song (and of course rap) lyrics in school books and in public debates about the content and context of television programming and its audiences. In these sociocultural contexts, education is constituted as a process through which on learns about one's "surroundings" (*mazingira*), comparing them to other contexts and evaluating the difference. This concern with an awareness of one's transforming surroundings and the claim that participation in popular culture constitutes a critical means of developing such acumen are prominent themes in hip hop globally and in Arusha. Groups who fashion themselves as practitioners of reality-based rap often emphasize the role of consciousness raising in their performances, and so see hip hop as an educational vehicle. Such consciousness raising is often linked to the Nation of Islam, which has a significant following in American hip hop. Consider the 5 percent nation, which "refers to the idea . . . that at any given time, only 5 percent of any population are politically aware enough to be influential" (Krims 2000: 96–97). In keeping with this claim, many hip hop performers self-consciously seek to constitute this 5 percent nation in order to shape a wider politics. The extent that these specific ideas inform the global development of hip hop, even among explicitly Muslim rappers and audiences, is open to considerable debate (Swedenburg 2001). In Arusha, as I indicated above, many Muslim youth are aware of the religious affiliations of hip hop celebrities, and further, they embrace the Muslim identity of those (Wu-Tang Clan, NaS, Mike Tyson) who identify with the Nation of Islam. The theological particulars of the Nation of Islam are, to my knowledge, irrelevant in the Tanzanian case, but what is absolutely crucial to hip hop in this context is its concern with consciousness raising as a political project. In Arusha, this notion of awareness is captured in self-descriptive term used by many who follow hip hop: *MaMental*. This is a Kiswahili neologism derived from the English word *mental*, which has currency in some hip hop circles as a term that refers to intellectual activity and so indicates understanding or insight.[5] This autonym might thus be approximated as "the knowing ones" or "the thinkers." Those who take part in hip hop performance in urban Tanzania clearly understand themselves to be working to develop a form of consciousness, a theme that resonates with wider understandings of popular culture practice in Arusha. This stance is condensed and objectified in the mental condition of these youth.

The critical self-awareness embraced by these hip hop participants illuminates a more general concern with authenticity and the real, and the proper modes of expressing or representing them. These urban youth characterize the relevance of their own actions in terms of knowing qualities. Their acts are valid and legitimate so long as they seek to achieve and communicate an awareness of the world. In this way, reality and its representation go hand in hand. Popular expressions or voices are real insofar as they articulate an awareness of and insight into changing circumstances; the real itself is defined as the object of thinking and knowing as valued actions. These concerns with tireless thinking as a means of keeping it real further suggest a crucial aspect of authenticity as it is understood and acted on in Arusha. For if thinking and being conscious are vital to sustaining a commitment to reality, this implies that reality is threatened by a pervasive lack of awareness, a vast unknowing. And in urban Tanzania, this threat to the real from ignorance or unthinking action is a deeply felt problematic that characterizes a great many contemporary lives.

Losing Your Way, and Keeping It Real

The force of this concern with the fugitive character of reality, the threat of ignorance, and the value of the authentic is apparent in the many religious pursuits and practices found in Arusha. Pentecostalism in Aru-Meru has attracted the most scholarly attention (Baroin 1996; Stambach 2000b), but there is also a renewed interest in Islam that is motivated and structured in broadly similar ways. The testimony of two young men I know—one affiliated with the Assemblies of God and the other a Sunni Muslim, each of whom has confronted a spiritual crisis—indicates how the real and ways of knowing it are grasped as part of contemporary religiosity. The first man, Michael, who is in his late twenties, works as a security guard in town and has become a preacher in his church. He came to the Assemblies of God, he said, after years of a wayward life. He had been a trader in the black market all across Tanzania for many years and had lived, in his own words, a life of "debauchery and nonsense" (*usherati, na maisha ya ovyo*). His life changed when his father fell ill and Michael was called home by his family. Back in Aru-Meru, Michael began to hear about the activities of the Assemblies of God, who "had answers to all the questions about what to *do* in life." This contrasted with the Lutheran faith, which never offered any concrete solutions. "They don't care!" he told me. "If you come with questions they just tell you to pray, but they won't help." Pentecostals, on the other hand, showed him that the Bible has answers to everything that can happen "as you live your life." A young woman in his village had been instantly cured of demonic possession by the utterance "*Yesu ni Bwana*" (Jesus is Lord) at an Assemblies of God prayer meeting. "Today," says Michael, "this woman has become a success and has given birth to many children."

The next account comes from a younger man, Ahmed. Ahmed comes from the oldest Muslim residential zone in Arusha, from a family with more financial means than many but of wildly shifting economic fortunes. He lives in a matrifocal compound presided over by his mother's mother, along with his mother. Ahmed has attended classes in tourism at one of the numerous technical colleges that offer such classes in the area. But most importantly to him, he has had the opportunity to attend secondary schools in Kenya, an opportunity that he lost, by his own account, because of his bad behavior. His mother, however, told me that he was unable to continue in school because the family could no longer pay the school fees.[6] I had known Ahmed to be a dedicated "thug" (his own word), a denizen of one of the numerous barbershops that have sprung up all around town, places of informal gathering and meager economic prospects for thousands of young men. But I also found in the summer of 2000 that he had become a devout Muslim, attending prayers at his neighborhood mosque five times a day. When I asked Ahmed why he had taken up his faith, he told me that he had returned to Islam after getting kicked out of school for the last time the previous year. He told me that he had "lost [his] way" (*nimepotea njia*) and that he was returning to what he had known since he was a child. All of the trouble he had gotten into at school, especially the sin of smoking *bhangi* (pot), had not improved his life at all. "Life changes (*Maisha yanabadilika*)," he told me, "and these changes make you search for the right way (*njia ya kweli*)." On a subsequent occasion, Ahmed took me to his mother's sitting room, where he showed me texts, published in Kuwait, on how to pray and the proper meanings of Islam. He told me he has known the proper rites since he was a child, but he enjoyed seeing them published in an imported text and written in English.

These accounts recapitulate a number of key religious themes. The centrality of the Bible, for example, as a text where all of experience is found exemplifies the textual absolutism also attributed to the Koran. The way that a Kuwaiti text written in English situates Ahmed's direct bodily praxis in a global context also recalls the significance of education as a mode of forging connections between disparate circumstances. In each account, the truth of an authentic reality is held to be incontestable. Undoubtedly there are important dimensions of these men's histories that should be distinguished; these men's religious experiences are not identical, nor are they simply tokens of a common type. But they do point to a shared set of concerns, a way of characterizing existential crises and their practical resolution, that informs each of these perspectives. For both Michael and Ahmed, what they determine to be the real is arrived at through a specific way of knowing that confirms both the truth of what they know and the authenticity of their expression of this knowledge (in the form of Michael's preaching or Ahmed's daily prayers, each modes of voicing their faith). Each man described coming to an awareness of the truth through his encounter with falsehood and nonsense. Each lost his way and became aware of that deviation by coming back, returning to the proper condition to which he had access all along. In Michael's case, he returned home only to be born again, while Ahmed rediscovered a Muslim practice that he had known since childhood. Although Michael self-consciously rejected his past Lutheranism as inadequate and Ahmed embraced a familiar faith, in both instances, the real was an entity that had always been present and that they had only to recognize in order to acquire. At the same time, what allowed this recognition to take place was the aberration—the debauchery, the *bhangi*, the nonsense—through which they came to a clearer understanding. It is as though losing one's way validated and authenticated the value of the real to which one returned. Moreover, the themes of aimlessness and nonsense as dimensions of knowledge confirmed, yet again, the apocalyptic premise that the real is at risk. And so such experiences of deviation were routinely incorporated into renewed understanding of the truth and frequently characterized the authenticity of the voice. Such voices spoke with greater authority—that is, they were more real—because of how they came to their insights into that reality, the *hali halisi*, as it is lived today. Again, the real and ways of representing it are mutually constituted.

These concerns are paramount both in a revitalized spirituality and in the popular music of Arusha. Consider what was probably the song that received the most airplay across Tanzania in the summer of 2000, "Chemsha Bongo" (literally, "Boil Your Brain" or "Think Hard"), by Hard Blasterz Crew. The very title of the song immediately denotes the value of thinking and knowing; it also connotes ties to place through its association with *Bongo*, or "brain," a colloquial term for Dar es Salaam, an appellation that further indicates the centrality of thinking to popular cultural practice. This song was the first track from the album *Funga Kazi* ("Finish the Job"), which plainly implies the qualities of hardness and toughness predominant in this kind of reality rap. The song begins with the chorus[7]:

> Savior, I offer my soul, free me from this chaos
> If I fool with this life today, I'll go to bed hungry
> Think hard before you are trapped, you'll be amazed
> Think hard before you are trapped, you'll be astonished.

The chorus neatly encapsulates the crisis (a world of "chaos" and "foolishness") that might be resolved by thinking through one's predicament, in the hopes of salvation. The lyrics of "Chemsha Bongo" elaborate on this process, describing in detail the world of chaos and a failure to properly think about the consequences of such nonsense. The song describes the life of a young man, J, who comes from a loving, modestly well-to-do home and who is drawn through his desire for "the sweetness of life" (*utamu wa maisha*) to forget his respect for his parents and elders. Instead, he pursues a life of beautiful women, crates of beer, and a posse of followers (*wapambe*, literally "those who decorate"). Eventually, these infinite desires lead him to the pursuit of crime, a life on the run in Zanzibar, and the accumulation of debts. His friends who once celebrated his arrival at the bars and clubs now say, "*cheki J arosto amesha zeeka,*" "check out J, he's already grown old."

In the concluding verse of "Chemsha Bongo," J's parents are killed in a bad accident, and J's first thought is one that actually cheers him up ("*Nikajipa moyo*"): "I knew I'd inherit wealth because of this disaster" ("*Nikajua nitarithi mali kutokana na hayo maafa*"). Suddenly J is overcome with astonishment by his relatives. In an act akin to divine intervention ("*Vilianza kutokea vizingiti na sielewi vilipo ibuka,*" "They started to break through the floodgates, I don't understand where they popped up"), all his remaining family members begin fighting over money, and he realizes, too late, that he is as good as dead himself. Horrified by this epiphany, J addresses his listeners and reminds them of the importance of religious devotion

> Rich people, pray to God before you depart
> Man is like a flower, he sprouts and he dies,
> And money is like a devil, if you have it you can never be found worthy.

The song concludes with a horrifying vision of corporeal damnation:

> Friends I cry I've already been undone
> Right here I smell of sweat, I'm entirely spoiled
> My body is like a piece of cassava that's been scraped down.

Next is an ecumenical call for renewed spiritual commitment in order to avoid the disasters that J himself faced:

> Its true what they say about the Prodigal son,
> The Bible and Koran, they say the remorseful are forgiven
> Angry citizens still want to take me for a thrashing
> They wanted to burn me, they've soaked me in oil
> Say your prayers and search every hour and every minute
> Don't hope to find, my brother, what I found.

The poetic structure and the central textual features of "Chemsha Bongo" produce a narrative that creates an authentic voice. The narrator, J (which many listeners will recognize is the actual nom de guerre of the rapper, Nigga J), reports directly on his own experience. He begins by reporting that he will condense his entire life in these verses ("*Kwa kifupi,*" "In short"), beginning with the way he was raised. J's childhood is focused especially on education and is clearly situated in a social world of parents and wise elders. Yet the very comforts of his life plant the seeds of his ultimate undoing: "*Maisha yalikuwa matamu nilisahau yote haramu*" ("Life was sweet, I forgot all that was forbidden"). This statement, which occurs early in the lyrics, establishes the central tension in the overall narrative: in effect, J's life is shaped by this forgetting. The significance of this forgetting is made concrete in a series of contrasts: his parents and elders, present in the initial and concluding verses, are replaced by the "chicks" (*mademu*) and "posse" (*wapambe*) whom J runs with in the body of the song. Poetically, J's life is motivated by "sweetness," in contrast to the foul stench of those who would restrain or impede him. This sweetness is literally embodied in the foods J enjoys and provides for his crew, especially roast pork and beer (*kiti moto na bia*)—foods that are specifically forbidden (*haramu*) and so directly exemplify what he has forgotten. Ultimately, these same poetic devices are inverted as J's very body and blood emit the odor of death, and his body, which formerly enjoyed the expensive foods of the sweet life, becomes "like a piece of cassava that's been scraped away," the cheapest, most common, and most flavorless of foods.

Underlying these contrasts, and in many respects at the root of J's forgetting, is the fate of J's "intelligence" (*akili*). J's begins his life showing his intelligence, with him heading straight to school. This intelligence, though, soon gives way to the power of money. Although elders cleverly advise him by "speaking in riddles," money "was like a hammer" (*Fedha kwangu ni kama nyundo*) used to destroy all in his way. Facing a life of crime to maintain the lifestyle he has pursued, J is cut off from the wealth of his parents. The parents try to shift the focus of his ambitions:

> Only my parents tried to show me that my inheritance is education
> I decided that you study in order to get money.

From this moment forward, J's life is in rapid decline. He eats his wealth, and women who once fell all over him now laugh at how he has aged. "Poverty comes knocking" (*Umasikini umepiga hodi*). In the end, J's fatal transformation is revealed as his "head starts to spin" (*Akili ilianza kuniruka*, literally "My intelligence passed over me"), and his relatives bitterly fight over the money of their dead kin. "*Kwa kifupi*"—in short, as J would have it, love of money destroys the possibility of learning. It is only after he has been destroyed by this monetary pursuit, literally undone, that he is able to offer a lesson for others, one that reaffirms, in the "name of truth," the power of prayer, the need for repentance, and perpetual devotion to God. In so doing, J further reaffirms the centrality of education and intelligence to acquiring the real, by rendering his own life as an illustration—indeed, an embodiment—of this process. A further illustration of this point is that J has now gone solo with a hit release, *Machozi, Jasho, Na Damu* (Tears, Sweat, and Blood) with a new moniker: Professor J. Moreover, the voice through which he articulates these changes exemplifies the total process of education, one that has forgotten the truth, that has lost its way, and that is fully achieved on its return to an ever-present and authentic reality.

Although "Chemsha Bongo" was, and remains, one of the most popular rap songs in Tanzania, it was by no means unique in its explicit and strikingly apocalyptic message. All of the informal crews in Arusha, young men who composed lyrics or who performed at rap concerts and competitions in town,[8] told me that they liked to listen to and create verses about *dini* (religion). One duo with whom I worked for several weeks calls

April 28

INTS 3560 – Globalization and International Security

Topic Three Question - Governance, Order, and Information in a Networked World

INSTRUCTIONS: In 2 to 4 pages (1 inch margins, double spaced), answer the question below. Please make sure your name and the course name are on the top of the page as well as an indication that you are answering the Topic 3 question. No title pages, covers, binding or other treatments required. If you directly quote from someone or some source, please identify that source either via a footnote/endnote or an internal citation & bibliographic reference at end, but unless you quote or borrow directly, there is no need for sources or references. This should be your take on the question.

WRITING HINT: First person is discouraged as it is your essay and stating it's your opinion or your views is redundant.

DUE: Monday May 5 at the start of class

TOPIC THREE QUESTION:

The biggest criticism of Morozov's book The Net Delusion is that while he does a great job making the counter- argument about global information networks/the internet and freedom, his way forward, to practice cyber-realism, is at best under-developed. Referencing the book's own arguments, explain what cyber-realism would be in practice. To put it another way, if Morozov is right about the problem, what is the solution and/or correct approach?

themselves Chronic Mobb. This group consists of two young men, both eighteen years old, one of whom goes by Nesto Dogg, the other, Spidah Killa. When I first met Nesto, he was living with his mother and grandmother in a small pair of rented rooms in one of the most notoriously dangerous areas of town near the open-air market. Nesto was still finishing primary school, working intermittently at a barbershop near his home, and hoping to find a way to get to secondary school. His father, who lived in Dar, had taken a second wife, leaving the members of Nesto's house to scramble for resources where they could. The following year, I met up with Nesto when he performed with Spidah at a local weekly rap competition. He told me he had not been able to continue with school, but that he and Spidah, who had long been friends, were still barbering and regularly going to the tanzanite mines at Mererani *"kutafuta mkwanja"* ("looking for cash"). Spidah and Nesto were taken with stories about people who had struck it rich in the mines, and they were equally amused by reports of how easily these fortunes were blown. Nesto's mother had also taken to working "in the bush" (*porini*), a vernacular term for working at the mines, in her case not as a miner but as an aspiring gem trader.

Chronic Mobb, like many crews in Arusha, generally describe the "message" (*ujumbe*) of their verses in terms of the "lessons" (*mafundisho*)

Crew posing at a rap competition

Chronic Mobb

and "intelligence" (*akili*) through which they hope the audience will "become aware" (*watakuwa "mental"*). A number of groups further linked these concerns with religion, and they concretized this connection, as did Chronic Mobb, by beginning their performance with widely recognized Christian hymns. The song by Chronic Mobb I want to consider takes its title from such a hymn, "Katika Viumbe Vyote Vilivyo Umbwa" (Of all Creatures Created). It begins with the two-line hymn itself,

> In all of God's creation
> Man was created above all others

that Chronic Mobb sings several times before launching into their original verses. Nesto told me they like to use the hymn in order to "stir up" and "enliven" (*kuchangamka*) the audience, a technique that had the effect of generating audience participation on most of the occasions I saw Chronic Mobb perform. This performative quality is plainly the message of their verses as well. "Katika Viumbe Vyote" is not presented as a narrative, and Nesto and Spidah do not describe their own conditions as object lessons in the way J does. Still, there are clear parallels between this rap and "Chemsha Bongo" in the immediacy of experience as this is represented in the verses. In each of the two verses, performed by Nesto and Spidah in sequence, the rappers address their audience through reference to their own bodily condition. In turn, these bodily conditions are grasped as generic human conditions and so presented as indisputable evidence of our created condition. Nesto begins by lamenting how "sad" and "tired" he is, and he warns, "Let's not be stupid" (*tusiwe akili fyatu*), instead recognizing that we were actually created. Like J, who forgets his initial condition of intelligence, Nesto asserts that "we don't remember" who created us and what that requires of us. Creation is confirmed as both real and orderly, with man above all others, and God above him. The initial lines of Spidah's verse reiterate these claims, urging people to remember their created condition and directly describing the hierarchy of the human body ("With a head to think with, and eyes to see/A nose for smelling, ears to hear") as self-evident proof of this creation.

Having established the forgotten fact of creation, Nesto and Spidah go on to detail the ways that this creation is directly subverted in contemporary life:

> But even though the Lord created us
> I see the disgrace of men lying with men
> Until chicks are barren,
> And even little girls have abortions.

Nesto further denounces the inversion of age hierarchies, with "kids beating their mother" and "old folks tripped up." Spidah's verses follow the same pattern of inversion of the proper order:

> We have ears, but we don't hear
> Prophets guide us but we don't follow.

In both verses, the persuasive force of the claims is the reality of our own created bodies. Nesto sees and meets the corporeal disgraces he describes, and Spidah's lament is the subversion of the body itself ("We have ears, but we don't hear"). In turn, both Nesto and Spidah call for a renewed bodily connection to divinity, "speaking from the heart" so that we will "put his will in our hearts." Although J offers his own life course as exemplary evidence of his spiritual claims, Nesto and Spidah (who would seem to exempt themselves from responsibility for the horrors they decry) validate the realness of their assertions through the body, showing how the body is tangible proof of God's creation, how the presence of evil is manifest in the deviant condition of the contemporary body, and how the body offers us a means to address these failures and remember our created condition.

Real Value

In verses like those of "Chemsha Bongo" and "Katika Viumbe Vyote," the themes of religious devotion and spiritual crisis are hard-hitting and direct. There is no mistaking the call for an immediate return to divine guidance in a troubled world. Indeed, both Hard Blasterz Crew and Chronic Mobb make ecumenical pleas for the necessity of faith, extolling the Bible and Koran, churches and mosques, acting in "the name of Jesus," and asking for a Muslim blessing (*omba dua*). Not all of Tanzanian hip hop is so manifestly concerned with religious matters, but it is clearly one of the dominant themes in popular urban music. As the work of Remes (1999), Perullo (2005), and Stroeken (2005) reveal, rap music has become immensely popular across Tanzania, and locally produced rap has even been seen as a distinctively local product known as *bongo flava*. Rap is widely seen as "an important means for marginalized Tanzanian youth to address mass audiences" (Perullo 2005: 77). The theme of corruption is widely popular today, one of the many *ujumbe mkali* ("strong" or "fierce" messages) of bongo flava. Here too, corruption is seen as "Hali Halisi," as Mr. II raps in his composition of the same name (cited in Perullo 2005: 81):

Siasa ni mchezo mchafu	Politics is a dirty game.
Wanataka umaarufu.	They just want to be famous
Wanasiasa wa Bongo wengi waongo.	Lots of Tanzanian politicians are liars.

Here, the theme of corruption is described as both an unvarnished examination of the harsh truth of "reality"—*hal halisi*—and a false face that distorts reality itself. I would argue, therefore, that the power of rap performances like "Hali Halisi," "Chemsha Bongo," and "Katika Viumbe Vyote" illustrates the extent to which religiosity itself has been rendered meaningful and pertinent through its mutual constitution with hip hop, and undoubtedly other globalized modes of cultural production. The themes of losing your way in a world of nonsense and returning to or remembering a more complete truth are certainly long-standing narratives in both Islam and Christianity. Navigating these movements by the use of intelligence and education through which you become conscious of your life's condition is now a standardized strategy exemplified in spiritual chronicles, soap opera fans' self-accounts, and rap lyrics. All of these motifs strongly resonate with the fundamental purpose of keeping it real, which pervades hip hop sensibilities wherever they are found. Equally important is the fact that these broadly shared, categorical understandings are concretized in the actual performance; these are not merely semantic parallels, for they are underpinned by distinctive pragmatics. The realness of these accounts is more than a conceptual assertion, or even an avowal of faith. It is embedded in the forms of articulation through which the voices making these claims are created, so as to partake of the realness they bespeak. The authentic character of their ontological positions is plainly exhibited in the representation of that reality. This wedding of representation to reality is illustrated by J's account of his own forgetting and his consequent physical destruction, and in Chronic Mobb's equally embodied poetics, which demonstrates facts of divine creation in the forms of human suffering, experience, and evil.

These features of the voices deployed in these raps are further grounded in the musical poetics of these performances, which are notably concerned with hardness, toughness, and endurance, qualities especially beloved by young, un(der)employed men and exemplified in the names Hard Blasterz Crew and Chronic Mobb (*chronic,* according to Nesto and Spidah, signifying tireless effort and diligence). The musical features of these rapper performances—a rapid delivery or flow to the verses, the dense clustering of note values driving a percussive rhythm forward, and the layering of heavy beats with light dissonant electronic sounds (there is a keyboard accompaniment to Hard Blasterz Crew)—all generate hardness (Krims 2000: 71–75). This hardness is further contrasted with other popular musical genres in Tanzania, especially *taarab,* which rappers and their fans claim is "weak" and "soft." This hardness indicates the commitment of the performers and is intended to suggest, as do the textual features of their lyrical forms, a directness of expression and the unmediated character of experience. The truth of the reality that these verses describe is meant to be intrinsic to their very utterance.

The global proliferation of popular cultural products like hip hop, evangelical Christianity, or Muslim reform are characterized not by a celebratory embrace of pluralistic choices, but by a firm attachment to an ontological truth, an assertion of the presence of authentic forces at work in human experience. In this sense, these cultural forces are akin to what Geschiere and Nyamnjoh (2000: 423) describe as "a general obsession with autochthony," a quest to secure a vague, unspecified access to an originary force that establishes clear lines of political inclusion and exclusion. This obsession, like the workings of hip hop and popular religiosity in Arusha, are seen as "the flip side of globalization" (Geschiere and Nyamnjoh (2000: 424) as mobility and dispersal are paired to the formation of new and more impermeable boundaries. The claims of urban Tanzanian religiosity expressed in hip hop are both more profound, and in some ways more troubling, than the identity politics of autochthony. These Tanzanian claims insist not simply on difference at the levels of identity (indeed, they sometimes call for a certain ecumenicism, uniting all who follow God), but also on a new grounding in a truer reality. They also call for distinctive ways of knowing that reality, for ways of using one's intelligence under conditions as they actually are. What is troubling about this pronounced affirmation, this attachment to the real as an authentic way of being and doing, is the precarious nature of reality as it is defined. It is no surprise to find, in a discourse that makes the very commitment to keeping it real the only legitimate mode of action, that challenges to sell-outs, selfishness, and insincerity abound. But the crisis decried in Arusha is not simply a failure to toe the line of a doctrine. Rather, it is the threat—or perhaps the promise—that reality itself is under siege. Hard Blasterz Crew and Chronic Mobb offer explicitly apocalyptic accounts of the world as they find it. This message is part of their hardness, their directness, their realism. Moreover, this apocalyptic prospect is tied to the way of knowing reality, of using one's intelligence and being educated, that this mode of reality rap defends. Indeed, in the case of Chronic Mobb, it could be said that the truth that they call for "MaMental"—the knowing ones—to embrace is the consciousness of our pending obliteration. We must confront reality as it is, and that reality is that the end of the world is near, but those who ask forgiveness for their sins will go to heaven. Although Hard Blasterz Crew seem less worried about the end of the world, the critical act they call for is asking forgiveness. In either case, a final judgment looms.

How can we account for the tenuous nature of reality? Why is the apocalypse so potent and present a force in the lives of these young Tanzanian men? Apocalyptic pronouncements are nothing new in the worlds of either Christendom or Islam; yet simply assimilating these current dynamics to that recurrent legacy tells us little that is particular either to this specific historical moment or to the concrete terms in which the end of days is understood and expressed. At the same time, it would be reductionist in the extreme to appeal to globalization, late capitalism, neoliberalism, or any of the other social scientific rubrics through which contemporary political economies are decried as the underlying source of these profoundly spiritual and ontological claims These verses may lament economic and social marginalization, but they are most concerned to educate humanity about our impending doom. Most importantly, if we want to read these popular movements as veiled critiques of shifting structures of political economy, we must also recognize that these movements are captivated by the possibilities of these shifts. Hard Blasterz Crew plainly shows the considerable allure of *mademu* and *wapambe*, chicks and a posse, crates of beer and gold-rimmed Benzes, even as they fear their influence. Spidah Killa and Nesto Dogg declaim the importance of asking a blessing and begging forgiveness for our sins, yet they gear up each month to dig in the local tanzanite mines, hoping for that huge score, one that they fully expect will evaporate as soon as they grab it. Perhaps it is this latter dynamic that reveals something of the apocalyptic force of the present moment and manifests its contradictory characteristics in the experience of youth. More than simply the material constraints and abjection of global economic reforms, it is the nature of the possibilities they offer—the impossible dreams, the concreteness of excess, the massive jackpot—that seem exquisitely and uniquely real, yet simultaneously, indeed necessarily, evanescent. This is value meant for destruction, a windfall intended for obliteration. More than economic limitations, the current moment institutes a mode of materializing and signifying value that is all-consuming and always consumed. I am hesitant to offer such tidy explanations for the apocalypse. Yet such a perspective alerts us to particular ways of being and doing that are increasingly commonplace in our world, modes of knowing the truth and acting on it, of representing the world and keeping it real.

Chemsha Bongo

Chorus: Mwokozi nitoe roho niepuke hili balaa

Maisha nilichezea leo hii nalala njaa

Chemsha Bongo kabla ujapagaa ukashangaa

Chemsha Bongo kabla ujashangaa ukaduwaa

Kwa kifupi nimekulia kwenye maisha ya kitajiri

Wazazi wangu walinipenda walinipa lile na hili

Na tangu nikiwa mdogo nilionyesha kwamba nina akili

Sio siri nilikimbia umande kusoma sikuona dili

Maisha yalikuwa matamu nilisahau yote haramu

Ilitakiwa uwe na hadhi fulani upate japo salamu

Washkaji niliwapita maskani kama vijisanamu

Wazee wenye busara walisema kijana hana nidhamu

Hawakuniumiza kichwa niliamini hawata nilisha

Hawata nivisha

Na hawajui utamu wa maisha

Mimi ndio mimi mwendo mdundo

Wengine niliona uvundo

Niliamini naweza kula muwa pasipo kukuta fundo

Walisema mafumbo

Fedha kwangu ni kama nyundo

Na kila aliyenighasi sikusita kumjibu utumbo

Nilibadili mikoko mbali mbali ya kifahari

Chorus: Savior, I offer my soul, free me from this chaos

If I fool with this life today, I'll go to bed hungry

Think hard before you are trapped, you'll be amazed

Think hard before you are trapped, you'll be astonished.

In brief, I was raised with a comfortable life

My parents loved me, gave me this and that

And since I was little I showed my smarts

It's no secret I ran off early, saw no point in school

Life was sweet, I forgot all that was forbidden

You had to have some respect even to be greeted

I passed by friends' homes like they were pictures

The wise elders said that boy has no manners

They didn't hurt my head, I decided they wouldn't stop me

They won't stunt my growth

And they don't know the sweetness of life

I indeed am the beat of the drum

Others stunk to me

I decided I could eat sugarcane without finding the knot

They spoke in riddles

My money was like a hammer

And if anyone bugged me I'd answer 'em in the guts

I took down the tough guys

I loaded crates of beer while my posse would wash the car
Chicks went crazy for me, fat ladies liked me
I had two young babes wherever I went
I was known as Billionaire Bill Gates the chicken elder
Crews called for me, hey you, here's the party
And if anyone bugged me I'd give 'em a buck
Whoever boasted wouldn't be getting fed
We went where we liked, today Oyster Bay tomorrow Mikocheni
I'd change bars, today the Sleepway tomorrow Macheni
Elders would advise me, but I said forget that
And if there's nothing to do, go push a cart!

Every club I went into the posse had already arrived
'Cause they were sure to get some roast pig and beer
Chicks threw themselves at me each one trying to grab me
Others came behind saying "J we feel faint"
I had a custom every time I left a bar
When I said everyone drinks free no one was surprised
One day I was living with a chick, Zuwena
Don't let 'em say otherwise, this player had cash
I was parking my Mercedes Benz Convertible, yeah
It was black with gold rims, and not too cheap
The posse was chillin' in four red Range Rovers
I had a bad attitude, laughing like a white man

Nilikuwa napanga crate za beer wapambe waoshee gari
Mademu walijigonga mashangingi walinipenda
Nilikuwa na toto mbili kila kiwanja nilichokwenda
Niliitwa Billionaire Bill Gates mzee wa kuku
Wapambe walipembelea wewe mambo iko huku
Na kila aliye nighasi sikusita kumpatia buku
Aliye jifanya kiburi hakutafuna japo ruzuku
Tulikuwa tukihamahama leo Ofbey kesho mikocheni
Nilikuwa nabadilisha bar leo Sleepway kesho kwa macheni
Wazee walinishauri nikasema wanga niacheni
Na kama hamna shughuli kasukumeni mikokoteni

Kila club niliyoingia wapambe walishangilia
Kwa kuwa walipata hakika kula kiti moto na beer
Mademu walinigombania kila mmoja kunikumbatia
Wengine walikuja kwa nyuma "J tunakuzimia"
Nilikuwa na desturi kila kiwanja nafunga bar
Nilipo sema wote kunyweni bure hakuna aliye shangaa
Siku moja nilikuwa nikiishi na demu mmoja ukipenda Zuwena
Asikwambie mtu jibaba nilikuwa na hela
Niliku nimepark Mercedes Benz Convertible ebo
Ilikuwa nyeusi rim za gold si ya hela kidogo
Wapambe walikuwa wametanda na Range Rover nne nyekundu
Nilikuwa naongea kwa nyodo huku nikicheka kizungu

I created havoc, and any bullshit we wanted

We took on "gentlemen" and left them as pickpockets

I broke the rules of the road and the traffic cop laughed it off

He knew if he stopped the traffic the boss would be on him; money talks

No one pushed me around, and anyone who bugged me would rot in Segerea [notorious Dar prison]

But then my folks tried to show me my inheritance is education

I decided that you study in order to get money.

So I didn't see the point, 'cause I was prideful, and my brothers hated me

Me the bighsot and my family rejected me

Now I start to eat my wealth until I was cryin'

I sold my three cars and was left with just the chaser

Life started to change, my debts grew

So there came a time I had to run and hide in Zenj (Zanzibar)

All the places I went before I could no longer go

All those chicks and posses started treat me like a brute [lit. "pagan"]

They all ran me off, and worse, laughed at me saying

"Check out J that loser's already grown old"

I started pawning my stuff even my furniture

I lived like a groundhog I didn't show on the streets

Poverty comes knocking I'm living without hope

I don't know who'll feed me, people, I've got troubles

Nilifanya vurugu za mwaka na ushenzi tulivyotaka

Hadi tunatoa team waungwana walibaki nyaka nyaka

Nilivunja sheria za barabarani na traffic alichekelea

Alijua akizuia msafara boss wake atamfokea fedha iliongea

Hakuna aliye nisogelea na kila aliye nighasi aliozea segerea

Ila wazazi walinihusia kwamba urithi wangu ni elimu

Niliamini unasoma ili upate fedha

Hivyo sikuona umuhimu kwa kuwa nilikuwa kiburi ndugu zangu hawakunipenda

Mtukutu jeuri familia yangu ilinitenga

Nilianza kula mtaji nionekane bado natesa

Niliuza gari zangu tatu na nyumba nikabaki na chaser

Maisha yalianza ku-change madeni yakawa mengi

Hivyo kuna wakati nilikimbia na kwenda kujificha zenj

Viwanja nilivyozoea hivi sasa nikawa siendi

Wale mademu na wapambe wote wakaanza kuniona mshenzi

Wote walinikimbia na mbaya zaidi walinicheka walisema

"Cheki J arosto amesha zeeka"

Nikaanza kuweka bond mpaka vitu vyangu vya ndani

Niliishi kama digidigi sikuonekana mtaani

Umasikini umepiga hodi kuishi sasa sikutamani

Sijui nilie na nani jamani nipo mashakani

There was a bad accident and my parents were killed
I knew I would inherit wealth from this disaster
I took heart, I was the ghost who rose from the dead
Although I had eyes, whoa, I was blinded
They started to break through the floodgates, I don't know where they popped up

Stepchildren and stepmothers were claiming high status
Uncles and aunts all started up too
My head started to spin
The stench of blood became rotten
They were fighting over money, I saw it was better to die.
Rich people, pray to God before you depart
Man is like a flower, he sprouts and he dies.
And money is like a devil, if you have it you can never be found worthy
To cross the earthly threshold takes the comforting hand of God

Friends I cry I've already been undone
Right here I smell of sweat, I'm entirely spoiled
My body is like a piece of cassava that's been scraped down
"You ain't supposed to laugh," people of the world, truly I am remorseful
In front of God and this world I believe the doors will open.

Ilitokea ajali mbaya wazazi wangu wote wakafa
Nikajua nitarithi mali kutokana na hayo maafa
Nikajipa moyo mimi ni mzuka niliye fufuka
Ingawa nilikuwa na macho kumbe nilikuwa nimepofuka
Vilianza kutokea vizingiti na sielewi vilipo ibuka

Watoto wa nje na mama wa kambo walipandisha hulka
Wajomba na mashangazi wote wakawa wamecharuka
Akili ilianza kuniruka
Hharufu ya damu ilianza kunuka
Waligombea mali nikaona ni kheri kufa
Matajiri ombeni kwa Mungu kabla ya kuondoka
Binaadamu ni kama maua kwani huchanua na kunyauka
Na fedha ni kama shetani ukiwa nayo huwezi tukuka
Dunia kizingiti yataka mkono wa Mungu kuvuka nenda kwa mapoz

Mwenzio nalia nimesha umbuka
Hapa nilipo nanuka kikwapa siwezi mchafu kunuka
Mwili wangu ni kama kipande cha muhogo jinsi nilivyo pauka
"hutakiwi kucheka" walimwengu kweli najuta
mbele ya Mungu na hii dunia naamini milango itafunguka

Jina la kweli mwana mpotevu nanuka Bible na
Qur-aan vinasema msamehe anayejuta
Wananchi wenye ghadhabu bado wananipeleka puta
Walitaka kunichoma moto walisha niloweka kwenye mafuta
Fanya sala na kutafuta kila saa na kila dakika
Usitake yakukute ndugu yangu yaliyo nikuta.

Lyrics by Moses E.R.C.esq

It's true what they say about the Prodigal son, the Bible
and Koran, they say the remorseful are forgiven
Angry citizens still want to take me for a thrashing
They wanted to burn me, they've soaked me in oil
Say your prayers and search every hour and every minute
Don't hope to find my brother what I found.

Katika viumbe vyote

Verse La Kwanza (Nesto)

Chorus: Katika viumbe vyote vilivyo umbwa
Binadamu kaumbika kuliko vyote[1]

Nasikitika napo kumbuka
Mpaka machozi yananitoka
Kama kuishi tumechoka!
Basi, tuache kuropoka
Tusiwe akili fyatu ka Kaboka

We, binadamu, kweli umeumbika
Lakini wengi hatukumbuki
Ni nani aliyetuumba
Ardhi hata na mbingu
Ni yeye pekee Mungu
Nakulani we Shetani,
Nitolee kiwingu nyuma yangu
Napata kizungu zungu
Kwa machungu, na omba dua kwa uchungu

Ee mwenyezi mungu

Chorus: In all of God's creation
Man was created above all others

I'm sad when I remember
Til tears fall from my eyes
How tired we are of this life!
Okay, enough of this nonsense,
Let's not be stupid like Kaboka [a cartoon character]

People! Really you *were* created,
But too many of us don't remember
Who it was that created us
Along with Earth and Heaven.
It is only God himself
Who cursed the Devil
And put darkness behind us.
I get so dizzy
From the pain, I pray for a blessing for this pain

Oh! Almighty God

---

[1] This verse is a widely known Christian hymn, which Chronic Mobb sings to get the crowd into their rhymes.

Nisamehe dhambi zangu
Nije kwako siku kufa kwangu.
Lakini pamoja na mola katuumba
Naona norma madume kuwa wachumbe
Mpaka mademu kuwa magumba
Hata kitoto kutoa mimba
Tumechoka kuyumba yumba
Kulogana tu kwa ndumba

Hii safari inatisha
Bora maovu kujakatisha
Nasi tuswali "swala isha"
Kwani dunia ni nusu kyama
Kutanana kitoto cha mpiga mama
Katafunua mtama.
Ni norma hakuna woga wala huruma
Roho mbaya kama Osama
Mpaka mbuzi kupigwa para
Kizee kupigwa ngwara

Ooh! kila kona
Mabalaa yamezagaa
Usionee dagaa
Onea kambale

Forgive me for my sins
That I may rest in peace the day I die.
But even though the Lord created us
I see the disgrace of men lying with men
Until chicks are barren,
And even little girls have abortions.
We are tired of complaining
Bewitching each other like evil sorcerers

This trip is scary
Better give up these evil ways
And say our evening prayers
Cause the end of the world is near
Meeting a kid that beats his mother
Slamming her to the ground
It's a shame! there's no fear or pity
There's evil souls, like Osama
So even goats are screwed for kicks
And old folks are tripped up.

Ooh! On every corner
Shattered dreams spread all around.
Don't chase after those little kids
Go for someone more mature.

Ita: Mamenta! Eee! *Jibu:* Eee!

I: Msujudie mola wako, ee! *J:* Eee!

I: Usamehe dhambi zako! Ee! *J:* Eee!

I: Siku ya kifo kwako, we! *J:* Eee!

I: Uende pea peponi, ee! *J:* Eee!

Versela Piti (Spidah)

Chorus: Katika viumbe vyote vilivyo umbwa
Binadamu kaumbika kuliko vyote

Binadamu kiumbuka ulipo toka
Katika viumbe vyote vilivyoumba
Binadamu kaumbika kuliko vyote
Kichwa kufikiria hata na macho kuona
Puwa kunusia, masikio kusikia
Mdomo wa kulia
Mikono kushika
Miguu kutembelea.

Tunamasikio lakini hatusikii
Manabi waliusia lakini hakuwafuati
Kufurahia rukazani msikitini
Kuingia kanisani kuzamia
Nahata mola kumsujudia

Call: Conscious ones! Ee! *Response:* Ee!

C: Respect your Lord, ee! *R:* Ee!

C: Ask forgiveness for your sins! *R:* Ee!

C: On the day you die, you! *R:* Ee!

C: You'll get to heaven, ee! *R:* Ee!

Chorus: In all of God's creation
Man was created above all others

People! Remember where you come from
In all of God's creation
Man was created above all others
With a head to think with, and eyes to see
A nose for smelling, ears to hear
Mouth for eating
Hands to grasp
Feet for walking.

We have ears, but we don't hear
Prophets guide us but we don't follow
Be happy to hold to the mosque
To dive into your church
And even to respect the Lord

Na moyoni tuweke nia
Tuache cheza na vitabu vya dini
Haya yote ni mambo ya dunia yatakwisha
Tufuate na mafundisho ya dini
Tuisome dini ni undani

Spidah nazama kunywefani
Sitaki utani
Natoa yote moyoni ili sote twende peponi

Tumfunge kamba shetani tumlani
Awudhu bilah mina shaitwani rajim[2]
Tumfunge kuzimwi kifo kuwe adimu pamoja na adimu
Ushinde katika jina la Yesu
Sote ni wamoja hata na dini ndiyo moja
Tunamtegemea mungu mmoja
Lakini wengine watunga hoja
Kupingana ndiyo maana tunagombana

Let's put his will in our hearts
Let's quit playing with these sacred texts
All of them tell of the end of the world
Let's follow the lessons of religion
And prayer will be our shelter

Spidah I'm telling you for real
I don't like joking
I'm speaking from my heart so we can all get to heaven

Tie up the devil and curse him!
Awudhu bilah mina shaitwani rajim
Snuff out death till it's hardly there
You'll succeed in the name of Jesus
We're all the same and religion is all one
We all depend on one God
But some are opposed
This conflict is why we fight

---

[2] A line of Koranic verse calling for protection from demons.

Conclusion

I returned to Arusha after a three-year absence in the Christmas season of 2003. I felt the usual mixture of anxiety and anticipation that is typical of longer-term field research; eager, of course, to catch up with everyone and see how the town had changed, but uncertain about the fate of many friends and associates with whom it was difficult—at best—to keep in touch. My time in Arusha that year was entirely too brief; but my experiences at that time crystallized for me many of the pressing questions that I've addressed throughout this work. What I found in my conversations around town confirmed the sense of contradiction, dynamism, and fragility that I have argued are increasingly characteristic of the lived experience of neoliberal reforms in Tanzania, and certainly elsewhere.

Undoubtedly the most dramatic transformation in Arusha was a major reorientation of both commercial and residential space right at the heart of town. In 2001, the municipal council began implementing a plan designed—as almost every one I spoke with in town described it—to "clean up" Arusha. A few roads were repaved, and plans are afoot as I write to install streetlights in the downtown area. But the principal transformation of the city was the complete removal and relocation of the town bus stand at the heart of Arusha's commercial zone. The stand was relocated to an area nearer the outskirts of town, by the open-air Kilombero market. Indeed, this was an area of town where a good deal of development was taking place, of a kind eminently predictable in the current political economic era. Just across Sokoine Road, running southwest out of town, was the huge, well-lit, securely patrolled Shoprite Grocery, the largest food retailer in Africa, with its headquarters in the Western Cape province of South Africa. This was the friendly face of the South African capital in postsocialist Tanzania, a capital that is more notorious, especially in and around Arusha, for its takeover of Tanzanian Breweries, along with its attendant retrenchments, and its lucrative mineral rights concessions from the Tanzanian state, which has allowed the AfGem corporation to dominate the mining and marketing of tanzanite, whose consumers are almost exclusively American. The Shoprite sits adjacent to a strip mall, removed from the main street, lined with, among other amenities, several cappuccino bars, an ice cream parlor, and a boutique where designer bridal gowns can be rented by the hour. The relocation of the bus stand, suitably shielded from the view of Shoprite's customers, has had a major impact on the economic fortunes of many in Arusha. The Kilombero area was a warren of semipermanent shanty housing that nonetheless housed a good number of people, many of whom worked in the market. A large swath was cut through this housing as the offices and informal enterprises associated with the bus companies—and of course the buses, minivans, and cabs—came to occupy the area. In addition to displacing the residents of this already tenuous region, the municipal plan to clean up the town also removed the equally dense array of bustling shops and trades in the former bus stand. I found that most of the businesses operating in the old stand had not had the resources to relocate to the new stand, and a great many people who made their living in this zone simply had to search for other forms of income.

This spatial transformation incorporates in miniature a host of interconnected processes that form the broader background to popular practices in Arusha. An influx of capital, facilitated by corporate-state agreements (like cleaning up the town for the sake of attracting more capital), has lead to the expansion of so-called opportunities associated with consumption. Those who were least directly able to participate in these opportunities (no one that I knew had ever shopped at Shoprite, let alone rented a wedding gown, or could ever hope to acquire AfGem-mined tanzanite) were, of course, most directly affected by these citywide changes. Their livelihoods and homes were quite literally uprooted by these all too immediate processes.

At the same time, I was heartened to find that many who lived and worked in regions that were not substantially different from the stand at Kilombero had managed to endure, even thrive. A group of young women I knew working as seamstresses continued to find work. They also managed to produce a future for themselves. Many were able to marry, to have children, and to train more seamstresses in successful projects of apprenticeship. Many of these women benefited from small grants that targeted women's development, and they enjoyed the extended support of religious organizations, or had family members who could offer child-care, housing, or other forms of aid. My good friend Saidi, the painter operating under the nom de plume Nevada Art, was also able to sustain himself well. He had trained several young painters over the course of several years, enjoying the benefit of their labor, and had secured enough resources for himself to provide bridewealth that allowed him to marry in his mid-twenties. He, too, enjoyed the support of his family, as he was able to house himself on land provided by his brother, where he lived rent free for several years. It should be clear, however, that none of these factors could distinguish those who had managed to experience social reproduc-tion from those who had not enjoyed such success. I knew many young people, especially young women, who worked in the informal margins of consumer services as barbers, hairdressers, barmaids, and *daladala* transport conductors and who also had family support, many with at least some secondary education, and yet struggled to maintain an income that could support themselves (and often their dependents) from month to month. I can only offer anecdotal evidence, with nothing like a long-term grasp of the ways these lives will continue to unfold. Still, I would suggest that it makes little sense to try to predict which indicators contribute to a modicum of success and which are more likely to produce continuous struggle. Rather, it seems evident that an increasingly broad population find themselves living in circumstances in which either of these prospects is a distinct possibility for their future.

These circumstances, and the lived experience emergent within them, are characteristic of the neoliberal conditions that have seen the proliferation of markets targeting potential consumers and transnational movements of capital that have contributed to their expansion—as well as reoriented the commercial and residential arrangement of Arusha—and conduced to a greater overall instability. In particular, the forms of value realized under these political economic reforms, which are both a source of aspiration and subjected to critique as evanescent and illegitimate, are expressed and made concrete in the sense of uncertainty widespread in Arusha today. There is an intense awareness of the spectral pleasures of self-fashioning of the sort that has become commonplace in postsocialist Tanzania. Again, the mining economy is exemplary of these possibilities. This industry provides a fallback—or at least an imagined one—for a huge number of people in Arusha. Men and women, young and old, in town told me a standardized story: if everything else goes south, I can always go to the mines. Many young men do just that, and it is not uncommon to see bands of men, boys among them, tromp through town in work gear in a cloud of shimmering dust, just back from digging in neighboring Mererani. But many women, most with children to provide for, also talked with me of their time in the bush, pricing gems and looking for deals with young diggers, networking feverishly among the myriad dealers. Indeed, I had many discussions with middle-aged mothers about various grades of ruby, highs and lows in world markets, and the deleterious effects of AfGem on tanzanite prices. As a means of generating value, mining is a course of last resort, but it is also a common denominator, and in that sense iconic of the current moment. The appeal of quick cash in the gemstone economy is self-evident to everyone. But so are its risks—and these are not merely the imminent dangers of wildcat mining. Just as powerful in the imagined value of gemstones are the reports of extravagant consumption that almost always accompany reports of huge strikes. There are notorious accounts of lavish expenditures in highly spectacular forms, local thugs who sink their windfalls into tourist hotels, bush Maasai who finance decadent strip clubs. Inevitably, all of these extravagances end in financial ruin. The stereotypical gesture of young men joking about how quickly fortunes disappear as soon as they are made is to dramatically slide the full length of a finger under the nose, suggesting that big paydays are snorted away in drugs and similar indulgences.

Pairing dreams of opulence with tales of ruin is as least as old as Rumpelstiltskin (Schneider 1988). Such accounts are especially widespread in Africa, where reports of incomes earned through morally ambiguous means are destined to be "hot," "bitter," and generally unproductive money (Shipton 1989; Walsh 2003; Weiss 1996). In the neoliberal era, the capricious character of this kind of wealth has been widely linked to widespread anxieties about occult economies. Mining is a paradigmatic procedure in a world where the production of value is highly enigmatic, where "the mysterious mechanisms of the market hold the key to hitherto unimaginable riches" (Comaroff and Comaroff 1998b). I think these accounts are exemplary of neoliberal disquiet, but they are not, in any straightforward way, moral condemnations of current economic conditions. However, these reports are telling indicators of a great many peoples' experience of Tanzanian neoliberal reforms in the past decade. Whether the allure of the market is necessarily an invitation to absolute corruption is an unanswerable question, but the fact that these concerns are so persistently linked (remember the popularity of used clothing and the suspicion of women who wear them, the glorification of global images in the form of thugs and *wajeuri* that celebrate and confirm one's own oppression, or the false idols of fame and fortune decried in Tanzanian rap) tells us something about the way that those who are living with the implementation of widespread adjustments grasp their implications and possibilities. In part, these possibilities are the price that is exacted for positioning one's self as a subject on a globalized stage (Foster 2002). I think, more specifically, that these potentialities are experienced as a sense that the stakes in any activity are extremely high. Many people feel themselves to be living on the cusp of success and failure[1]; they can either scratch out a living looking for a life, or they can hope to reap unimaginable wealth by unforeseen and incalculable techniques. But there is little to choose—or realistically pursue—between these polar options. Perhaps this is why these opposites are so frequently grasped as two sides of the same coin, and why, as in the mining boons, they are so quickly obliterated: success is seen only as a temporary condition that leads almost inevitably to failure.

The preeminence of this form of value production, characterized by a polarization of possible outcomes and oriented toward the immediacy of self-fashioning through mass consumption, highlights the status of youth, both as a social category and problematic condition. In part, this is undoubtedly because the cultivation of the self as an aspect of identity, which is now promoted and globalized any number of ways and is deeply embedded in mass modes of consumption, is so strongly associated with youth. As a social category, youth are targeted as consumers, and more significantly, they are iconic bearers of the dynamic possibilities of consumption as a means of self-production. Thus, the pleasures of consumption are routinely touted (a routine that is at least as long-standing as modernity itself; see Cook 2004; Foster 2002) as youthful. The ways the market emphasizes youth while simultaneously excluding them from access to the values available in the market is a potent, deeply felt contradiction of neoliberal culture today.

There is an even more fundamental predicament that goes to what might even be considered the ontological condition of youth. The modes of temporality that are embedded in neoliberal social practice often radically undermine a sense of temporal unfolding; in particular, these practices make it distinctively difficult to grasp the prospects of the future in the present (Weiss 2004). Beyond the well-known effects of time compression (Harvey 1989), an actual disjunction between the present and the future is witnessed in the most compelling institutional forms of capitalism today. The premium on being perpetually wired so as to have access to up-to-the-second information facilitates the much lionized flexibility of capital, which in real terms often amounts to the sudden transnational movement of enormous sums of wealth. Just-in-time production regimes and rampant currency and commodity speculation, centerpieces in any model of late capitalism, are symptoms of this more general temporal orientation. Under such conditions, it is all but impossible to understand one's present activities as oriented toward constructing, let alone securing, a desirable future. Further, this hollowing out of the future is part of the lived experience of the current moment. The common sense of value as access to the means of consumption gives all economic practice a sense of pressing immediacy, in which all that matters is *kushika mkawanja,* "scratching out a living," either in the fraught hope of making ends meet or in order to participate in the presentist styles, gestures, and significations of self-presentation and performance. This relentless emphasis on the now redounds to make a problem of youth. If youth are held in so many respects to embody the possibilities of the future, it follows that as the prospect of the future is increasingly opaque and in doubt, so too are youth found invariably to be in crisis (Weiss 2004).[2] The constraints experienced by and imposed on youth bespeak a wider configuration of material and meaningful forces at work in the world today—forces that, even as they move almost instantaneously through circuits that span time and distance, are increasingly felt by so many to undermine their capacity to secure a solid grasp on their own future.

This tenuous hold on processes of temporal unfolding—configured, implicitly, in coordination with the simultaneous sense of spatial incorporation and marginalization in a new global order—frames the practices and experience of young men and women in Arusha today. I have tried to detail some of the potentials and constraints of this contemporary situation without succumbing either to a critique of political economy that sees only dependency and frustrated reaction to an order of domination or to a celebration of the creativity that Africans have generated independent of the harsh realities they daily confront. The contradictions in popular cultural performances belie either of these positions, for even marginalization and oppression can be embraced as potent signs of endurance, struggle, and near-transcendent personhood; and the imaginative production of local communities of semiotic virtuosity can themselves be founded on the promotion of radical inequalities, notably a pronounced sexism. In the final analysis, this assessment of Arusha popular cultural practices argues that struggling with these contradictions is a call for belonging in modes that are recognizable and relevant to those making that call.

In his provocative call for a theory of value, David Graeber (2001, here following Terry Turner) argues that the most important dimension of a politics of value is the struggle to define what value *is*. My evaluation of Arusha's popular culture is in keeping with that more general view, as I hold that the attempt to articulate not only a right to participate in a globalized order of action, but a definition of the very terms of that participation is the paramount political dynamic in contemporary society. What alternatives are there to the juridical claims of entitlement, to demands for an international recognition of forms of sovereignty that are of limited relevance to quotidian life? How can the power of the market be challenged or transgressed? These are vexing problems, in part because of the strong appeal of the very sociopolitical forms that nonetheless have left significant misery in their wake. What the work of popular culture in Arusha (and undoubtedly elsewhere) reveals is that fantasies can make tangible a sense of alternatives. Even the most banal and repressive of fantasies requires an imaginative effort. Although imagination in and of itself need not be lauded, it is indispensable to the production of a viable future. Current neoliberal conditions that render the future so vulnerable make the work of imagining all the more necessary. What the actions of the barbers and hairstylists, sign painters and seamstresses, minivan conductors and video fans in Arusha today demonstrate is that confronting the limitations of the current moment also requires all of us to consider its possibilities.

Notes

Introduction

1. Note that proliferation is not the same as success. If anything, the sheer number of *vinyozi* were in such stiff competition with one another that many of them collapsed (often literally) not long after they opened.

2. The term *bongo* in Arusha is, to my knowledge, used to refer to Dar as a whole—although those more familiar with the capital's neighborhoods may be referring more specifically to Ubongo, a residential area that is home to many university faculty. My thanks to Amy Stambach for pointing out this alternative possibility.

3. Consideration of the use of the term *space* in much critical theory and theories of popular culture can be useful compared with the Swahili understanding of space as "opportunity" or "opening." This is a comparison I intend to pursue in future work.

4. The socioeconomic position of women salon workers is less fortunate than for most barbers. See chapter 5 for further discussion of these circumstances.

5. The parastatal sector accounted for 24 percent of nonagricultural wage employment (Due et al. 2000: 2).

6. I am grateful to Jean Comaroff for her insights into these processes.

1. Themes and Theories

1. See chapter 6 for more detailed discussion of cosmopolitanism.

2. Mitchell's work has also been subject to significant critique; see Magubane (1971) and Ferguson (2002).

3. A study of cosmopolitanism on the Copperbelt, writes Ferguson (1999: 109), must take into consideration "not only . . . the considerable effects of political colonization, but also . . . the cultural colonization that comes with the economic dominance of the Western multinational corporation, the distinctive valuation of skills and styles proper to the capitalistic workplace, [and] the powerful effects of Western styles of schooling"—all of which seems true, but leaves open the question of what the "effects" of Zambians's contribution to this process might be.

4. On the uselessness of resistance as a mode of ethnographic writing and a similar critique of anthropological celebrations of (certain forms of) agency, see Ortner (1995) and Durham (2000).

5. These concerns, though, are by no means irrelevant in Tanzania or Arusha (Weiss 2004).

2. Enacting the Invincible

1. The terms *House Nigga, Field Nigga, Street Nigga,* and *boss* are all English terms in this Swahili conversation.

2. I discuss these notions of consciousness and its relationship to one's environment more extensively in chapters 6 and 7.

3. Taxis are remarkably expensive; a basic ride within the city limits costs what someone earns in a day and a half. Taxis, which are relatively abundant in Arusha, clearly survive on the tourist and NGO trade, as is evident from the regions where they are most commonly found: near the bus stand, in the parking lot of major hotels, in the vicinity of the Arusha International Conference Center.

4. Although *vijana* (sing. *kijana*) refers to "youth" in much official discourse, as in, e.g., the ruling party's Youth Wing (Umoja wa Vijana) the phrase *vijana na wasichana,* "young men and young girls," is more frequently heard in news reports and conversation.

5. See Remes (1999) for discussion of the relevance of police harassment of youth to popular music in Tanzania.

6. The mapping of (implicitly) racialized divisions under British colonial rule resonates today, as African and Asian businesses are largely located in the zones established in the '30s.

7. Consider the way that threats of shaving dreadlocks demonstrates police pettiness and incompetence, and not their coercive force.

8. "Zanzibar: Violence Condemned, Tanzanian Security on the Rampage," Human Rights News, http://www.hrw.org/english/docs/2001/01/31/tanzan199.htm (accessed Sept. 2, 2008).

Portraits 1

1. This follows the suggestion of Peter Geschiere, which I gratefully acknowledge.

2. Later in the book, I will focus on the lives of other men and women who do not work in barbershops.

3. I treat Hussein's discussion of his memories of his mother in more detail in chapter 4.

3. Thug Realism

1. By 2000, "Kosovo" marks had reverted to Nike swooshes and Fila dashes.

2. One of the more remarkable features of the shops is the way in which a strikingly narrow and similar set of images (African American rappers, basketball players, supermodels) can sustain a broad array of recognized styles. In other words, the forms themselves do not dictate the fashions created with them.

3. These are clearly objectifying processes, and they are absolutely central to the shops. However, these displays, as I discuss below, are informed by a social practice rooted not in images but in a set of embodied dispositions.

4. In my time visiting over fifty barbershops in Arusha, I did know only one woman who worked as a barber. Her work was a fact commented on as remark-

able by all who met her, and her shop was widely known as the one where a woman was a barber.

5. I am indebted to Amy Stambach for pointing out this connection to me.

6. As Stambach (1999) and Tripp (1996) note, any number of NGOs and development agencies sponsored women-owned beauty salons as a means of targeting women's development in the 1990s.

7. See Askew (1999) for an excellent discussion of the variability of Swahili social organization; she demonstrates that such matricentric ties have an enduring significance in Tanzania.

8. This experimental attitude is confirmed for many of the Muslims I know in reports form the Internet about scientific practice in the West inspired by readings of the Koran. Aside from the way the Internet is now contributing to the reformulation of Muslim communities, the Internet as a technological achievement is also given legitimacy by this attitude.

9. Local styles of dress, especially the appropriation of *mitumba,* or used clothing, is characterized by a similar dynamic. In spite of the fact that young men and women in Arusha are familiar with the most popular American and European brands of clothing—especially sportswear such as Nike and Reebok, Fila and FUBU—and can frequently purchase cast-off examples of these brands, many people remain convinced that the clothes available to them are only pale imitations of the "real" brands that (they imagine) pervade Euro-American markets.

4. The Barber in Pain

1. My differentiation between identity and personhood as aspects of subjectivity is plainly an analytical construction. In practice, the ability to act on the world is ineluctably wedded to social agents' sense of who they are, and how others know and recognize (and authorize) the agents acts: persons have identity, and this informs their personhood. Nonetheless, I think it is useful to distinguish between the range of potential actions possible in a given context, and the enactment of particular actions that come to define, and so differentiate, particular kinds of actors.

2. For a compelling discussion of the ways that women's hair styling in contemporary Tanzania has been shaped by public discourse about Tanzania's marginality, its efforts at economic self-reliance, and contemporary efforts to become "modern" under conditions of liberalization, see Stambach (1999).

3. The importance of barbershops as centers of sociality in the African diaspora has been widely noted; to my knowledge, there is little work that has been done on barbershops in East Africa.

4. In Luhaya, as well, "worries/troubles" are characteristically described as "thoughts," *ebitekelezo.* Here, the term is not a cognate of the Swahili, so the term is not simply borrowed by Haya speakers to describe their troubles. This suggests, if tentatively, that the link between thoughts and worries is a widespread semantic association in East Africa.

5. Jamaa is a charismatic movement in Congo (see Fabian 1978).

Portraits 3

1. As an aside, I think it's interesting to note that of young couples who had purchased land for home construction, none of them described these plots as a

shamba, or "field," but only as a *sehemu,* a "piece," or "section" of land—although most of them grew vegetables on the land before construction (which might never happen). This suggests the nature of the aspiration implied in such home construction, which is oriented *away* from the rural forms of production—and the generational connections these entail—of a farm and toward the open-ended possibilities of an empty plot.

5. Gender (In)Visible

1. See Makhulu (2004) for a similar process viz. "photo idioms" on the Cape Flats.

2. This practice may be more characteristic of Arusha than the Swahili coast; see Parkin (2000).

3. See Munn (1990) on Gawa sorcery for a similar dynamic of self–other interpenetration.

4. See the discussion of *kijiwe* in chapter 3 for discussion of male appropriation of female space.

5. But see also my discussion of dreadlocks and completely shaved heads in chapter 3.

6. Learning from Your Surroundings

1. Das is not endorsing this definition but poses it as a "formulation in culture theory" (Das 1995: 170) that social anthropology should work to critique.

2. Although the study of participation roles and frameworks has been especially central to the study of language, my contention is not that we should adopt a linguistic model to social life; it is rather that language use is only one form of complex social interaction that can productively be addressed through a study of the various modes social actors participate in. In my view, participation relates to fields of action, of which language is one possibility.

3. Whether these assumptions actually tell us very much about actual serial audiences is highly contestable. My point is that these formal features of broadcasting are conventions that are understood to stand in some kind of relationship to the audiences they presume.

7. Chronic Mobb Asks a Blessing

1. Nkwame, Valentine March, "School Girls Collapse in Fits of Hysteria," *Arusha Times,* March 16–22, 2002.

2. Indeed, as we shall see for some in Arusha, the distinction between these positions is paramount, while for others the lines of delineation are much more fluid and contextual.

3. Here I would add that the exaggerated masculinity of barbershops—which has an interest in hip hop as a central theme—bespeaks an attempt to give purpose to male bodies and relations in a neoliberal world where the men's productive capacity is extremely tenuous (see also Buford 1993 and Cole 2008).

4. I would add that I had remarkably similar discussions about the scientific and mystical character of the Bible with Pentecostal Christians in Arusha.

5. See, for example, the UK group Fun-Da-Mental. In Arusha, this term is also incorporated into the names of local rap groups, and it also appears in rap lyrics.

6. Primary education is fully funded in Tanzania, but secondary schools—especially those in Kenya—require fees.

7. See the appendix for full text in Swahili and English translation.

8. There are a number of venues in Arusha where rap competitions for local crews are held. A few nightclubs and hotels with performance venues will occasionally host local hip hop artists. The rap competitions I attended took place in a small club associated with the downtown movie theater. Local groups performed on consecutive weekends for a small cash prize sponsored by the club owners. Some rappers from Arusha—most notably X Plastaz (whose members were barbers in town)—have signed with producers from the Netherlands and have received international recognition.

Conclusion

1. I owe much of my thinking on this notion that life is lived on the cusp of success and failure to the highly stimulating advanced seminar on "Youth and Globalization" held in April 2004 in Santa Fe.

2. I am indebted to Jean Comaroff for discussion of this connection between youth and the future in neoliberal culture.

References

Abrahams, Ray. 1987. "Sungusungu: Village Vigilante Groups in Tanzania." *African Affairs* 87: 179–96.

Abu-Lughod, Lila. 1991. "Writing Against Culture." In *Recapturing Anthropology*, ed. Richard Fox. Santa Fe: SAR Press.

———. 1997. "The Interpretation of Culture(s) After Television." *Representations* 59: 109–34.

Allison, Anne. 2000. *Permitted and Prohibited Desires: Mothers, Comics, and Censorship in Japan*. Berkeley: University of California Press.

———. 2006. *Millennial Monsters: Japanese Toys and the Global Imagination*. Berkeley: University of California Press.

Appadurai, Arjun. 1991. "Global Ethnoscapes: Notes and Queries for a Transnational Anthropology." In *Recapturing Anthropology: Working in the Present*, ed. Richard G. Fox. Santa Fe: School of American Research Press.

———. 2004. "The Capacity to Aspire: Culture and the Terms of Recognition." In *Culture and Public Action: A Cross-Disciplinary Dialogue on Development Policy*, ed. Vijayendra Rao and Michael Walton. Stanford: Stanford University Press.

Argenti, Nicolas. 2005. "Dancing in the Borderlands: the Forbidden Masquerades of Oku Youth and Women (Cameroon)." In *Makers and Breakers: Children and Youth in Postcolonial Africa*, ed. F. De Boeck and A. Honwana. Oxford: James Currey.

Argyle, John. 1991. "Kalela, Beni, Asafo, Ingoma and the Rural-Urban Dichotomy." *African Studies* 50, no. 1–2: 65–86.

Armstrong, Edward G. 2004. "Eminem's Construction of Authenticity." *Popular Music and Society* 27, no. 3: 335–55.

Asad, Talal. 1983. "Notes on Body Pain and Truth in Medieval Christian Ritual." *Economy and Society* 12, no. 3: 287–327.

Askew, Kelly. 1999. "Female Circles and Male Lines: Gender Dynamics along the Swahili Coast." *Africa Today* 46, no. 3–4: 67–102.

———. 2002. *Performing the Nation: Swahili Music and Cultural Politics in Tanzania*. Chicago: University of Chicago Press.

Austin, J. L. 1962. *How to Do Things with Words*. Oxford: Clarendon Press.

Axel, Brian Keith. 2002. *From the Margins: Historical Anthropology and Its Futures*. Durham, N.C.: Duke University Press.

Bakhtin, Mikhail. 1998. "Carnival and the Carnivalesque." In *Cultural Theory and Popular Culture: A Reader,* ed. J. Storey. Athens: University of Georgia Press.

Barber, Karin, ed. 1997. *Readings in African Popular Culture.* Bloomington: Indiana University Press.

Baroin, Catherine. 1996. "Religious Conflict in 1990–1993 among the Rwa: Secession in a Lutheran Diocese in Northern Tanzania." *African Affairs* 95: 529–54.

Bastian, Misty L. n.d. "'Take the Battle to the Enemies' Camp': Militarizing the Spirit in Nigerian Neo-Pentecostal Christianity." Unpublished MS, Department of Anthropology, Franklin and Marshall College.

Bauman, R. 1977. *Verbal Art as Performance.* Prospect Heights, Ill.: Waveland Press.

Beidelman, T. O. 1997. *The Cool Knife.* Washington, D.C.: Smithsonian.

Berg, C. 1951. *The Unconscious Significance of Hair.* London: Allen and Unwin.

Boddy, Jannice. 1989. *Wombs and Alien Spirits: Women, Men, and the Zar Cult in Northern Sudan.* Madison: University of Wisconsin Press.

Blunt, Rob. 2004. "'Satan Is an Imitator': Kenya's Recent Cosmology of Corruption." In *Producing African Futures: Ritual and Reproduction in a Neoliberal Age,* ed. B. Weiss. Leiden: Brill.

Bourdieu, Pierre. 1977. *Outline of a Theory of Practice.* Cambridge: Cambridge University Press.

———. 1984. *Distinction: A Social Critique of the Judgement of Taste.* Trans. Richard Nice. Cambridge, Mass.: Harvard University Press.

———. 1991. *Language and Symbolic Power.* Ed. John Thompson, trans. Gino Raymond and Matthew Adamson. Cambridge: Harvard University Press.

Brown, M. F. 1996. "On Resisting Resistance." *American Anthropologist* 98, no. 4: 729–49.

Buford, Bill. 1993. *Among the Thugs.* London: Vintage.

Burke, Timothy. 1996. *Lifebuoy Men, Lux Women: Commodification, Consumption, and Cleanliness in Modern Zimbabwe.* Durham, N.C.: Duke University Press.

Ciekawy, Diane, and Peter Geschiere. 1998. "Containing Witchcraft: Conflicting Scenarios in Postcolonial Africa." *African Studies Review* 41, no. 3.

Cole, Jennifer. 1998. "The Uses of Defeat: Memory and Political Morality in East Madagascar." In *Memory and the Post Colony: African Anthropology and the Critique of Power,* ed. R Werbner. London: Zed Books.

———. 2004. "Fresh Contact in Tamatave, Madagascar: Sex, Money, and Intergenerational Transformation." *American Ethnologist* 31, no. 4: 573–88.

———. 2008. "Fashioning Distinction in Urban Madagascar." In *Youth: Mediating the Social Imagination,* ed. J. Cole and D. Durham. Santa Fe, N.M.: School of American Research.

Cole, Jennifer, and Deborah Durham. 2006. *Generations and Globalization: Youth, Age, and Family in the New World Economy.* Bloomginton: Indiana University Press.

Comaroff, Jean. 1985. *Body of Power, Spirit of Resistance.* Chicago: University of Chicago Press.

Comaroff, Jean, and John Comaroff. 2004. "Notes on Afromodernity and the Neo World Order: An Afterword." In *Producing African Futures: Ritual and Reproduction in a Neoliberal Age,* ed. B. Weiss. Leiden: Brill.

Comaroff, John L., and Jean Comaroff. 1993. *Modernity and Its Malcontents: Ritual and Power in Postcolonial Africa.* Chicago: University of Chicago Press.

―――. 1999a. *Civil Society and the Political Imagination in Africa*. Chicago: University of Chicago Press.

―――. 1999b. "Occult Economies and the Violence of Abstraction: Notes from the South African Postcolony." *American Ethnologist* 26: 279–301.

―――. 2000. "Millennial Capitalism: First Thoughts on a Second Coming." In *Millennial Capitalism and the Culture of Neoliberalism*, ed. Jean Comaroff and John L. Comaroff. Durham, N.C.: Duke University Press.

Cruise O'Brien, Donal. 1996. "A Lost Generation? Youth Identity and State Decay in West Africa." In *Postcolonial Identities in Africa*, ed. R. Werbner and T. Ranger. London: Zed Books.

Cook, Daniel Thomas. 2004. *The Commodification of Childhood: The Children's Clothing Industry and the Rise of the Child Consumer*. Durham, N.C.: Duke University Press.

Das, Veena. 1995. "On Soap Opera: What Kind of Anthropological Object Is It?" In *Worlds Apart: Modernity through the Prism of the Local*, ed. D. Miller. London: Routledge.

Das, Veena, and Deborah Poole. 2004. *Anthropology in the Margins of the State*. Santa Fe: School of American Research Press.

De Boeck. Filip. 1006. "Postcolonialism, Power and Identity: Local and Global Perspectives from Zaire." In *Postcolonial Identities in Africa*, ed. R. Werbner and T. Ranger. London: Zed Books.

de Certeau, M. 1984. *The Practice of Everyday Life*. Berkeley: University of California Press.

Derrett, J. 1973. "Religious Hair." *Man* 8: 100–103.

Dinwoodie, David. 1997. "Authorizing Voices: Going Public in an Indigenous Language." *Cultural Anthropology* 13, no. 2: 193–223.

Due, J. M., A. E. Temu, and A. A. Temu. 2000. "Privatization in Tanzania. A Case Study, 1999." Research report, Department of Agricultural and Consumer Economics, University of Illinois; Department of Agricultural Economics and Agribusiness, Sokoine University of Agriculture, Morogoro.

Durham, Deborah. 2000. "Youth and the Social Imagination in Africa." *Anthropological Quarterly* 73, no. 3: 113–20.

Dyson, Michael Eric. 2001. *Holler If You Hear Me: Searching for Tupac Shakur*. New York: Basic Civitas Books.

Engelke, Matthew. 2007. *A Problem of Presence: Beyond Scripture in an African Church*. Berkeley: University of California Press.

Fabian, Johannes. 1978. "Popular Culture in Africa: Findings and Conjectures." *Africa* 48, no. 4: 315–34.

―――. 1983. *Time and the Other: How Anthropology Makes Its Object*. New York: Columbia University Press.

―――. 1996. *Remembering the Present: Painting and Popular History in Zaire*. Berkeley: University of California Press.

―――. 1998. *Moments of Freedom: Anthropology and Popular Culture*. Charlottesville: University of Virginia Press.

―――. 1978. "Popular Culture in Africa: Findings and Conjectures." *Africa* 48, no. 4: 570–71.

Fair, Laura. 2001. *Pastimes and Politics: Culture, Community, and Identity in Post-Abolition Urban Zanzibar, 1890–1945*. Oxford: James Currey.

Ferguson, James. 1999. *Expectations of Modernity: Myths and Meanings of Urban Life on the Zambian Copperbelt.* Berkeley: University of California Press.

———. 2002. "Of Mimicry and Membership: Africans and the 'New World Society.'" *Cultural Anthropology* 17, no. 4: 551–69.

Ferme, Mariane. 2001. *The Underneath of Things: Violence, History, and the Everyday in Sierra Leone.* Berkeley: University of California Press.

Forman, Murray. 2002. *The 'Hood Comes First: Race, Space, and Place in Rap and Hip-Hop.* Middletown, Conn.: Wesleyan University Press.

Forman, Murray, and Mark Anthony Neal. 2004. *That's the Joint! The Hip-Hop Studies Reader.* New York: Routledge.

Foster, Robert. 1999. "Melanesianist Anthropology in the Era of Globalization." *Contemporary Pacific* 11, no. 1 (140): 1–33.

———. 2002. *Materializing the Nation: Commodity Consumption and Commercial Media in Papua New Guinea.* Bloomington: Indiana University Press.

Foucault, Michel. 1977. *Discipline and Punish: The Birth of the Prison.* Trans. Alan Sheridan. New York: Vintage.

Friedman, Jonathan. 1990a. "Being in the World: Globalization and Localization." *Theory Culture and Society* 7: 311–28.

———. 1990b. "The Political Economy of Elegance: An African Cult of Beauty." *Culture and History* 7: 101–25.

———. 2000. "Globalization, Class and Culture in Global Systems." *Journal of World-Systems Research* 6, no. 3: 636–56.

Fuglesang, Minou. 1994. *Veils and Videos: Female Youth Culture on the Kenya Coast.* Stockholm: Coronet Books.

Geertz, Clifford. 1973. "Deep Play: Notes on the Balinese Cockfight." In *Interpretation of Cultures.* New York: Basic Books.

Gell, Alfred. 1988. "Anthropology, Material Culture and Consumerism." *JASO* 19, no. 1: 43–48.

Geraghty, Christine. 1991. *Women and Soap Opera: A Study of Prime-Time Soaps.* Cambridge: Polity Press.

Geschiere, Peter. 1997. *The Modernity of Witchcraft: Politics and the Occult in Postcolonial Africa.* Charlottesville: University of Virginia Press.

———. 2003. "On Witch-Doctors and Spin-Doctors: The Role of 'Experts' in African and American Politics." In *Magic and Modernity: Interfaces of Revelation and Concealment,* ed. B. Meyer and P. Pels. Stanford, Calif.: Stanford University Press.

Geschiere, Peter, and Frances Nyamnjoh. 2000. "Capitalism and Autochthony: The Seesaw of Mobility and Belonging." *Public Culture* 12, no. 2: 432–52.

Gibbon, Peter, ed. 1995. *Liberalised Development in Tanzania.* Uppsala: Scandinavian Institute of African Studies.

Gilroy, Paul. 1994. "After the Love Has Gone: Bio-Politics and Etho-Poetics in the Black Public Sphere." *Public Culture* 7, no. 1: 49–76.

Glassman, Jonathon. 1995. *Feasts and Riots: Revelry, Rebellion, and Popular Consciousness on the Swahili Coast, 1856–1888.* Portsmouth, N.H.: Heinemann.

Gluckman, Max. 1963. *Order and Rebellion in Tribal Africa.* New York: Free Press of Glencoe.

Goffman, Erving. 1981. *Forms of Talk.* Philadelphia: University of Pennsylvania.

Graeber, David. 2001. *Toward an Anthropological Theory of Value: The False Coin of Our Own Dreams.* New York: Palgrave.

Gupta, Akhil, and James Ferguson. 1997. "Beyond 'Culture': Space, Identity and the Politics of Difference." In *Culture, Power, Place,* ed. Akhil Gupta and James Ferguson. Durham, N.C.: Duke University Press.

Hannerz, Ulf. 1996. "The Local and the Global: Continuity and Change." In *Transnational Connections: Culture, People, Places.* New York: Routledge.

Hanks, William F. 1995. *Language and Communicative Practices.* Boulder, Colo.: Westview Press.

Hansen, Karen Tranberg. 1999. "Second-Hand Clothing Encounters in Zambia: Global Discourses, Western Commodities, and Local Histories." *Africa* 69: 343–65.

Harvey, David. 1989. *The Condition of Postmodernity. An Enquiry into the Origins of Cultural Change.* Cambridge, Mass.: Basil Blackwell.

Hymes, Del. 1974. *Foundations in Social Linguistics: An Ethnographic Approach.* Philadelphia: University of Pennsylvania Press.

Jenkins, Henry. 1992. *Textual Poachers: Television Fans and Participatory Culture.* New York: Routledge.

Kaplan, Martha, and John Kelly. 1994. "Rethinking Resistance: Dialogics of 'Disaffection' in Colonial Fiji." *American Ethnologist* 21, no. 1: 123–51.

Kelsall, Tim. n.d. "Subjectivity, Collective Action and the Governance Agenda in Arumeru East." Working Paper 42. QEH Working Paper Series.

Kerner, Donna O. 1988. "The Social Uses of Knowledge in Contemporary Tanzania." Ph.D. diss., City University of New York.

Krims, Adam. 2000. *Rap Music and the Poetics of Identity.* New York: Cambridge University Press.

Lamb, Sarah. 2000. *White Saris and Sweet Mangoes: Aging, Gender, and Body in North India.* Berkeley: University of California Press.

Lambek, Michael. 1998. "The Sakalava Poiesis of History: Realizing the Past through Spirit Possession in Madagascar." *American Ethnologist* 25: 102–27.

Larkin, Brian. 1997. "Indian Films and Nigerian Lovers: Media and the Creation of Parallel Modernities." *Africa* 67, no. 3: 406–40.

Lawuyi, Olatunde Bayo. 1997. "The World of the Yoruba Taxi Driver: An Interpretive Approach to Vehicle Slogans." In *Readings in African Popular Culture,* ed. Karin Barber. Bloomington: Indiana University Press.

Leach, Edmund. 1958. "Magical Hair." *Journal of the Royal Anthropological Institute* 88: 147–64.

Lefebvre, Henri. 1991. *The Production of Space.* Trans. D. N. Smith. Cambridge: Blackwell.

Lewis, J. Lowell. 1999. "Sex and Violence in Brazil: Carnival, Capoeira, and the Problem of Everyday Life." *American Ethnologist* 26: 539–57.

Lewis, Laura. 2003. *Hall of Mirrors: Power, Witchcraft, and Caste in Colonial Mexico.* Durham, N.C.: Duke University Press.

Liechty, Mark. 2002. *Suitably Modern: Making Middle-Class Culture in a New Consumer Society.* Princeton, N.J.: Princeton University Press.

Lienhardt, Godfrey. 1961. *Divinity and Experience: The Religion of the Dinka.* London: Oxford University Press.

Linnebuhr, Elisabeth. 1997. "Kanga: Popular Cloths with Messages." In *Readings in African Popular Culture,* ed. Karin Barber. Bloomington: Indiana University Press.

Lowenhaupt-Tsing, Anna. 1993. *In the Realm of the Diamond Queen: Marginality in an Out-of-the-Way Place.* Princeton, N.J.: Princeton University Press.

Mageo, Jeannette Marie. 1994. "Hairdos and Don'ts: Hair Symbolism and Sexual History in Samoa." *Man* 29: 407–32.

Magubane, Bernard. 1971. "A Critical Look at Indices Used in the Study of Social Change in Africa." *Current Anthropology* 12: 419–31.

Makhulu, Anne-Maria. 2004. "Poetic Justice: Xhosa Idioms and Moral Breach in Post-Apartheid South Africa." In *Producing African Futures: Ritual and Reproduction in a Neoliberal Age,* ed. B. Weiss. Leiden: Brill.

Malkki, Liisa. 1997. "Children, Futures, and the Domestication of Hope." Humanities Research Institute. University of California, Irvine.

Marx, Karl. [1852] 1978. *The Eighteenth Brumaire of Louis Bonaparte.* In *The Marx-Engels Reader,* ed. Robert Tucker. New York: Norton.

———. 1906. *Capital: A Critique of Political Economy.* New York: Charles H. Kerr.

Masquelier, Adeline. 1999. "Debating Muslims, Disputed Practices: Struggles for the Realization of an Alternative Moral Order in Niger." In *Civil Society and the Political Imagination in Africa: Critical Perspectives,* ed. John L. Comaroff and Jean Comaroff. Chicago: University of Chicago Press.

———. 2001. *"Prayer Has Spoiled Everything": Possession, Power, and Identity in an Islamic Town of Niger.* Durham, N.C.: Duke University Press.

Matongo, Albert B. K. 1992. "Popular Culture in a Colonial Society: Another Look at the Mbeni and Kalela Dances." In *Guardians in Their Time,* ed. S. N. Chipungu. London: Macmillan.

Mbembe, Achille. 1992. "Provisional Notes on the Postcolony." *Africa* 12: 3–37.

———. 1997. "The 'Thing' and Its Doubles in Cameroonian Cartoons." In *Readings in African Popular Culture,* ed. Karin Barber. Bloomington: Indiana University Press.

———. 2001. *On the Postcolony.* Berkeley: University of California Press.

Mercer, Kobena. 1994. "Black Hair/Style Politics." In *Welcome to the Jungle: New Positions in Black Cultural Studies.* New York: Routledge.

Merleau-Ponty, Maurice. 1962. *The Phenomenology of Perception.* London: Routledge and Kegan Paul.

Meyer, Birigt. 1998a. *Translating the Devil: Religion and Modernity among the Ewe in Ghana.* Edinburgh: Edinburgh University Press

———. 1998b. "Commodities and Power of Prayer: Pentecostalist Attitudes Toward Consumption in Contemporary Ghana." *Development and Change* 29: 751–76.

Meyer, Birgit, and Peter Geschiere, eds. 1999. *Globalization and Identity: Dialectics of Flow and Closure.* Oxford: Blackwell.

Miller, Daniel. 1992. "*The Young and the Restless* in Trinidad: A Case of the Local and the Global in Mass Consumption." In *Consuming Technologies: Media and Information in Domestic Spaces,* ed. E. Hirsch and R. Silverstone. London: Routledge

———. 1994. *Modernity: An Ethnographic Approach.* Oxford: Berg Press.

Mitchell, J. C. 1956. *The Kalela Dance: Aspects of Social Relationships among Urban Africans in Northern Rhodesia.* Manchester: Manchester University Press.

Mitchell, Tony, ed. 2001. *Global Noise: Rap and Hip-Hop outside the USA.* Middletown, Conn.: Wesleyan University.

Munn, Nancy. 1990. "Constructing Regional Worlds in Experience: Kula Exchange, Witchcraft and Gawan Local Events." *Man* 25: 1–17.

———. 1996. "Excluded Spaces: The Figure in the Australian Aboriginal Landscape." *Critical Inquiry* 22, no. 3: 446–65.

Nelson, Diane. 1999. *A Finger in the Wound: Body Politics in Quincentennial Guatemala.* Berkeley: University of California Press.

Ngwane, Zolani. 2004. "'Real Men Reawaken Their Fathers' Homesteads, the Educated Leave Them in Ruins': The Politics of Domestic Reproduction in Post-Apartheid Rural South Africa." In *Producing African Futures: Ritual and Reproduction in a Neoliberal Age,* ed. B. Weiss. Leiden: Brill.

Obeyesekere, G. 1981. *Medusa's Hair: An Essay on Personal Symbols and Religious Experience.* Chicago: University of Chicago Press.

Ortner, Sherry. 1995. "Resistance and the Problem of Ethnographic Refusal." *Comparative Studies in Society and History* 37: 173–93.

Parkin, David. 1995. "Blank Banners and Islamic Consciousness in Zanzibar." In *Questions of Consciousness,* ed. A. Cohen and N. Rapport. London: Routledge.

———. 2000. "The Power of Incompleteness: Innuendo in Swahili Women's Dress." In *Rhétoriques du quotidian,* ed. B. Masquelier and J.-L. Siran. Paris: L'Harmattan.

Peligal, Rona. 1999. "Locating an Urban African Community in the History of Arusha, Tanzania, 1920–1967." Ph.D. thesis, Columbia University, New York.

Perry, Imani. 2004. *Prophets of the Hood: Politics and Poetics in Hip Hop.* Durham, N.C.: Duke University Press.

Perullo, Alex. 2005. "Hooligans and Heroes: Youth Identity and Hip-Hop in Dar es Salaam, Tanzania." *Africa Today* 51, no. 4: 75–101.

Piot, Charles. 1999. *Remotely Global: Village Modernity in West Africa.* Chicago: University of Chicago Press.

Pollock, Sheldon, Homi K. Bhabha, Carol A. Breckenridge, and Dipesh Chakrabarty. 2000. "Cosmopolitanisms." *Public Culture* 12, no. 3: 577–89.

Potter, Russell A. 1995. *Spectacular Vernaculars: Hip-Hop and the Politics of Postmodernism.* Albany: State University of New York Press.

Ranger, T. O. 1975. *Dance and Society in Eastern Africa: 1890–1970: The Beni Ngoma.* Berkeley: University of California.

Remes, Peter. 1999. "Global Popular Music and Changing Awareness of Urban Tanzanian Youth." *Yearbook for Traditional Music* 31: 1–26.

Riles, Annelise. 2003. "Introduction: When Knowledge Fails—Encountering the Mundane." *Documents: Artefacts of Modern Knowledge,* ed. A. Riles. Durham, N.C.: Duke University Press.

Rubin, Deborah S. 1996. "'Business Story Is Better than Love': Gender, Economic Development and Nationalist Ideology in Tanzania." In *Women out of Place: The Gender of Agency and the Race of Nationality,* ed. B Williams. New York: Routledge.

Sahlins, Marshall. 1989. "Cosmologies of Capitalism: The Trans-Pacific Sector of 'The World System.'" *Proceedings of the British Academy* 76: 1–51.

———. 1999. "Two or Three Things that I Know about Culture." *Journal of the Royal Anthropological Institute* 5, no. 3: 399–422.

Schneider, Jane. 1988. "Rumpelstiltskin's Bargain." In *Cloth and Human Experience,* ed. A. Weiener and J. Schneider. Washington, D.C.: Smithsonian.

Schumaker, Lyn. 2001. *Africanizing Anthropology: Fieldwork, Networks, and the Making of Cultural Knowledge in Central Africa.* Durham, N.C.: Duke University Press.

Setel, Philip. 2000. *A Plague of Paradoxes: AIDS, Culture and Demography in Northern Tanzania.* Chicago: University of Chicago Press.

Shipley, Jesse Weaver. 2004. "'The Best Tradition Goes On': Audience Consumption and the Transformation of Popular Theatre in Neoliberal Ghana." In *Producing*

African Futures: Ritual and Reproduction in a Neoliberal Age, ed. B. Weiss. Leiden: Brill.

Smith, James. 2001. "Of Spirit Possession and Structural Adjustment Programs: Government Downsizing, Education, and Their Enchantments in Neoliberal Kenya." In *Producing African Futures: Ritual and Politics in a Neoliberal Age,* ed. B. Weiss. Leiden: Brill.

Shipton, Parker. 1989. *Bitter Money: Cultural Economy and Some African Meanings of Forbidden Commodities.* Washington, D.C.: American Anthropological Association.

Silverstein, Michael. 1993. "Metapragmatic Discourse and Metapragmatic Function." In *Reflexive Language,* ed. J. Lucy. New York: Cambridge University.

Spear, Thomas. 1997. *Mountain Farmers: Moral Economies of Land and Agricultural Development in Arusha and Meru.* Oxford: James Currey.

Spitulnik, Debra. 1993. "Anthropology and Mass Media." *Annual Review of Anthropology* 22: 293–315.

———. 2000. "Documenting Radio Culture as Lived Experience: Reception Studies and the Mobile Machine in Zambia." In *African Broadcast Cultures: Radio in Transition,* ed. R. Fardon and G. Furniss. Oxford: James Currey. Westport, Conn.: Praeger.

Stallybrass, Peter, and Allen White. 1986. *The Politics and Poetics of Transgression.* London: Routledge.

Stambach, Amy. 1999. "Curl Up and Dye: Civil Society and the Fashion-Minded Citizen." In *Civil Society and the Political Imagination in Africa,* ed. J. L. Comaroff and J. Comaroff. Chicago: University of Chicago Press.

———. 2000a. *Lessons from Mount Kilimanjaro: Schooling, Community, and Gender in East Africa.* New York: Routledge.

———. 2000b. "Evangelism and Consumer Culture in Northern Tanzania." *Anthropological Quarterly* 73, no. 4: 171–79.

Stroeken, Koen. 2005. "This Is Not a Haircut: Neoliberalism and Revolt in Kiswahili Rap." *Image and Narrative* 11. Available at: http://www.imageandnarrative.be/worldmusicb_advertising/koenstroeken.htm. Accessed July 5, 2008.

Swedenburg, Ted. 2001. "Islamic Hip-Hop vs. Islamophobia Aki Nawaz, Natacha Atlas, Akhenaton in 2001." *Global Noise: Rap and Hip-Hop outside the USA,* ed. Tony Mitchell. Middletown, Conn.: Wesleyan University.

Synnott, Anthony. 1993. *The Body Social.* London: Routledge.

Tripp, Aili Mari. 1996. *Changing the Rules: The Politics of Liberalization and the Urban Informal Economy in Tanzania.* Berkeley: University of California Press.

Turner, T. 1980. "The Social Skin." In *Not Work Alone,* ed. J. Cherfas and R. Lewin. Beverly Hills, Calif.: Sage.

———. 1993. "Anthropology and Multiculturalism: What Is Anthropology that Multiculturalists Should Be Mindful of It?" *Cultural Anthropology* 8: 411–29.

Turner, Victor. 1967. *The Forest of Symbols.* Ithaca, N.Y.: Cornell University Press.

Urla, Jacqueline. 2001. "'We Are All Malcolm X!' Negu Gorriak, Hip-Hop, and the Basque Political Imaginary." In *Global Noise: Rap and Hip-Hop outside the USA,* ed. Tony Mitchell. Middletown, Conn.: Wesleyan University.

Vail, Leroy, ed. 1989. *The Creation of Tribalism in Southern Africa.* Berkeley: University of California Press.

Walsh, Andrew. 2003. "'Hot Money' and Daring Consumption in a Northern Malagasy Sapphire Mining Town." *American Ethnologist* 30, no. 2.

Wacquant, Loïc. 1998. "The Prizefighter's Three Bodies." *Ethnos* 63, no. 3: 325–52.

Weiss, Brad. 1996. *The Making and Unmaking of the Haya Lived World: Consumption, Commoditization and Everyday Practice.* Durham, N.C.: Duke University Press.

———. 1999. "Good-for-Nothing Haya Names: Powers of Recollection in Northwest Tanzania." *Ethnos* 64, no. 3: 397–420.

———. 2001. "Getting Ahead When We're Behind: Time and Value in Urban Tanzania." Paper presented at the annual meeting of the American Anthropological Association. Washington, D.C., November 2001.

———. 2004. "Contentious Futures: Past and Present." In *Producing African Futures: Ritual and Reproduction in a Neoliberal Age,* ed. B. Weiss. Leiden: Brill.

West, Harry G., and Todd Sanders. 2003. *Transparency and Conspiracy: Ethnographies of Suspicion in the New World Order.* Durham, N.C.: Duke University Press.

White, Hylton. 2004. "Ritual Haunts: The Timing of Estrangement in a Post-Apartheid Countryside." In *Producing African Futures: Ritual and Reproduction in a Neoliberal Age,* ed. B. Weiss. Leiden: Brill.

White, Luise. 1997. "Cars Out of Place: Vampires, Technology, and Labor in East and Central Africa." In *Tensions of Empire: Colonial Cultures in a Bourgeois World,* ed. F. Cooper and A. Stoler. Berkeley: University of California Press.

Wilder, Gary. 1999. "Practicing Citizenship in Imperial Paris." In *Civil Society and the Political Imagination in Africa,* ed. J. L. Comaroff and J. Comaroff. Chicago: University of Chicago Press.

Wilk, Richard. 2003. "Colonial Time and TV Time: Television and Temporality in Belize." In *Television: Critical Concepts,* ed. Toby Miller. Routledge.

Žižek, Slavoj. 1997. *The Plague of Fantasies.* London: Verso.

Index

Tracking Globalization

BRAD WEISS is a professor of anthropology at the College of William and Mary. His previous books are *The Making and Unmaking of the Haya Lived World: Consumption and Commoditization in Everyday Practice* and *Sacred Trees, Bitter Harvests: Globalizing Coffee in Colonial Northwest Tanganyika*. He is editor of *Producing African Futures: Ritual and Reproduction in a Neoliberal Age* and executive editor of the *Journal of Religion in Africa*.